# The Awakening of Milbuk

# The Awakening of Milbuk

## DIARY OF A MISSIONARY PRIEST

**A.E. Amaral**

authorHOUSE

*AuthorHouse™*
*1663 Liberty Drive*
*Bloomington, IN 47403*
*www.authorhouse.com*
*Phone: 1 (800) 839-8640*

*Published by AuthorHouse  12/22/2015*

*ISBN: 978-1-5049-5358-0 (sc)*
*ISBN: 978-1-5049-5357-3 (e)*

# DEDICATION

*To my wife, Maria,*
*Our five children,*
*& Hannah*

*To the Community of Milbuk,*
*To whom I am forever grateful.*
*And to the people of Malisbong,*
*Both Living and Dead*

*May we remember and pray*
*For them all*
*For all the Ghosts of the Forgotten.*

# CONTENTS

# PREFACE

Forty years have come and gone and of all the places where I lived and worked, one place keeps coming to mind each and every day of my life…Milbuk. This place was not the idyllic King Arthur's Camelot, though at times, I felt that life there was somewhat pleasant and serene. And as I attempted to write the story of this town far away in distance and in memory, it seemed to me to have disappeared from the face of the earth like the fabled Atlantis. It didn't seem important anymore to anyone except to me. But it wasn't always that way.

The story is a familiar one told before, of a people caught up in the turmoil, suffering and death of war. The resource I have for narrating these tragic events is in the recall of those experiences hidden deep within the crevices of my mind. My thoughts and emotions at the time, and the remembering of the events are somewhat clouded by the distortions of the passing years. The only thing I know is that these events certainly happened and absolutely shaped the outcome of my life, for I was there. I have chosen to dramatize some of the events of which I was not an eyewitness. Yet, this in no way lessens the truth of what happened.

The names in this narrative have been changed to protect the innocent, even though they have nothing to fear in the telling. The names of the bringers of death and destruction are unknown in most cases. Nevertheless, they will recognize the story of their evil deeds. The victims of their atrocities, long since dead, are their witnesses. Their voices will again come to life and speak. And I, with the fading memory of an old man, need to put to rest these *ghosts of the forgotten*.

A.E. Amaral

# CHAPTER 1

# *Seeds of Vengeance*

I t was Saturday evening, June 29, 1974 as Dimalub Maulana sat motionless on a small narrow plank of wood bridging the floor of the large speedboat. His arms were folded across his chest and he was deep in thought. The powerful, in-board Volvo motors propelled the swift, finely balanced, double out-rigger banca through an area of the Celebes Sea called Moro Gulf. Except for a momentary stop to refill the fuel tanks, Commander Dimalub would travel the almost 300 kilometers non-stop to his destination. He and his five companions had secretly left Basilan Island shortly after sunset to avoid any Philippine naval gunboats patrolling that part of the sea. The sea was relatively calm on this moonless night in June. The warmth of the sun's heat could still be felt in the early evening breeze. This first part of the journey would last for nine to ten hours giving Dimalub time to meditate on the following day's plans, time to remember the recent events of the past that necessitated such a trip in the first place.

Dimalub was a "dreaded" Moro, a son of a Muslim Datu from Jolo, proud of his heritage as a Tausug. He had attended the Notre Dame of Jolo Catholic College. This school was built and managed by a missionary order of Priests called the Oblates of Mary Immaculate. They were not concerned with directly proselytizing the Muslims but rather in providing them with strong, educational skills that would hopefully enable them to enrich their people in this most southerly and neglected part of the Philippines. The college also

1

helped to foster better community relations between the Muslim majority and the small fledgling Christian groups, immigrants to this populous city of 98,000 people. This is a place where real estate development, such as public housing, schools, training facilities and even solid waste management, is conducted by the Catholic Church. The Oblates have priests who double as architects and builders, as well as physicians and dentists.

But for the events of the last six years, this young Muslim man would have followed in the footsteps of his father and become deeply involved in the politics of Jolo City and maybe one day a national leader of his people. His education had given him the ability to see beyond appearances and to delve deeply into the root causes of the problems afflicting his people. He was disillusioned with the central government in Manila because of the injustices committed against his people, a complex of grievances. He was also angry with the local politicians who continued to rule in the old manner of the original sultans, feudally and corruptly using private armies, and approving back door deals with Manila to expand their personal fiefdoms with little regard for the ordinary people's needs. But nothing moved him more than what happened shortly before his graduation.

On March 18, 1968, 28 Muslim army trainees on the island of Corregidor were massacred by the Armed Forces of the Philippines. One of the young recruits killed on that evening in March was Dimalub's first cousin. He remembers how excited his cousin, Hamid was about the promise not only of a monthly allowance, but also over the prospect of eventually becoming a member of an elite unit in the Philippine Armed Forces. That meant, among other benefits, guns, which Muslims regard as very precious possessions. So from August to December 1967, the young recruit underwent training on the island of Simunul in the Sulu archipelago. The name of his commando unit was Jabidah.

This elite unit of Muslim Filipinos was to be part of a special government operation to wrest control of a disputed territory in Malaysia called Sabah. Ever since independence in 1946, the government of the Philippines had eyes on the island of Sabah.

Malaysia did not receive its independence from the British until the early 1960's. Even under President Macapagal, the Philippines claimed Sabah as a territory. The reasoning was this: the former Sultanate of Brunei ruled over the island of Sabah and once held sway over the territories of Sulu and Mindanao. It would seem natural that these territories should remain intact and be relinquished to the authority and dominance of the Philippines. The importance of obtaining this island was not for the benefit of the Muslim peoples who inhabited Sabah but rather in the quest for the hidden resource called OIL. So, early in his first administration, President Ferdinand Marcos decided to go along with a plan devised by his military advisors to take advantage of the struggling Malaysian government by destabilizing the political framework of the island. The operation was called "Merdeka".

On December the 30th of 1967, the 135 Muslim recruits boarded a Philippine Naval vessel for the island of Corregidor in Luzon for "specialized training." This second phase of the training turned mutinous when the recruits discovered their true mission. The recruits began to realize that the government plan would mean not only fighting their brother Muslims in Sabah, but also possibly killing their own Tausug and Samal relatives living there. Additionally, they had already begun to feel disgruntled over the non-payment of the promised P50 pesos monthly allowance. The recruits then demanded to be returned home. For the Jabidah planners, it seemed that there was only one choice.

As the sole survivor later recounted; the plotters of the massacre led the trainees out of their Corregidor barracks on the night of March 18, 1968 in batches of twelve. They were taken to a nearby airstrip. There, the military executioners massacred the trainees with automatic gunfire. Jibin Arula, the survivor, said that he heard a series of shots and saw his colleagues fall. He ran away from this horrific scene towards the mountainous hill ringing the island and rolled off the edge into the sea. He recalled clinging to a plank of wood and was able to stay afloat until rescued that morning by fishermen from Cavite.

The truth of the massacre took some time to emerge. When the story became public, Muslim students in Manila held a week long protest vigil over an empty coffin marked 'Jabidah' in front of the presidential palace. They claimed that "at least 28" Moro army recruits had been murdered. There was a firestorm in the Philippine press, attacking not so much the soldiers involved, but the culpability of a government administration that would ferment such a plot, and then seek to cover it up by wholesale murder. Court-martial proceedings were brought against twenty-three military personnel involved. Although the exact number of deaths still continues to vary depending upon the source of the reference, there is no denial of the fact that Corregidor was host to a massacre on that night. The Jabidah Massacre was just another in a string of acts of discrimination and outrage against the Bangsamoro people (i.e. Muslim Filipinos living in that area of the Philippines, believed to be ancestral land).

The incident inflamed the Muslim communities to the extent that former rivalries among the politicians of the various Muslim ethnic groups were forgotten. Plans for a concerted movement to seek independence were formed. In May of 1968, Datu Udtog Matalam, a prominent Maguindanaon political leader, formed the Mindanao Independence Movement (MIM). Young Muslim men readily joined the movement and were organized into a youth section and sent for military training in Malaysia. Their leader was Nur Misuari, the young college professor and political science lecturer at the University of the Philippines in Manila, who had returned to Mindanao and Jolo after Jabidah.

Dimalub had been wearing the camouflage uniform of a guerilla fighter for the last three years. He had joined the rebellion and secessionist movement shortly after listening to a speech in the main Jolo Mosque given by Nur Misuari, also a Tausug. Misuari preached a unity among all Muslims in the Philippines, no matter what language they spoke or to what ethnic group they belonged. He called this concept of Muslim Unity, Bangsamoro. It didn't take much convincing for Dimalub to join up with this new secessionist group of Nur Misuari, the Moro Nationalist Liberation Front (MNLF).

Now as Commander Dimalub, he had the responsibility as a guerilla leader of the MNLF.

For the last two years, Dimalub had been operating on the island of Jolo, taking side trips to Malaysia to offer assistance in the training of new recruits. He considered himself fortunate to have been trained by some of the best freedom fighters in the camps situated in the country of Libya. He was being groomed for greater responsibilities. Then it happened. On February 7, 1974, government troops began an offensive against the rebel held city of Jolo, the capital of Sulu and the center of Muslim culture and tradition. Dimalub was involved in one of the largest conflicts between the MNLF and the Armed Forces of the Philippines.

The Philippine Administration in 1974, under President Ferdinand Marcos, was hell bent on a total war solution to its "Muslim Problem", calling the insurgents "communists", whom, Marcos said, were intent on overthrowing the government of the Philippines. There would be no quarter given to any insurgent. The "Burning of Jolo City" was a dramatic example of the government's policy of total war and total cover-up. Since 1970, rebel elements of the Moro National Liberation Front under the leadership of Nur Misuari had been successful in various sorties against the army, driving them from key Muslim towns on Jolo. This island was the center of the secessionist movement to form an independent Muslim state. President Marcos had been unsuccessful in pacifying these areas. His frustration grew. So, in January of 1974, the Armed Forces of the Philippines committed 36 battalions of soldiers, along with naval boats and aircraft, for the purpose of assaulting alleged rebel camps on the island of Jolo. Secessionist groups had been occupying important towns on the island without challenge. The intent of the military operation was to dislodge the rebels and gain government control once again.

On February the 4th, rebel groups began to infiltrate the town of Jolo backed up by the support of the local police who numbered about a thousand. The town was patrolled by elements of Philippine Army Units and a group of "returned" rebels who had received new weapons from the Government after surrendering. This plan was an inducement in having these former rebels change sides in order to divide the allegiance of the different rebel groups.

The Government Army units closest to the town of Jolo were stationed at a camp near the airport. Just before dawn of February the 7th, the rebels attacked the Army. Loud explosions reverberated from one end of the city to the other, as mortar rounds were exchanged between the opposing sides. Two thousand Muslim rebels together with the police of Jolo became enmeshed in a house to house, door to door battle with troops of the AFP and the "returned" Muslim fighters who had changed sides. The rebels had warned the people of Jolo to flee from the city until the fighting was ended. But where could they go. Once the fighting started, it became clear that the people had no choice but to flee for their lives as best they could. The battle was ferocious and lasted for over three days.

Jolo was destroyed, burnt to the ground. The complete destruction of the city with a population approaching 100,000 people was such a catastrophe that the mere thought of the scale of destruction and death leaves the mind numb. And yet this "massacre" of civilians in particular and the enormous number of evacuees it generated, remained a secret for years. Government reports stated that the number of dead were about 500. The bureau chief of the Associated Press in Manila, Arnold Zeitlin, had reported that 10,000 people had died. This was told to him by a representative of Social Welfare in Jolo. For this reporting, Mr. Zeitlin was not permitted entrance to the Philippines eight months later when he was returning from vacation in Hong Kong.

A complete news black-out was in effect throughout the country and especially in those areas where the Armed Forces of the Philippines were actively engaged in military actions against the Muslims of the Southern Philippines. The death toll among the military was unknown as was the number of deaths among civilians and insurgents. Casualty figures were regularly under-reported. Complaints to the Muslim governments of the world concerning the "genocide" being perpetrated by the Marcos regime were often discredited as the rebel's ploy to distort the true facts. The government denied all allegations and offered its own version of what happened. The whole scene was a soap opera on the world stage.

Ten years later, after much research, it was determined that 20,000 civilians were killed in one night by the incessant shelling from naval ships and the bombing from aircraft. The inferno that consumed the crowded and tightly built town of Jolo created such a wall of fire that only ash was left in its wake. It is estimated that 60,000 people were made homeless during the battle. 40,000 or more settled in Zamboanga and thousands fled to the island of Sabah. This event pales in comparison to such enormous genocide as occurred in Germany, Croatia and in Rwanda. But this was the Philippines. Years later, people traumatized by such an event, still write of their experiences so ingrained within their memories.

Dimalub and his band of fighters first entered the city in the evening hours of January the 4th. His unit, one of many rebel groups, all numbering over a thousand, fought fearlessly to drive out the government troops, who for several months had been harassing the outlying villages on the island, searching out the rebel strongholds and driving the people from their homes. The rebels' intent on entering Jolo was to make a stand here in this principal city and to force the government to take their movement for secession seriously.

Upon arriving in the city, Dimalub went immediately to his father's home and pleaded with him to leave Jolo with the whole family until the fighting was over. His father refused to leave. Later, he relented and led his wife, sons, daughters, their children and other members of his family to the docks where friends of his had boats available to transport them to relatives in Zamboanga. When all the family were on board, the father bid them all farewell and headed back to his home in the city amid the tears and cries of his family. Dimalub had thought that everyone had left Jolo by boat and were safe. However, towards the evening of the 7th, as he was retreating from the city, he passed by his home and saw that it was completely demolished. A neighborhood friend recognized him and came running up to him. "Dimalub, your father is dead!" Shock and sadness crossed his face. Several of his unit accompanied him to the site. It didn't take them long to find the father's remains. Dimalub could hardly recognize his father, having been burned so terribly. He had barely time enough to dig a grave for his father and to recite the proper prayers before the area was over-run by government troops and former Muslim insurgents who had gone over to the government side for a few pesos and a new Armalite. Luckily, Dimalub and his men were able to escape and fight another day.

The evacuees from Jolo did not fare well in their flight. The refugee camps were squalid and haphazardly organized for the 40,000 or so Muslims evacuees from the Philippine island of Jolo. The journey between Jolo and the Malaysian island of Sabah was doubly dangerous for the fleeing refugees; dangerous because of the ill repair of many of the boats and dangerous due to the overcrowding of the crafts. Nevertheless they must leave. To remain would be certain death for some, torture for others, hunger and suffering for all. Every boat that could float was put into service for the panicked people who crowded the shores and beaches of Jolo. The nearby rumblings of the AFP Artillery and the bombs of the Air Force reminded them of the horror they witnessed as homes, families and friends were torn apart and destroyed before their eyes. Many barely escaped the horrible onslaught of the military. Now here they were fleeing from the only home they had ever known, fleeing from the very government who had sworn to protect them.

The Malaysian government had been sheltering Muslim dissidents and insurgents for years now. In fact, Malaysia was the conduit of funds and weapon supplies for the Moro Nationalist Liberation Front. Libya was supporting the ideals and goals of the MNLF by offering military training to its members and giving money to purchase weapons. The Muslim countries were sympathetic to the plight of the Philippine Muslims.

The new found Muslim consciousness and solidarity was reaching new and surprising heights. The OAPEC countries, the oil producing consortium of Arab, Muslim countries experienced a remarkable surge of power that blocked and frustrated the arrogance and domination of the Western powers. An oil embargo was placed upon the United States and some of its allies for the support that was given to Israel during the Yom Kippur War in its fight against its Arab neighbors. The embargo lasted five months and was lifted in March of 1974. Former political power strategies by the West were turned upside down. The OAPEC consortium was now dictating the terms of the deal and determining not only the price to be paid in terms of money, but demanding that fair treatment be given to the sizeable Muslim populations in these "Christian" countries. The Muslim countries did not want to hear that those countries dependent on their oil were mistreating their Muslim citizens. It was for this reason that men like Dimalub Maulana were able to continue their struggle against this oppressive government regime. The "Ummah" (Muslim solidarity) was all too real to him. He could feel the support of his Muslim brothers thousands of miles away.

## CHAPTER 2

# *Journey of Revenge*

This was Commander Dimalub's second such trip from Basilan to the shores of Sultan Kudarat. He and his crew had been traveling now for almost nine hours and the first rays of daylight were almost upon them. For the last hour, the speedboat had been cruising along the western shore of Mindanao, sixty kilometers south of Cotabato City. He and his men were now only a few minutes away from their first stop, the town of Palimbang. Here, he would beach the boat and hide away from the curious eyes of government troops. There were many Muslims in this area who were friendly to the cause of the MNLF. They would make sure that the boat would be well hidden and the cargo of weapons safe. Still, Dimalub would need to seek assistance and hospitality from Imam Druz Ali, even though he knew that the Mayor didn't have much enthusiasm for the goals of the MNLF.

It was a new day, Sunday, the last day of June. Upon arrival at the town of Palimbang, Dimalub and two of his men approached the house of Mayor Druz Ali. They were met by several of the Mayor's body guards who challenged them. One of the men recognized Dimalub from an earlier visit and welcomed him. It was almost 6:30 A.M. and the Mayor had yet to arise from his night's rest. The chief body guard knocked on the door of the house and one of the Mayor's sons answered the intrusion by shouting through the closed, barricaded door, "Who is it?" "What do you want?"

"It's Ahmed," the reply came back. "I need to speak with the Mayor now."

Ahmed was one of the Mayor's chief body guards assigned that evening to provide security during the night. "It had better be important," the son replied. The son went to the bedroom of his father and awoke him, "Papa, Ahmed has an important message to give you. It can't wait until later."

The Mayor opened his eyes and grumpily sat on the edge of his bed, looking for his sandals. "Tell Ahmed to come in."

The son opened the door and cautiously let Ahmed slide through the small opening he provided, closing the door and locking it immediately upon his entrance. "What is it, Ahmed," the Mayor impatiently demanded.

"Mayor, I'm sorry to disturb you but one of our "ronda" guards came upon a speed boat from Basilan. The men beached their boat about a half kilometer from here near the mangroves. You've met the leader of the group once before. The visitor said that you knew his father, a Datu and former politician from Jolo. His name is Dimalub Maulana, a commander of the MNLF. He needs to speak with you now. It's very important. He's outside the house, sir, with two of his companions."

The Mayor sat on the kitchen chair and quickly rose to his feet. "Bring him inside right away. I know his father and I've met this young man before. I'd better hear what he has to say."

The son opened the door and waved the two men inside the house. "Assalam alaikum," the Mayor greeted his visitors. "Alaikum Assalam," was their reply.

"Thank you for receiving me into your home so early in the morning. I'm here on a mission from the MNLF planning committee to begin operations in the province of Sultan Kudarat and in particular, here in the township of Palimbang".

"Oh my", the Mayor exclaimed. "Are we going to war with the Christians?"

"No, not directly," Dimalub answered. "We need to clear certain parts of the mountains of any settlers so that we can operate training

11

camps in the area and transport arms and supplies to the other rebel groups near Cotabato City. Also, we plan to disrupt the Weyerhaeuser logging operations so that the government will send troops to protect the logging concession. The people who will be affected by all this will, of course, be the Christian settlers who have come and taken over our land...our country. I know that the operations in your township will cause you some problems and money...but we know that such inconveniences are necessary for our people to obtain independence from this Marcos government. Our Muslim brothers are fighting and dying throughout Sulu and Mindanao. We need to widen the war so that the government Army units will be drawn away from some of our key objectives like Cotabato City and Jolo. This is a war of attrition. We must make it costly for the Philippine government to deny us independence and sovereignty. Do you have any questions?"

"Yes. What do you expect me to do?"

"I know that you have your own army of 'black shirts' to protect your interests. I am not asking you to join me in these operations. Continue to be a trusted public servant and maintain your good relationship with the Weyerhaeuser logging company. When the Army arrives to protect the interests of the logging concession, ingratiate yourself with them. Keep up your neutrality. They needn't suspect that you or I even met and talked about such matters. I have come to you out of respect and to inform you of our plans. You needn't be enthusiastic about our movement, but the day will come when you will have no choice but to join us in our plans for liberation. We appreciate all the assistance that you can give us."

"There is one more question I have," the Mayor said. "Can you give me any details about what you plan to do?"

"Are you sure you want to know? Are you able to keep a secret," Dimalub answered with extreme gravity.

The Mayor hesitated to answer and then said, "No, that's alright. I'll know about it when it happens. It will make it easier for me to say that I knew nothing of these affairs."

"Good," replied Dimalub. "Now what I need is a little food and some sleep. Can you recommend someplace where I may receive hospitality?"

"Forgive me," the Mayor replied, "for not offering you food and a place to stay sooner. Of course you and your companions will stay with me and my family. I will arrange a safe place for your boat and the other men."

"Thank you very much, Mayor. Your gracious hospitality and assistance will be mentioned to my superiors."

The Mayor was troubled all day long with this dangerous visitor in his home. Even when Dimalub eventually left, he did not sleep well that night. His mind was busy calculating the losses that he would suffer because of these military operations. Will he lose power and influence? Will the government blame him for implicitly cooperating with the rebels? How can he distance himself from such activity and still benefit? This will be a delicate balance. He was not convinced that such blatant terrorist attacks would bring the desired effect. These operations will only interfere in his plans for improving his wealth, status and power in the township. Mayor Druz Ali did not want to separate himself from the Philippine government nor did he want to anger and disappoint the rebels by his lack of cooperation. How to steer the middle course?

Within his heart of hearts, Mayor Ali resented these educated up-starts of the MNLF. Their wanton actions seemed to endanger everything he had worked for politically and "religiously". He was after all an important Datu, at least in his own mind, and a Muslim Imam to boot. Who were they to wield such power and to tell him what to do? These rebels may destroy everything I have worked for, he thought. Such was the Mayor's dilemma.

Commander Dimalub planned to leave Palimbang the following evening by 8:00 P.M. The Mayor had arranged for the purchase of gasoline so that Dimalub's men, who would be returning to Basilan, would not need to stop and refuel. All was going according to plan. At exactly 8:00 P.M., Dimalub and his men pushed off from the shores of Palimbang and headed out to sea. It would take less than an hour to reach Kulong-Kulong. The Mayor was glad to see them go and half-heartedly wished them success in their operations.

As Dimalub and his men approached the coastline near Kulong-Kulong, they could see the lights of the logging camp of Milbuk. The housing compound and the extensive mill area of the Weyerhaeuser Logging Company were brightly lighted and seemed a bit incongruous in such an isolated place. There were no roads in or out of this Municipality, much less from this isolated logging town. This was truly an out-of-the-way place that could only be reached by boat or small plane. No place on the coast of this new province of Sultan Kudarat had electrification for the people, except here. Isolated generators in certain towns could be found that gave temporary light and power to individual homes and businesses, but Milbuk had electric power 24 hours a day.

Five kilometers away, a single lantern hung on a pole on a small promontory at the top edge of the beach at Kulong-Kulong. The lantern swung gently in the breeze, back and forth, as if signaling to someone out at sea, penetrating the night and casting ghostly shadows on the sand. Commander Dimalub and his men passed beyond the place of the lighted beacon and finally made landing half a kilometer down the beach under the umbrella of darkness. The tide had reached fullness only a half hour before, but the water was still high enough for the boat men to maneuver the boat up close to the green mantle of grass that bordered the forest of coconut trees. Dimalub and his five companions quickly exited the boat, automatic guns at the ready, searching the shadows for any hostile movements. They plunged into the grove of trees and reconnoitered the area. The houses of the villagers lay over 500 meters down the beach.

It wasn't long till they could hear muffled voices and running feet nearing their position. And then silence. "Assalam alaikum!" a voice chanted on the night's air. Silence again. "Assalam alaikum", the voice repeated! All was briefly silent, then the reply from Dimalub, "Alaikum Assalam!" "Come forward!"

A young man, Ajol by name, dressed in camouflage khaki pants and a non-descript polo shirt, came forward, shouldering an AK-47 with a broad smile lighting up his face, "It's good to see you again, sir. We were worried that something bad may have happened. We were expecting you last night. It's good that you're finally here."

"We were delayed", Commander Dimalub replied. "We had to stop-over early in the morning at Palimbang to avoid government naval patrols. We hid the boat and were able to obtain more gasoline for the return trip. I informed the Mayor of our plans so that he would not be caught unawares when we begin our operations in the area. And so here we are. How is the recruiting going here in these barrios?"

"Just fine, sir", Ajol said. "The people here are very hospitable and we were able to recruit several dozen volunteers for training."

"Good! Call the rest of the men", Dimalub ordered, "and help us unload the weapons, ammunition and other supplies from the boat. We must hurry so that the boat may return to Basilan. Three of us will be staying here with you to train the recruits and plan some exercises for them. Now take me to the village Datu so that I may greet him."

Eight men appeared on the beach to unload the deadly cargo. There were AK-47s and boxes of ammunition for over 24 men. They all took some cargo from the boat and formed a line, following Ajol half a kilometer to a small house where several more armed men awaited them. The weapons were placed carefully in the far corner of the house. The rebel soldiers then settled down for the night in anticipation for the long journey to their mountain hideout and training camp early in the morning. Ajol left them there and proceeded with Commander Dimalub to the home of Datu Ibrahim Malik.

Datu Malik had not been enthusiastic about helping this secessionist group in their plans to overthrow the authority of the government. He had been active as a young man in fighting against the occupying Japanese as a guerilla fighter. He felt proud that the Philippines had attained independence from the Americans in 1946. For the last 25 years, he had lived quite comfortably, making a good living from the copra of this large coconut plantation left to him by his father. After Independence, his father was able to send Ibrahim to Manila, where he spent almost six years completing his studies and returning with a degree in commerce. As a graduation gift, his father arranged passage for him on a ship heading for the Arabian Peninsula. He would be one of the hundreds of Muslim Filipinos that year making the "Hajj" or pilgrimage to Mecca. Upon his return, Ibrahim was received by the village people as a respected man and a teacher or "Imam" for his community.

Four years ago, Datu Malik had been elected Mayor of Palimbang, beating out an old rival of his, the present Mayor, Druz Ali. The last election was somewhat of a farce. Malik lost to Ali by the narrowest of margins. Many felt that there had been irregularities in the voting. These alleged anomalies were never able to be proven much to the disappointment of the people. Datu Malik was a kind and just man, truly concerned about his people's welfare. He avoided making a big fuss about the irregularities and accepted the election results graciously so as not to anger the new Mayor, who out of revenge might cause harm to his people.

The Datu had been closing his eyes to the smuggling of arms for a few years now. It was not as if smuggling was something brand new to his town. In fact, most of the goods transported to Kulong-Kulong for sale at the local stores came through the countries of Malaysia and Indonesia. Smuggling was a government term that was placed upon goods coming into the Philippines without being taxed by Philippine Customs. The Muslims called what they did, TRADING! However, weapons were another matter. Datu Malik felt obligated to his fellow Muslims, especially in view of the injustices committed by the government army against his people. His only reservation was this. He was afraid that the destructive sword of war would come and visit his peaceful part of the world. He shuddered when he thought about the suffering that would come to his people if the government decided to retaliate against these rebels by visiting his town with their soldiers.

Nevertheless, Datu Malik welcomed Commander Dimalub to his home and afforded him hospitality. Dimalub assured the Datu,

"We will only stay the night and at first light we will be journeying into the mountains to establish our training camp. I will take good care of your young men. Be assured that we are fighting a just war against the government. This Ferdinand Marcos is about killing us all so that the land and its riches may be given to others. We are Muslims and this land belongs to us." Ibrahim Malik made no comment on Dimalub's speech but prayed that Allah would be with him and his men, protecting them from harm. The speed boat carrying the weapons from Basilan left shortly after delivering the deadly cargo. They would journey to Cotabato City for supplies and gasoline before returning to Basilan.

Early Monday morning, July 1st, just before the darkness of night was ending, Commander Dimalub left with twelve men from Kulong-Kulong and an additional eighteen recruits from Malisbong. They silently trudged over the hidden trail snaking through the mountains and jungles of this rain forest until they came upon an opening. Ajol and Dimalub carefully approached the crest of the hill and peered over the wide open plateau. Binoculars in hand, Commander Dimalub searched over the landscape for any signs of movement, human or otherwise. There were no people in sight. All was quiet. Carefully they proceeded in single file over the low lying hills, looking for any signs of human habitation. They did not want anybody to know of their presence. Soon they would be at their base camp, a place hidden in a valley, away from the prying eyes of people. Patrols would be sent out in pairs to reconnoiter the area and guarantee that on one would observe their activity.

For the first week of training, Commander Dimalub made certain that each of the new recruits was well aware of the reasons for the struggle against the government. He wanted each recruit to commit himself to the cause, so that the hardships, sufferings and sacrifices of the next few months would be willingly borne without complaint. These recruits must be willing to kill...to take another person's life in order to promote independence for the Muslim people. There must be no hesitation! Dimalub and his trained fighters were Tausug, Samal and Yakan. The recruits were Maguindanaon. Dimalub insisted, "It doesn't matter what language you speak or to what tribe you belong. We are the Bangsamoro People. We are Muslims and this is our land".

Besides indoctrination, the recruits were made familiar with the AK-47. It was a soldier-friendly weapon, often called the "peasant rifle". It was simple in design, reliable, and accurate. The rifle fired a 7.62 mm bullet either automatically or semi-automatically from a 30 round clip at a rate of up to 600 rounds per minute, and performed with accuracy at up to 435 yards. The trainees were taught to disassemble and assemble the weapon, insuring its cleanliness at all costs. None of the recruits were allowed to practice firing the rifle until all of them were thoroughly familiar with the weapon. The recruits were only permitted to fire the rifle on semi-automatic. This meant that they could fire the rifle only once, each time they pulled the trigger. Ammunition must be used sparingly. Under no circumstances were they to put the rifle on automatic. "Make each shot count: one shot, one kill", was the instruction drilled into them. There would soon be time for some 'real life' exercises in combat maneuvers and ambush techniques.

# CHAPTER 3

## A Lesson in History

From my earliest days, I always wanted to be a missionary priest in some far off country. I longed for the great adventure dreamed in the fantasy of youthful thoughts about foreign lands: the strange people, mysterious languages, magnificent landscapes and daring deeds. These all cascaded together in my mind as so many images manufactured by movie scenes, lives of the saints, and the brave tales of missionaries. China was at the top of my list. That vast expanse of land where half the earth's population lived was the most mysterious of places, a bizarre world of strange vistas and cities teeming with people. The Chinese themselves were often described as exotic and inscrutable. Their language was so foreign to Western ears and most incomprehensible. The adventure of it all! I was filled with great excitement and expectation for the quests that lay ahead of me. And so I, young Art Amaral, entered the Passionist Preparatory Seminary in Dunkirk, New York, a small town sitting along the shore of Lake Erie.

Yes, the adventure of it all, made the whole idea of being a missionary so exciting. I would be able to do great things for people who needed salvation. It definitely seemed like they needed to be "saved". Just look at the photos that the missionaries, home-on-leave, showed to us. And there were so many people. However, no sooner did I enter the Seminary when the whole of China was closed off to the West and to the thousands of missionaries of all denominations and religions who were cast out of the country. The year was 1955.

Disappointed with the loss of China as a mission field, I thought to myself, "Should I leave the seminary and join the Armed Forces?" What would I do now? There were no job prospects for a person with barely two years of college under his belt. Yes, there was nothing for me outside the seminary walls. Besides, I liked the academic life and the tranquility of the seminary, but most of all I enjoyed the time set aside each day for recreation and sports. Here I excelled. Being one of the better athletes in the seminary, I was good enough to play every sport and was a leader in organizing games ...games of all sorts. I loved the competition and the companionship. Yes, there was nothing better for me to do than to remain in the seminary and pursue my dream to be a missionary priest someday.

It was in my fourth year in the Seminary, during which Pope John XXIII invited the Passionist Congregation of the Eastern Province of the United States to take over the diocese of South Cotabato in the southern part of Mindanao in the Philippines. The year was 1958. My old desire to live the life of a missionary was re-ignited. I had read a lot about the Philippines in the context of what happened during the Second World War. One of my boyhood heroes was General Douglas Macarthur. Oh, the adventure of it all. I could hardly wait. It wasn't until seven years later that I was able to volunteer for assignment to the Philippines, a year after my Ordination to the Priesthood in 1964. I was 29 years old.

Almost immediately after arriving in Manila, I was headed off to language school. It was strange at first to hear people address me by my religious name of Marcellus, since for the past seven or eight years I had been called 'Duke' by my classmates and at times even by my teachers. This nickname was not after the actor, John Wayne. His fame as a rough and tumble cowboy sort of guy was not my style. The nickname described the fastidious and meticulous way I dressed and combed my hair. Thankfully, I lost that moniker when I arrived in the Philippines. My proper religious name was Father Marcellus Amaral.

I spent the next six months learning the culture and language of the people to whom I was assigned. On March 17, 1966, during dinner time, Father Harold Stout, the religious superior of the Passionist Fathers in the Philippines, looked up from his meal and stared intently at me. In his usual formal and authoritative style of speaking he made the following announcement. "Marcellus, I have arranged for you to attend a three day seminar at the East Asian Pastoral Institute at the Jesuit University in Quezon City. This is a new endeavor by the Jesuits to provide cultural, theological and sociological perspectives concerning the peoples of Southeast Asia among whom we missionaries work. Missionaries from India, Thailand, Borneo, Malaysia and the Philippines will be attending. I think that it is important for you to be there and learn as much as you can about the Muslim peoples living in our diocese.

The subject of the seminar is the *"History of the Expansion of Islam in Southeast Asia and its Relevance for Today"*. I know that your work in the parishes of South Cotabato will be to minister almost entirely to the thousands of Filipino Catholics, new settlers in the region. However, you need to know that we live and work in a land once occupied almost exclusively by Muslims. You won't see many Mosques in Dadiangas or Marbel, but there are communities of Muslims in surrounding areas. A couple of our priests are already actively working in Muslim areas, fostering good will among the people and assisting the Christian community to get along peaceably with their neighbors. So, enjoy yourself while you're here in Manila. When you arrive at your parish, you will be up to your neck in work with baptisms, marriages, religious instructions, hospital chaplaincy and so forth....Peoples from the Visayas and Luzon are arriving every day by ship and plane. This is the new frontier. Good luck!"

When April the 6th arrived, I took my place midway in the large conference hall. Sixty or seventy priests, religious sisters and brothers were in attendance. Many of them were American missionaries but there were also other European countries represented like Ireland, Italy, France, Belgium, and Germany.

The first day of the conference focused on the history of Islam and its meteoric spread through the countries once occupied by Rome and its Legions. The expansion of Islam through many of these once Christian dominated lands went hand in hand with the military success of the Muslim armies. The conference speaker for the day was a Jesuit historian, Father Felix Ordonez, a Spaniard, who spent almost twenty years teaching at the Jesuit College in Kuala Lumpur, Malaysia. He was well acquainted with his own country's history of occupation by the Muslim armies, an occupation that lasted for almost 900 years until they were driven out in the 1600s.

Father Ordonez had a heavy Spanish accent, but his English was quite good. After a few hours of listening to him, even I began to converse with others with the same accent. He began the lecture with a question.

"When I mention to you the word Arab, what comes to mind?"

We all stared in silence, wondering if he really wanted us to answer. He looked about the hall at the blank stares and answered for us.

"Do you not think deserts, camels, turbaned heads, flowing robes and the like? Yet there were Arab Muslims of old who were also indomitable seafaring people, whose journeys of trade spread far beyond the sands and oases of the Arabian Peninsula to the western shores of India and throughout the thousands of islands of the archipelagoes of Southeast Asia that today make up the nations of Malaysia, Indonesia and the Philippines. These Arab peoples even journeyed all the way to China and set up a very sizeable community at (Canton) the present day Guangzhou."

He continued,

"The Arab traders, of course, left behind selected members of their crew, who established trading communities among the indigenous people. When the boats of their kinsmen arrived each year during the season of monsoon, the goods to be traded and shipped back to their home ports would have already been prepared and ready for shipment. Such organization of course developed over the centuries into a smooth running cartel which monopolized the trading of spices and many other desired goods to the eager Mediterranean countries. The source of their goods was a well-kept secret as was the seasonal shifting of the trade winds in the Indian Ocean that made all this possible. It is no wonder then, that with the birth of Islam and its rapid spread throughout the Arabian Peninsula, the trading ports of these Arab seamen should develop into vibrant Muslim communities."

Everyone in the hall was now riveted to his every word as he described the centuries of Muslim influence.

Father Ordonez explained that, "After Islam took root in India, during the 12th and 13th centuries, merchants from the southern part of India, most of whom were Muslim, became a major proselytizing force in Southeast Asia, fashioning the special blend of commerce and missionary activity which was the chief character in the expansion of Islam throughout the archipelago."

"Malacca (Kuala Lumpur, Malaysia) was chief among those vibrant Muslim communities. During the 1400's Malacca became an important port for Asian international trade and a major commercial power. At the latter part of the 15th century and the beginning of the 16th century, this commercial hub also became a center for Islamic studies and the source for propagating the faith throughout Southeast Asia. Missionaries of Arab descent and Indian Muslims set out for Indonesia from Malacca in order to advance the fortunes of Islam. Many of the traders belonged to "Sufi" orders and their missionary zeal stands out when compared to the earlier Arab traders who did not concern themselves with missionary activity. The "Sufis" stressed the brotherhood of Islam or the "Ummah" for all who embraced the faith, making only minimalist religious demands on the performance of the laws (the "Sharia"), leaving room for pre-Islamic beliefs and a variety of customs. The Islamic doctrine appealed to the local populations as disseminated by the Sufi religious instructors. Many of the religious concepts were already found within the local populations especially those that tended toward mysticism. Islam was tolerant of many peculiar customs, even such customs as appeared to be contrary to Islamic ("Sharia") law."

"Over generations, it is evident that the spread of Islam began and prospered when the local chieftains converted to the religion because of the political and economic alliances which Muslim traders could provide. These advantages were based on Muslim solidarity that stemmed from belonging to the "Ummah". Southeast Asia was one of the last regions of the world reached by Islam. By 1565, the Spaniards had reached the Philippines from their South American bases. Both Spain and Portugal quickly realized that the spice trade they sought to monopolize was largely controlled by Muslim traders, whose centuries-long presence in the region had generated substantial Muslim populations and states."

Father Ordonez digressed a bit from his lecture to speak briefly about the influence that the "Crusades" of the 11th to 14th centuries had upon the colonizing efforts of the Spanish Conquistadors.

"Initially, the Crusades arose from a complaint by the Byzantine Emperor of Constantinople to Pope Urban II in 1095. The complaint stated that pilgrims from his country were being robbed and killed by bands of Muslim raiders who preyed upon the caravans. Europe at the time was in the process of developing stable communities into recognizable countries. However, there were domestic feuds among the leaders of these emerging principalities and kingdoms that were causing untold misery for the general population. The idea of forming a crusade of Christian rulers, leading their followers in a glorious defense of the Holy Places, hopefully would distract these petty rulers from killing one another.

The original idea for the Crusades was simple: to create an avenue of access to the Holy Lands so that the Christian pilgrims could travel to and return safely from their journey. Those who volunteered to join such an endeavor would be rewarded for their efforts. Spiritual indulgences would be granted to all participants as well as some temporal benefits as well, such as absolving a person from past crimes and obligations. Then, there were the unspoken benefits that would come from conquering enemy towns and cities. All this was possible for those who "took the cross".

Invitation to join a crusade came about by the preaching of a priest or bishop, envoys of the Pope to the various Western kingdoms. Volunteers were asked to take a vow to defend the Holy Places and each warrior received a cross from the hands of the Pope or his delegate and was thenceforth considered a soldier of the Church. The soldiers of the Crusades wore symbols of the cross on their tunics. There was no doubt that the trappings of battle on both sides evidenced a clash of religions. At least it would seem to be so.

The formality of the Crusades under the support and direction of the various Popes declined after 250 years. However, there were small individualized endeavors which were called crusades but were not sanctioned as such. This continued for the next 150 years. The first Crusade ordered by Pope Urban II set out in the year 1096. So by the 1600's it appeared that the Christian West had grown tired of this endless bloodletting against such a formidable opponent. It is interesting to note that the Spanish Conquistadors considered their global exploration of the "new" world as a crusade, not only to claim such land as they were able for the crown of Spain but to "bring the faith of Christianity" to the pagan hordes whom they conquered.

When the Spaniards finally arrived in the Philippines, they were able to subdue and suppress the natives in the Northern and Central Islands. The Muslim natives of the Southern Philippines were quite another matter. At first glance it would seem that these Muslims were truly a united people despite the fact that they were divided into 13 ethno-linguistic tribes. At certain times in their history, these tribes even conducted war against one another. What each tribe valued most was the autonomy and independence they had enjoyed for so many centuries and the pride they held in their own identity. Each tribe spoke a distinct dialect and practiced customs peculiar to them. Their adherence to Islam, though important, did not become a determining factor in uniting them until well into the twentieth century.

The continuing war with the Spaniards was less a religious conflict and more a political one. The Muslim tribes of the Southern Philippines did not want to lose their independence. They had never been subjugated by a foreign power. In fact, Islam came to them gently. No conquering army forced them to become adherents.

The Spaniards had another agenda. Winning battles against a defeated foe was only the beginning in Spain's plan to conquer new lands. Spain's strategy took the form of religious nationalism, (a curse in our own day), namely, the cross and the sword. Religion was used as a tool to control the population that may revolt if not trained to accept the yoke of their masters.

It was evident to the Muslims that the Spaniards would force them to become Christians. Christianity was preached to them as the only true religion and Islam, therefore, was a "false religion" to be stamped out at all costs. This plan of the Spaniards outraged the Muslims who became more determined to fight. Thus, the resistance did take on a religious tone, a "jihad" (holy war) with the battle cry, "Kamatay sampay kamarharhikaan" (Death until victory is achieved).

The Spaniards were perplexed over this strong resistance to their rule. What to call these stubborn people? All they could think of was their own experience of subjugation by the conquering Muslim armies that held power over their country for centuries. The Christians of Spain called the Muslim foreign occupiers of their country, Moors. And so the name "Moros" was given to the Islamic peoples of the southern Philippines, a name with negative connotations that branded these people as pirates, "juramentados", repulsive, sinister and the like. When the Americans wrested the Philippines from Spain, even their colonizing efforts met with fierce opposition that resulted in bloody conflicts and massacres, lasting from 1902 to 1913.

After hundreds of years of bloodletting in the name of religion, it is not surprising that the Muslims of the Philippines would hold us missionaries, if not in contempt, then in great suspicion. Three centuries of repression under the Spaniards, followed by almost 50 years of betrayal by the Americans, stored up within the consciousness of this people a sense of their distinctiveness. And so the beat continues. The new rulers of the Philippines from Macapagal to Marcos had learned little from the events of the past 400 years. *"The crusades are alive and well in the Philippines."* These words rung in my ears for days, wondering what part I would play in this ongoing game. I left those few days of seminar with a new awareness of my mission. It would be six years later that my assignment as parish priest would take me to a place where the majority of the people were Muslim. Here I would try to put into practice the plan of bringing harmony and understanding between Christian and Muslim. How I was to succeed or fail is the subject of this story.

# CHAPTER 4

# *A Troubling Choice*

My language and cultural studies were now over. The religious superior assigned me to the city parish of General Santos City or Dadiangas as it was formerly called. Here, I worked as an assistant pastor in a parish of over 50,000 people, assigned as a prison and hospital chaplain, coordinator of religious instruction in an ever-growing parish with thousands of children. My work week lasted a full six days and sometimes seven, from early morning to late at night. The one day I took off was spent at a neighboring priest's parish catching up on my sleep and taking time for some quiet conversation with another American. My first tour of duty lasted four years, after which I was furloughed back to the States for several months to visit family and friends. A new ruling came down for us Passionists concerning the names we religious adopted at our Profession. My religious name of Marcellus was now able to be changed back to my Baptismal name of Arthur. The choice was ours to make and I made it. I would thenceforth be known as Fr. Art Amaral.

My second tour as a missionary came at the latter part of 1969 and gave me the opportunity to travel throughout the Philippines in the quest for priestly vocations. For almost three years on recruitment work, I conducted spiritual retreats and days of recollection for students in the high schools and colleges throughout the Philippines. I traveled to the far northern cities of Tuguegarao in the province of Cagayan and to Tarlac in Ilocos Norte. My work brought me to the other provinces in Luzon. Many of my travels took me through the cities and towns of the Visayan Islands, like Cebu, Bohol, Negros Oriental and Occidental and throughout the length and breadth of Leyte even to the place where General MacArthur wadded on shore to fulfill his promise of "I shall return!" And of course, I visited the many towns in the southern provinces of Mindanao, traveling even to the outer limits of Philippine territory, to the City of Puerto Princesa on the Island of Palawan.

In these places, I conducted special days of spiritual retreat and test taking for the young men of college age who showed an interest in the priesthood. I was looking for bright, young and dedicated men to enter the seminary and eventually persevere through eight years or more of study and prayer to the day of their Ordination. And during the course of three years recruitment, I was able to provide a few good candidates for the Passionist Congregation, who were eventually ordained priests.

Upon completion of my three year's tour, I returned to the States where I visited with my family and friends and then went off to live in a House of Prayer in Morris Town, New Jersey. I remained in this Pentecostal House of Prayer for one month. Like a dried sponge, I soaked up the spiritual environment of the place and felt myself become renewed and strengthened for the task ahead. Now I was ready to return to the Philippines once more. Little did I realize how dramatic the next three years would be and how my life would be changed forever.

A month later, I sat alone in the small chapel of the Retreat House at Calumpang. I was completing a half hour of prayer and meditation before meeting with the religious superior, Fr. Harold Stout. He had decided to give me a choice between two different assignments. It was quite unusual for him to do such a thing. I could choose to be pastor of the suburban parish of Lagao, just outside the city limits of General Santos and situated in a very quiet place. There, I knew quite a few of the parishioners living near the main church. I had previously been assigned there temporarily for a few weeks to help the ailing pastor, Father Jerome Ryan, cover several barrios located some distance from the main church. There I celebrated Mass and conferred the sacrament of Baptism on scores of children during the annual fiestas. I really liked the people and the location of the parish with all its far flung barrios. The work could use up the time, energy and resources of several priests.

Or, I could choose to be assigned a hundred miles up the Western coast of Mindanao to a parish called Milbuk. This was the only parish that was situated outside of the Province of South Cotabato. Milbuk was a logging camp on the shores of the Celebes Sea. The logging concession belonged to the American Company of Weyerhaeuser Lumber. There were about 5,000 people living in and near the logging camp, 90% of whom were Catholic. Milbuk was part of the Town of Palimbang. Most of the population throughout the municipality was Muslim.

I remember listening to the stories about Milbuk told by the former parish priest, Father Hyacinth Welka. He had worked hard to develop and expand the Catholic Community High School of 400 students. He was an easy-going priest who fit in well with the laid back character of the Filipino people. Hyacinth was a people-person who would spend hours just being with his people and listening to their stories.

Then it happened. A dozen Christian families living in a small farming village, 12 kilometers from Milbuk, were attacked early one morning. The attackers were believed to be Muslim mercenaries, sent by Datu Druz Ali, the Mayor of the Municipality of Palimbang, to avenge the death of his nephew. Seven people were killed in the village. Their bodies were horribly mutilated. Several others were wounded. The rest of the small village fled into the nearby forest while several of the community ran ahead to Milbuk for help. The people of the barrio approached the parish priest for assistance. Father Hyacinth gathered several men from the local militia who quickly armed themselves and rode with the priest to the village. Upon his arrival, Father Hy parked the jeep in the center of the village. He observed the dead strewn here and there like discarded cardboard boxes. He reached down to grab at a pile of clothes and an arm fell out onto the ground. Some of the people had been butchered. Then, out of the jungle, several men appeared, cautiously approaching the priest and looking about for any attackers. Once the word got out that the priest was there, the few remaining people streamed into the village and surrounded him.

There was little that Father Hy could do but to console the families and bury their dead. He could speak with the Mayor of Palimbang, who was also the Imam (religious leader) of the town Mosque. Hyacinth wasn't convinced that anything he had to say would move the Mayor to resolve the dispute, even though this was his role as a Datu (Chief) among his people. Hy had a suspicion that perhaps the Mayor was behind this incident or at the very least knew about what had happened and maybe had even sanctioned it. Nevertheless, he would visit the Mayor's office the next day after the funerals and address the people's complaint with the Mayor himself.

The settlers didn't wait for the mayor's intervention. They believed that nothing would be done anyway. Like the past incidents of a year ago when a few settlers had been killed along the road and others mysteriously disappeared. The mayor did nothing. The incident at the village of Bulan was blatant and deliberate. The attackers simply rode into the settlement and opened fire on the inhabitants. Something had to be done now.

These settlers had friends and family living in Surallah, South Cotabato who belonged to a vigilante group who called themselves "ilaga" or rats in Hiligaynon. The "ilaga" were successful in combating terrorist-like efforts of some Muslims in their area who attempted to drive them from their lands. The government used these "ilaga" to supplement government troops sent into the area to control the uprising of rebel Muslim groups in the various towns and provinces. The AFP (Armed Forces of the Philippines) would supply weapons and ammunition to these paramilitary groups. The weapons had been "loaned" to the Philippines by the United States through J.U.S.M.A.G. (Joint U.S. Military Advisory Group). The weapons were Springfield and Garand (M-1) rifles that had been heavily greased, crated and stored for decades in U.S. warehouses.

The weapons were now ready to be used again in another war. These groups of "ilaga" quickly multiplied throughout North and South Cotabato forcing the Muslims to form their own roving bands of armed marauders that were called "the blackshirts".

The "ilagas" arrived at Milbuk a week later and secretly took up residence in the homes of the loggers. Father Hyacinth did not approve of the ilagas' killing ways but he thought that maybe a show of force might help the situation by convincing the Muslim killers that any further incursions and attacks would only intensify the conflict. This didn't work out. The "ilaga" made furtive forays into the outlying areas in and around the Muslim villages to identify the Muslim "policemen" who had attacked the farming village. A clash between the "ilaga" and the "policemen" erupted only a few kilometers from the Town of Palimbang itself. The Muslims suffered many casualties. It was only then that the Mayor stepped in to mediate a cease fire and become the great negotiator to the conflict. The Mayor used his office and prestige to bring a halt to the conflict. It was only learned later that the Mayor of Palimbang was the #2 man in charge of the local "blackshirts".

Land grabbing and revenge is what this conflict was all about. The settlers had purchased the land from its Muslim "owners" only to be told that the "real" owners would also need to be paid for the land. The settlers were not willing to pay again. There was no office in the township that recorded titles and deeds to land. Titles to land were unknown among the Muslims. Land holdings stayed within families for generations. Families just knew where their land began and ended. Any exchange or outright sale of land was made with a verbal agreement, usually with one of the local datus (community leaders).

This conflict lasted from beginning to end for about two years. The final stage of open fighting lasted for three months but had a profound influence upon the whole township, its people and its industry. At its worst, the fighting affected the everyday operations of the logging company. Whole mountain areas of the municipality were not accessible due to the unrest. Muslim men, who had worked in the veneer mill and in the mountains cutting down the trees, were forced out of their "well-paying" jobs because of the pressure applied by their Christian co-workers. What a disruption!

There were no Muslims at all working for the Weyerhaeuser Logging Company. There were no Muslim students attending classes at the Milbuk Notre Dame High School. It was evident that I needed to focus my work on restoring the lost harmony among the people of this community and to enable both cultures to appreciate one another. What an enormous task! And yet, in spite of these inherent problems of the assignment, I chose Milbuk!

Troubling Choice: (Top) Church, the Milbuk Notre Dame
High School, Clinic and Loggers Housing Compound.
(Bottom) Logging Company Veneer Mill and Log Pond.

# CHAPTER 5

# A Day in the Life

My bedroom was small and simple much like the monastic cell I had occupied for ten years before coming to the Philippines. A plain desk and chair stood in the space near the windows facing the street. A single bed lay flush against the right side of the room. There was a clothes closet on the left side as you entered the doorway. Straight ahead a double window clothed in simple drapes looked out at the fat, cylindrical water tower that collected the rain for drinking and cooking. The Notre Dame High School building was only thirty-five feet away. The room spoke of austerity and the simple life. It also spoke loudly of loneliness. The date was August the 17th, 1972, my first day in the town of Milbuk, an isolated logging camp, situated on the shores of the Celebes Sea in the Muslim Province of Sultan Kudarat, Mindanao. This mission assignment was unlike anything I had experienced before.

Each night I lay in the still darkness of my "cell" staring motionless at the ceiling. Now and again, a three inch chameleon or "gecko" would scamper across the ceiling and down the wall searching out insects. My cat preferred the wide open spaces of the living room area on the second floor of the convento just outside my bedroom. Here a dozen or more chameleons could be counted at one time scurrying up the walls and across the ceiling, running after elusive flying insects. The cat would sit motionless in the dark shadows of the room and patiently wait for one of the chameleons to lose its foothold on the ceiling and come crashing to the floor. The "gecko" would hardly have time to recover from the stunned trauma of the fall, when the cat would spring from its hiding place and within seconds cover the chameleon with its paw. Having procured this tasty snack with such cunning, the cat would seize the gecko with its teeth and with a rapid gyration of its jaws render the chameleon lifeless.

The cat now lay relaxed and pleased on the throw rug of the living room as it casually chewed and gnawed away at the reptile. Soon the gecko would be no more, disappearing within the cavern of the cat's stomach. The feline glanced up once again at the ceiling observing other potential prey then slinked off to its favorite hiding place, patiently listening for the tell-tale splat of another careless chameleon. This was a perfect habitat of sorts in which the chameleons kept down the number of insects in the house, especially the mosquitoes and where the cat played an important role in limiting the population of chameleons. It all worked out and I approved.

During the long evening hours, I would catch up on the international news of the day on the "Voice of America" from the short-wave radio on my desk. It was early one night, that I heard the shocking news. President Ferdinand Marcos had declared Martial Law throughout the Philippines. The date was September 23, 1972. The thought occurred to me in the silence, "What will ever happen to the people of this country now? If lawlessness has already caused such problems, how much more active will the adversaries of the Government be now?" I did not fear this unknown but rather perversely welcomed the inevitability of the conflict as an opportunity for adventure. My hand reached over to the table by the bed and I turned off the radio. The glass of Christian Brothers' Mass wine that I drank just a half hour ago was finally taking effect. The burgundy taste of the wine still lingered in my mouth. My eyes closed and my mind drifted into a peaceful dream mode that brought relaxation to my body. This was another night alone…another night in silence.

Early in the morning, upon rising, I would gaze out of the screened living room windows toward the vastness of the Celebes Sea, listening to the gentle laps of water at the beach's edge. Over to my right was a cropping of large mangrove trees that you could walk to over the coral reef at low tide. This coral reef extended out for more than 300 meters. The reef was a buffer that protected the camp from any strong waves that might arise during a storm. Large unevenly shaped boulders measuring five to six feet in width, had been carefully placed end to end on one another along the whole length of the shore, forming an eight to ten foot high sea wall directly in front of the supervisors' houses that lined the shore and in front of the High School. These boulders had been dynamited and unearthed from the mountains during logging road construction A small area of beach was left open in front of the priest's convento to form a landing for the pump-boat or banca. The priest's convento was built on concrete posts that elevated the whole structure almost 3 feet off the ground. Any unusual high tide or flooding would hardly touch the wooden structure of the building.

Four other people lived in the convento with me. Rudy Alameida was the school treasurer, book keeper and secretary. He was a single man in his late twenties, thin and somewhat gaunt. Rudy performed all his tasks with a great deal of fastidiousness. He made sure that the three high school boys who lived downstairs with him were likewise diligent in performing their duties. The three students (15-16 years of age) were "scholars" (working students) at Notre Dame. Part of the agreement to their living at the convento was to keep it clean and orderly inside and out. For this they received a free education, board and room.

For the first nine months of my stay in Milbuk, I lived and labored alone in this far off, isolated place. At exactly 6:00 A.M. each morning, I would exit the rear door of the convento and walk the 300 meters to the parish church to prepare for the daily celebration of Mass at 6:30 A.M. The church was dedicated to the Blessed Virgin Mary and called Our Lady of Perpetual Help. There would be about a dozen women attending the Mass. Afterwards, I would spend the next half hour in prayer and meditation. The silence of the church was interrupted only by the singing of the Philippine National Anthem and the saluting of the Flag by the more than 400 students assembled in lines before the front entrance of the Notre Dame High School. Morning classes started at 7:15 A.M., ending at 11:30 A.M. The students would go home for lunch and siesta, returning at 1:00 P.M for the afternoon session. After my meditation and breakfast, I would walk the short distance to the High School next door.

It takes money to run a high school even in this back water of a town in a third world country. Each student was charged tuition to be educated at the Notre Dame High School. The public high school was far away in the municipal town of Palimbang itself, some 12 kilometers away. Filipinos prize education. The families make the sacrifice to send their children to school. The bishop of the diocese did not support the Notre Dame Catholic schools. Each parish priest who ran a high school was obliged to raise tuition from the students' families in order to make it work. At the beginning of each quarter of the school year, I would speak to the parents of the students at the end of the Sunday Mass and rally them to make their tuition payments on time. Rudy would remind me when the tuition payments were low or tardy. Luckily, we made enough to pay the teachers that year. My goal was to raise the teachers' salaries to compensate for the fine work they were doing. I couldn't believe how little salary they received. Some teachers hadn't had a raise in salary for years.

When I first toured the school property, what I saw were buildings with peeling paint, decaying classroom walls, and rotting floor boards. This was definitely a dangerous place for children to be educated. The main school building was "L" shaped with a two story wooden structure at the center and a series of one story attached classrooms. There were several other unattached classrooms nearby. All in all, there were 10 classrooms. Forty to fifty students occupied each classroom. It was amazing how attentive the students were and how little noise emanated from such a large student body. This of course changed quickly during the recreation period, when the whole campus was transformed into a cheering, screaming mass of children, playing softball or a heated game of basketball. I was so proud of the respect and orderliness of the students. This was, no doubt, due to the teaching staff and to the parents who provided the proper guidance.

The buildings were finally repaired, renovated and painted during my first year at Milbuk. It had taken me almost six months of pleading and negotiating with the company manager, before Mr. Roberts finally approved all the materials needed for the repairs. He sent his chief engineer to tour the facility and take down the specifics of all that was needed for the repair and renovation of the school. It was considerable. I had volunteered to pay for the labor if the company could supply the materials. The manager was true to his word. All shapes and sizes of lumber were ordered. Finished pieces of plywood from the veneer mill were given to replace the ones destroyed by the termites and other wood eating insects endemic to the country. Over a hundred gallons of paint were made available to spruce up the buildings and to create a pleasant and safe atmosphere for the children of the loggers.

My role at the Notre Dame High School was to hire new teachers, dismiss those who were remiss in their duties, pay the salaries of the teachers and maintain the upkeep of the buildings. Any matters pertaining to curriculum and day to day operations were left to the Principal, Mr. Ricardo Tranco and later to his successor, Mrs. Lourdes Gaviola. Actually, the Principal and I were responsible for the hiring and firing of personnel. Together we interviewed prospective candidates and made decisions on their fitness. I made it my habit to visit the high school each day to make myself available to the Principal, teachers and students.

A Day in the Life: (Top) Fr. Art and parishioners on a trip to Wasag Log Depot by Weyerhaeuser launch.

(Lower left: Fr. Art and Fr. Hyacinth celebrating Holy Mass for the 1974 Graduating Class of Notre Dame.

(Lower right): The Notre Dame H.S. teaching staff enjoying a picnic and swim near the mangroves.

# CHAPTER 6

## *A View from the Top*

O ne of my favorite 'things to do' during my free time was to ride the light weight motorcycle (trail bike) up the mountain hill overlooking the logging camp. The hill was hardly a mountain, standing about 250-300 feet above sea level. The clearing gave me a good view of the whole town. The Celebes Sea stretched west to the Island of Jolo, 240 miles away, the center of the Muslim secessionist group, the Moro Nationalist Liberation Front (MNLF). The Island of Basilan lay northeast of the Jolo archipelago, only 150 miles west of Milbuk. Many of the loggers had previously worked for the Basilan Logging Company, cutting down the abundant forests and preparing the logs for shipment to Japan and other nations. About 1968, Weyerhaeuser Logging Company took over the franchise from the former Basilan Logging Company and decided to concentrate all its logging energies in Milbuk since trouble with the Muslim separatists made it difficult for them to remain in Basilan.

As I strained my eyes across the vastness of the Celebes Sea, I could see nothing in the distance, only the outline of the horizon where sky meets sea some 36 miles away. On certain nights, "pump boats" (motorized bancas) or specially equipped speed boats would arrive from Jolo or from the Island of Basilan to a village only 4-5 kilometers away, called Kulong-Kulong. Here, the boats would unload smuggled goods, weapons and ammunition. At night, whenever I looked from the screened porch of the priest's house (convento), I could see the light of the large lantern that was hung out on the beach in front of the barrio of Kulong-Kulong. This village was on a point of land that jutted out into the Celebes Sea. Nobody interfered with this business done in the dark. The curiosity was enormous among the people but nobody wanted to risk their life to satisfy the itch to know.

Milbuk itself lay below nakedly open to the eye. There were no groves of coconuts to shield the industrial complex of the logging mill. Only a sparse number of trees were sprinkled among the rows of single storied homes (bungalows) within the living area of the camp. There were more than two hundred and fifty of these houses neatly arranged in double clustered rows with narrow streets intersecting each cluster. Before Weyerhaeuser came to develop the logging concession, the land which the town of Milbuk occupied was formerly a marshland, covered with mangrove trees, but now filled in with the soil from the nearby hills. The logging camp lay over a 66 acre swatch of land (about the size of 50 football fields) divided into two sections, the living area or camp and the mill complex. The living area encompassed the homes, schools, medical clinic, church and recreational facilities. The logging mill complex itself included the power plant, saw mill, the veneer factory, maintenance buildings and the log pond. And then there was the airfield, which was situated south of the Veneer Mill Complex, about a kilometer and a half distance away. The Company boasted two airplanes which they sorely needed for the transport of needed parts and supplies for the large fleet of trucks and Mill machinery. And of course, the logging supervisors needed access to the main airport in Davao in order to maintain contact with its main office in the Philippines.

Milbuk was Weyerhaeuser's chief operating area for the export of Philippine mahogany and the manufacture of "veneer", the inner core of finished plywood. Weyerhaeuser was no fly-by-night operation but a well-planned and organized exploitation of one of the Philippines most valuable resources, its lumber. "Lauan" is the largest internationally traded tropical hardwood product in the world. Lauan plywood is used for the facing of interior doors, for the backing of wood and faux-wood paneling, for the interior walls of truck bodies, RVs and trailers, shipping containers, sub flooring, movie and theater set construction, cabinet interiors and backing, furniture backing and drawers, picture frame backing and crafts. You get the idea. Look around your house today and there are literally dozens of products made from Lauan.

Renewable resource that it is, there was hardly any effort at reforestation. Lauan production began in earnest in the 1930s when Japanese logging companies began targeting the forests of the Philippines. The Weyerhaeuser Company picked up an early logging franchise during this period also. Other U.S. companies saw the benefits in land acquisition such as Dole and Del Monte for the production of pineapples and Firestone for the growing of rubber trees.

With the advent of Japanese hostilities in 1941, the Second World War provided some respite for the abundant forests. However, it was the development of a new method of making plywood that doomed the forests of the Philippines. This method used a rotary blade and turned the logs laterally (like a roll of paper towels), rather than slicing them side-to-side. This allowed the loggers to target all the large trees in the forests. The time and the money spent in creating the hundreds of miles of roads through the virgin forests of Mindanao were well worth the effort. The giant land moving machines had cut into the jungles and carved out the roads that would bring the bounty of logs to the mill.

Some logs were set aside in the huge pond and fastened together to be hauled by barges to waiting ships in the harbor. Other logs were removed from the log pond and placed onto a conveyer that brought the mahogany logs into the cutting machines. Here the logs were stripped of bark, shaped by the rotary blades and sliced into thin layers. These thin layers of lauan were further cut into uniform, pieces of veneer and brought together into sections for gluing. The whole process was fascinating. Both the logs and veneer were shipped to foreign ports.

The ones who suffered directly from the logging operations were the mountain natives, the Manobos, indigenous inhabitants of the forests. They never had a voice in the matter. Without complaint, they would move their village from place to place like nomads, whenever the noise and denuding of the forests drew near. And with the felling of the trees came the destruction of the "ecosystem". The forest animals on which the Manobos relied for food fled before the onslaught of the machines. The water sources became contaminated. The top soil for subsistence farming was quickly washed away by the rains, since there were few trees left standing. Indigenous peoples living in the countries of Southeast Asia have been severely impacted by the wood export industry and so have the rainforests of these countries.

Sitting on my trail bike and looking south from my lofty perch, I could view the flat expanse of coastal land covered by plantations of coconut trees reaching from the edges of the sandy beaches to the low-lying hills of the mountains. Beneath the branches of the coconut groves lay the mysterious, hidden villages of the Muslims.

Copra, a product of the coconut palm, was the chief cash crop all along the coast of Mindanao. From Milbuk, traveling south to the mouth of Sarangani Bay, a distance of 65 miles, there was a continuous forest of coconut groves and plantations, both large and small. Often, when passing through areas in which coconuts were being harvested, one could stop and gaze upon the activities of the workers. It was like a circus with its high wire acts. You could see slender, taut, muscular and tawny young men, barefoot and wearing only shorts, scamper up the high branchless, leaning trunks of coconut trees to heights of 50 and 60 feet, some even rising to 80 feet. Armed with a single curved knife, they would surgically sever the umbilical like cord attached to a bunch of coconuts from the topmost crown of the tree. A low, base-like boom echoed repeatedly throughout the plantation as coconut after coconut fell heavily to the ground below. There is no safety net for these acrobats. As soon as they had cleared a tree of fruit, these athletes of the palms hastily descended the slender, ringed trunk and quickly scaled another leaning tower of coconuts.

Once the coconuts had been cut down from the trees, the workers below gathered them up in wooden push carts and dragged them to large open spaces near the shore or along the side of the plantation where each mature nut was cut in half by the blade of a sharp bolo knife (machete). The halved coconuts were then spread over the wide open ground exposing the white meat of each nut to the air and sun. This initial process of drying lasted for several days. Close by the open space, fire pits were dug and filled with the husks of the coconut, the thick fibrous covering that surrounds the familiar single-seeded nut. The burning husks become like glowing embers of charcoal, creating a kiln for drying the meat. A grid is placed over the fire pit, on which the halved nuts are placed. A simple covering, usually a sheet of corrugated iron is set up over the kiln to protect the meat of the coconut from rain. The shield also helps to radiate the heat down to the meat to hasten the drying process. The meat is made up of 50% water and 30-40% oil. Well dried copra will contain only 4-5% of moisture and about 68% oil. The most valuable part of the coconut is the "copra", namely the dried section of the coconut's meat, valuable for the oil extracted from it. It takes 30 coconuts to obtain 10 pounds of copra (4.5Kg.). The Philippines is the leader in the production of copra.

What I remembered best is the smell that was emitted from the kiln during the drying of the coconut meat. The aroma is somewhat sweet and quite distinct. The experience always brings pleasant memories and sensations much like the smell of pine needles in a forest.

It's no wonder that the coastline along this side of Mindanao was so heavily forested with coconut trees. Coconut palms flourish best close to the sea on low lying areas a few feet above high water and where there is circulating groundwater and ample rain fall. It takes 15 years for a tree to reach full bearing. When it does, a coconut palm can yield up to 100 nuts a year, even though 50 nuts a year is considered good. Fruits require a year to ripen. Yields continue profitably until trees are about 50 years old. Plantations such as I view from my vantage point on this hill contain thousands of coconut palms.

I next turned my gaze to the north beyond the camp. The main road ran straight along the coast line from Milbuk to Palimbang, the center of the municipal government of the township. The road was invisible beneath the sheltering palm trees that stood like military sentinels all along the way. The company serviced the road each month by sending out road graders to smooth out the bumps and humps created by the logging trucks and the almost daily deluge of rain.

The sight of the road reminded me of my first encounter with the Muslim Mayor of Palimbang, Datu Druz Ali. The meeting took place six months after my arrival in Milbuk. I had planned this trip for several weeks and was anxious to insure that my encounter with this man would be successful. It was evident that I would need someone who knew the Mayor well and would serve as my assistant if there were need of an interpreter. I discussed my plan with members of the parish. There was no doubt in their minds that George Valencia was the man for the job.

George worked for the lumber company as a trouble shooter and public relations representative. He spoke Maguindanao, the chief dialect spoken by almost all the Muslims in Mindanao. George could also communicate with the Manobo tribes in their own language, though not as well. He was a college graduate, a single man of about 32 years of age, born in Cagayan de Oro, in the northern Mindanao province of Misamis Oriental. He was a product of the Jesuit College there. The Province boasted of several large logging companies which George no doubt knew about, one of which was Weyerhaeuser. Friendliness was his middle name and this trait was disarming to most people especially the women. He could really engage people in conversation. His role in the Company was to inform the various communities of scheduled logging operations in their vicinity. Like a politician, he would convince the leaders of the village communities of the benefits that the company was bringing to them by logging. Of course, the barrio captains and datus of the various villages were only interested in what the company would give to them personally. Gifts would be offered to keep the leaders happy. Some of the inhabitants would even be given temporary jobs to satisfy them.

The day of the appointment with Mayor Ali was April the 11th, 1973. I had celebrated Holy Mass for the small community of women and after a brief period of meditation, returned to the convent. George Valencia was already waiting and joined me for breakfast. After quickly eating cold fried eggs, rice and a cup of coffee, we descended the stairs and boarded the parish jeep. The vehicle was not all that reliable, but there was no other way of getting there except by public transportation. That meant sitting in an open jeepney with up to eight other people, with the prospect of being crushed like a sardine and shaken to death over a washboard road.

After navigating the bumps and holes for thirty five minutes, we turned left off the main logging road and down a narrow dirt road that ran through sparsely treed fields. There were no houses to be seen as we traveled this lonely stretch of road for about a ½ of a kilometer. Then up ahead could be seen the small group of homes huddled together along the left side of the road extending for about 300 meters. These were the homes of the few Christian families living in the town of Palimbang, the municipal seat of government. Across the street from this group of homes was the small wooden chapel or church where Holy Mass was celebrated each month for the members. The church held no more than 40 people. There were eight rough-hewn wooden benches running horizontally down the body of the chapel divided in two equal groups with a small middle aisle.

From the front door of the chapel you could clearly view the wide spacious plaza that opened up to a sandy beach overlooking the Celebes Sea. The Catholic chapel was just off the fringe of this plaza on the far upper left corner as you looked out to sea. There, to the far right, loomed a large and beautiful Mosque that covered half an acre of land. The Mosque was close by the shore. Up from the Mosque, across a narrow road, stood the large one story municipal building housing the Mayor's Office. The building was built on an elevated piece of land. A wide majestic stairway led to the main entrance of the municipal building. It surprised me how big and well-built the municipal building was for such a small town and a sleepy one at that.

My presence in Palimbang on this day was to meet the man that so many people talked about in whispers. Mayor Ali was a power in the township. He was also the imam (or prayer leader and teacher) at the Mosque and exerted much influence among his Muslim brothers because of his position. There were many rumors about this man and the stories were not flattering. Of course, the tales I heard were from the Christians not from other Muslims. Now I planned to see for myself what kind of man this was.

There were knots of people talking quietly on the grassy knoll that flowed down from the edge of the stairs that led inside the Municipal building. George and I made our way through the small crowd of people loitering on the steps at the entrance to the building. There was a small foyer just past the main doors. The entrance to the Mayor's office lay just to the left inside the foyer. A policeman watched closely as each person entered the double-door entrance way.

As we passed through the doorway we found ourselves in a very large hall that ran nearly the length and width of the building itself. All around the room, there were built-in benches. To our amazement all the benches were filled with men dressed up in their Muslim finery. There must have been close to 60 men waiting there, sitting quietly and occasionally whispering something to the person beside them. For all the people present in this hall, there was hardly any noise, just a low hum of conversation. Were they all waiting to speak with the Mayor? Was the Mayor about to announce some earth shattering news or give away thousands of pesos?

An aide to the Mayor approached George and me respectfully and escorted us across the hall as the eyes of each person fell upon us.

"What is the nature of your visit?" the aide inquired of George in Maguindanao.

George replied, "The new Catholic Priest of Milbuk wants the privilege of introducing himself to the Honorable Mayor and to greet him."

There, near the far corner of the hall was a large, mahogany colored executive sized desk that had been placed horizontally along the side of the wall. Behind the desk, Mayor Druz Ali was dispensing wisdom, favors, orders and permission. He was a well-dressed man in typical white Muslim attire, looking more like a religious cleric than a Mayor. There were no women in the room or around the building. This was an all-male affair. It appeared to me that Mayor Ali was exercising his duties of office like an ancient Muslim Sultan holding court before his subjects. Needless to say, I was quite impressed and a bit intimidated.

The traditional political structure of Filipino Muslim society focused on a Sultan who reigned as both a secular and a religious leader and whose authority was sanctioned by the Koran. Mayor Ali was not a Sultan but he did incorporate into his personage an authority that was both secular and religious. The Mayor was the Imam or religious cleric and leader of the large Mosque that stood predominant in the town square of Palimbang. Mayor Ali was the "Datu of the datus". The "datus" were communal leaders who measured power not by their holdings in landed wealth but by the numbers of their followers. This was most important in the plans and machinations of this man in his dealings with the people of the Township. In return for tribute and labor, the Datu provided aid in emergencies and advocacy in disputes with followers of another datu or among members of the community. Thus, through his "agama" or court…an informal dispute-settling session…the Mayor as the chief Datu became the tool for the smooth functioning of Muslim society. He was a powerful authority figure. God forbid, that someone, anyone should insult or disrespect Mayor Ali. It was tradition that the Datu might demand revenge ("maratabat") for the death of a follower or upon injury to his pride or honor.

The datus continue today to play a central and dominant role in Muslim society in the Philippines. In Muslim Mindanao, the datus still administer the "sharia" or sacred Islamic law through the "agama" or court. The Mayor was all about achieving the goal of expanding his circle of followers and accumulating wealth in the process. How much of this wealth, if any, was used to provide aid, employment and protection for his less fortunate constituents is anybody's guess.

I stood smiling but silent before the desk of the Mayor. His aide spoke quietly into the ear of the seated "Sultan" as the Mayor stared at me, the priest of Milbuk, intently. He rose slowly from his chair. I introduced myself and offered my hand in greeting, "Your Honor, my name is Father Art Amaral and I am so pleased to meet you. I hope that our meeting today will benefit all our people".

The Mayor thanked me without smiling. He was not a tall man. He was of average height and build for a Filipino. His eyes were focused and betrayed intelligence and cunning that would later be clearly in evidence. Mayor Ali sat down again on his "throne" and I was invited to be seated by the side of his desk.

The Mayor spoke to me, "How can I help you, Father?"

"I only have one request, Mayor", I answered. "I would like to suggest that you and I bring our two peoples together in a "Prayer for Peace and Reconciliation" meeting. We could hold this Prayer meeting at one of the Muslim barrios close to Milbuk. There is a village only a kilometer or so to the north along the main logging road. Do you know of this place?"

"Yes, I know of the place", the Mayor replied with interest.

I continued, "I want to have this communal prayer meeting in the hope of healing the wounds of the past two years. Both your people and mine have suffered greatly and too many have been killed for nothing. I want you to know, Mayor that I intend to invite any Muslim student who wishes to attend the Notre Dame High School to apply for the coming school year. These students will be offered scholarships. This means free tuition and books. I feel that it is so important for Muslims and Christians to live together in peace and harmony. If our peoples see that you and I support this project, they will attempt to live once more in peace with one another". I was speaking to the Mayor as Imam and religious leader of his people, not as the Mayor of Palimbang.

However, the Mayor was thinking of the priest's suggestion and plan, not as a religious leader but as a politician.

Deliberately, a slight smile appeared on the Mayor's face and he replied, "Father Art, I welcome your suggestion. Let me meet with my aides and plan what date and time would be convenient for both of us. The place you mentioned would serve our purposes well. Thank you for coming to me. I would appreciate it if you kept me informed of any problems that you may have. I will send a message to you through one of my aides concerning the date of this meeting."

And with that I rose from my chair and graciously thanked the Mayor with a firm handshake. I swung around military like and walked happily out of the hall, the smile on my face broadening as I thought how well the meeting went.

View from the Top: (Top) Weyerhaeuser Veneer Mill Complex and Log Pond looking out on Milbuk Bay. (Lower Left) Power Plant and "Campo Dos" with road leading south to Barrio Malunggay and the airport.

(Lower Right) The main housing site or "Campo Uno" looking out on the Celebes Sea with a Japanese logging boat anchored off shore awaiting the transfer of logs and veneer.

# CHAPTER 7

# *Help Wanted*

To this day, I don't know how any of my fellow priests who preceded me could have worked for so many years alone in a parish without any assistance from other like-minded religious. On several former assignments, I had been privileged to work with a missionary group of religious Sisters who were called the Oblate Sisters of Notre Dame, founded about sixty years ago by an Oblate missionary priest from Rhode Island. These religious Sisters were assigned to various parishes throughout the Provinces of North and South Cotabato. They conducted programs of religious instruction for both the children and the adults of the parish, preparing them for the sacraments of Penance, Holy Communion and Matrimony. They ran seminars for the adult parishioners to enliven their faith and assisted the parish priest whenever he would celebrate the Mass and Sacraments in the outlying villages, especially during the times of fiesta. Pastors were indeed fortunate to have such Sisters as associates in their work.

After six months at Milbuk, I began to plan for such assistance in this parish. The work was too great for just one person. With this in mind, I journeyed to Cotabato City and made an appointment with the Superior of the Oblate Sisters at their motherhouse in Tamontaka, a locale just outside Cotabato City.

It was March of 1973, when I arrived at the motherhouse of the Oblate Sisters to explain the needs of the parish. I was warmly welcomed. Mother Superior and two of her consultants sat down with me as I described the parish of Milbuk and laid out my plans for the revitalization of this isolated community. After giving a thorough presentation, they asked me numerous questions especially how I planned to accommodate any Sisters that might be assigned there. They gave me a tour of the facility and then led me into their dining hall. There, crowded around two long tables were a group of about 15 young women all dressed in the garb of the Oblate Sisters. These young ladies were novices, only weeks away from their day of profession. What I had explained to Mother Superior and her consultants, so I again described to the Novices concerning the many challenges I faced.

"There is a High School of almost 500 students. I need a trained religious Sister to review, renew and supervise the religious education of the student body. There is a large elementary school within the logging camp filled with almost a 1000 students in need of catechesis to prepare them for the sacraments of Penance and Holy Communion."

I continued.

*"The parish of Milbuk embraces the whole township of Palimbang that has a population of 43,000 people. There are more than 30 barrios/sitios (large and small villages) throughout the township. It is true that the township is predominantly Muslim. However, there are enclaves of Christians living not only at Milbuk but in at least five other sizeable communities. There must be at least 7-8000 Christians living in the parish and most of them live within a three kilometer radius from the logging camp at Milbuk. I also need someone who can understand and speak Maguindanao. There is a need to foster good relations between the Muslim and Christian communities and to repair the harm done over the past three years during a time of bloody conflict."*

The novices were visibly excited and interested by my presentation, asking many questions. Then one of the young ladies raised her hand and softy replied, "I understand and speak Maguindanao." I replied, "Would you be interested in coming to Milbuk?" Shyly, she glanced at the Mother Superior and said, "Yes, I am interested." Her name was Sister Ana Laurente.

A few weeks later, I received a letter from the Mother Superior saying that one of her consultants would be visiting Milbuk by launch from Cotabato City. Two Sisters arrived in early April to take a tour of the parish. I told them that I would provide a suitable house as a residence for the Sisters and be responsible for their transportation needs to and from Milbuk. Also, I would provide whatever monies they needed for the purchase of food and other necessities. Within two weeks, I received a letter from the Mother Superior saying that three Sisters would be assigned to Milbuk. Details of their departure and arrangements for escorting them to Milbuk would be forthcoming.

In early June of 1973, I met the first Oblate Sisters assigned to Milbuk at the Oblate Sisters' Convent in General Santos City situated on the campus of the Notre Dame of Dadiangas College. Sister Lourdes Abary, the superior of the missionary group introduced herself and then presented the other two members, Sister Elizabeth Veloso and Sister Ana Laurente, the former young novice who said she understood and spoke Maguindanao and was interested in coming to Milbuk. We set out very early the next morning by jeepney (public transportation) and traveled over 65 miles to the town of Maitum, arriving about 2:00 P.M. There, we were able to hire a reliable pump-boat (banca) to take us by sea the rest of the 30 miles to Milbuk. The sea was rather choppy. We did make good time, finally arriving at the dock at Barrio Malunggay, a good sized village adjacent to Milbuk. We walked the final kilometer to the camp, under the curious and watchful stares of the people.

The staff at my house welcomed the Sisters. I brought the Sisters to the spacious and private second floor of my house and showed them the three rooms they could occupy while their own house was being completed. I slept downstairs in one of the vacant rooms that I used for an office. It would take almost another month before the Sisters would be able to move into their new home. Once completed, the one story house would be more than adequate for their needs and comfortable as well. The house was built 20 meters from the shore in front of a wall of logs and boulders. The living room and kitchen windows opened out onto a pleasant view of the Celebes Sea.

How lucky I was to have such wonderful and talented religious women working in the parish. The superior of this small missionary group, Sister Lourdes was an older sister, perhaps in her forties. She was kind hearted and jovial, with an ever ready smile, always with a word of encouragement. The married women of the parish took to her quite readily. She was a good listener and attracted many admirers because of her kindnesses. Sister Elizabeth was an energetic person, with a lively sense of humor and a keen intellect. She was to be my catechist in chief, responsible for guiding and supervising the religious education of this community. Elizabeth loved to teach and conduct seminars among the people. There was a great deal of organization and thought behind everything she did.

And then there was Sister Ana, a soft-spoken and reflective young woman in her early 20's. Her work was to be my liaison with the teachers most of whom were women, to counsel and support them in their work. She was also to act as counselor to the student body, providing them with the opportunity of telling her their troubles and concerns. Sister Ana had another important job within her small community, namely, shopping for food and preparing the meals, which she performed quite well. All in all, this community of Oblate Sisters, possibly the first in this new province of Sultan Kudarat, proved to be a great asset to the parish. The whole community in and around Milbuk seemed to come Alive after only six months of their presence. At the beginning of May, 1974, two of the Sisters from the first group were assigned to other parishes and two new Sisters arrived at Milbuk. The second group of Oblate Sisters arrived from Cotabato City by launch, after having spent two weeks at the Mother House in Tamontaka. At this place and time, all the assembled Sisters met and celebrated their community and spent one week in religious retreat to enliven their spirits and empower themselves to return to their work with missionary zeal.

The three Sisters in this second group were Sisters Helen Molina, Cynthia Barrales and Ana Laurente. Sister Helen was the superior for the group. A rather smallish person, her stature belied her courage and assertiveness. When she spoke, she did so with a quiet authority. People listened to her words since her demeanor was so approachable. She laughed easily and made everyone feel comfortable in her presence. When others spoke, she listened with a sensitivity and compassion that made the person feel that what they said was important, and that they really mattered. Sister Cynthia took over as religious counselor to the students who readily identified with her. She was such good fun. Sister Ana, who now returned for her second year in Milbuk, was now supervising religious instructions and accompanying me to the outlying villages where I celebrated Mass. Sister Ana would translate and interpret my sermons in the prevailing language of the people, either in Tagalog, Cebuano or a combination of both. She was fluent and hardly missed a beat. Her sermons were far more effective than mine.

Help Wanted: (Top) The occasion was the visitation of the Oblates of Notre Dame's Superior General, Sister Rosalinda Ong, to observe the work of the first Sisters assigned to Milbuk. From left to right top: Sister Elizabeth Veloso, Sister Rosalina Ong, and Sister Teresa Abary. Bottom row is Sister Ana Laurente, the newly professed Oblate Sister.

(Bottom photo) Sister Teresa and Sister Ana on a journey to one of the villages of the Manobo tribe.

# CHAPTER 8

# *"Katawhang Lumad"*

On the Island of Mindanao there lived groups of indigenous peoples who were neither Muslim nor Christian. They had lived over a thousand years on these shores but with the arrival of the various migrations of peoples from other islands in the archipelago, these "natives" of Mindanao retreated from the coastal areas into the forests and mountains of Mindanao. These indigenous peoples were later classified into 18 ethno linguistic groups. It was only in 1986, that representatives from fifteen of these various tribes came together as a unified group to address their common grievances to the government. At that time they decided to refer to themselves by a common name that would signify their unity and enable them to address their common grievances as an indigenous people. The name they chose was "Katawhang Lumad" or native (indigenous) peoples. This appellation was a combination of two Cebuano words, since this dialect was the most common language among them besides their own peculiar dialect. The Lumads that inhabit the forests and mountains of the township of Palimbang are the Cotabato Manobo, certainly one of the poorest and most neglected of the tribes.

These people first came to my attention when a sick, Manobo child was brought to the convento by one of the parishioners. She was accompanied by the little girl's mother. I took the mother and child to the doctor at the company's medical clinic and asked him if he could attend to her.

"Hey doc, are you busy today?"

"No, not too many patients today, Father. Come on in."

Dr. Gaviola had been hired by the logging company almost right out of medical school. He was a handsome young man who had some experience in the emergency room of a city hospital. A bright and dedicated doctor, he was all alone in the clinic except for three young women who served as nurse's aides. They were hardly trained in this profession so that most of his day was spent in teaching them the rudiments of nursing. Otherwise, if he didn't spend the time training them, they would be of no use to him when and if the need arose. Doctors of his caliber and intelligence do not last long in these situations. There were no opportunities for growth and learning that comes from conferring with older more experienced doctors in large medical facilities. I was sure that Dr. Gaviola wouldn't last for more than a year or two. And that would be a shame.

Dr. Gaviola and I would talk most days when I would visit the patients in the clinic. The clinic had a large dormitory like room with the capacity for about eight beds. There were never more than two or three patients at any one time in the clinic. Needless to say, the doctor was able to provide the little girl with the medicine to restore her health. I then asked the Manobo woman through an interpreter where she lived. That was the beginning of my work among this aboriginal tribe.

After working with the Manobos for about a year, I proposed a plan for the education of their children. I would establish a home on the campus of Notre Dame High School staffed by two live-in teachers who would act as surrogate moms. They would supervise them in their education at the local public elementary school, located just across the other side of the campus. All their clothes and food would be provided to them free. The parents were enthusiastic and so were the kids.

The Manobo children's home would foster the Manobo culture and language. At the same time, the children would mix and mingle with the local children and learn the ways, culture and language of these people. To this end, I constructed a large two room house measuring 25 by 48 feet. The house was divided into 2 large sections. One room housed the Manobo girls and the other room was a dormitory for the young boys among them. The twenty children were pretty much evenly divided in gender. The boy's room served also as a classroom and a common room during recreation time. The two teachers had a small partitioned room in the girls' quarters where they slept.

Each child was given two sets of clothes. One set was used for school. The second set was used for after school and sleeping. Each morning at about 6:00 A.M., the children would take a bath in the sea nearby. They would return to the yard outside the home and would shower with fresh water, using soap to clean their hair and skin. Then they would dry off and place their school clothes on, clothes that had been washed and hung the previous afternoon. Upon returning from school, the children would remove their school clothes, wash and hang them, then they would all take a bath in the salt water of the Celebes Sea. Upon returning to the yard outside their dormitory, they would shower and cleanse themselves with soap. Within a month, the children's skin was dramatically transformed. The skin disease from the dirt and grime of their existence in the forests was gone. Coupled with the nutritious food that they were given at meal times, the children's very appearances changed. I supplied the food the children needed and the teachers prepared the meals.

My daily schedule demanded that I visit the two teachers who were assigned as surrogate mothers to the 20 Manobo children. The two teachers were on the staff of the Notre Dame High School. Cecilia Ramos taught history and Lisa Alcera was the nutritionist. Their schedule was arranged so that they could cover two of their classes each day and spend the rest of the time monitoring the twenty children who were in school all morning and part of the afternoon. The Manobo children would take an hour and a half break at 11:30 A.M. for lunch and siesta. The two teachers were on hand to feed them and help supervise them at their chores. When I arrived at their house, the children had just returned from school. They came running up to me laughing and full of life. Some of the kids touched me on my arms as I extended my hands to gently pat the tops of their heads. I loved being with the children, watching them play so happily without thoughts of survival.

The Manobo children were all in the first grade, even though their ages ranged from seven to thirteen years. They lived in the mountains with their families who subsisted on root crops, berries, wild deer and pigs. This was the first time anyone of them in their family had ever gone to school. Nobody in the Christian community seemed to care. Manobos were considered by the lowlanders to be stupid, dull people. What could they learn? Dirty, disheveled and ragged looking, these natives simply passed through the community without anybody's notice. They were invisible people. Now you see them...now you don't...disappearing into the shade and darkness of the forests.

I remember the first morning after the children had arrived in the camp to begin their schooling. The date was May 29, 1974. The children's' dormitory had not yet been completed. It would take several more days to finish all the work. In the meantime, the children were sleeping and eating downstairs in the convento using the two vacant rooms that had been offices at an earlier time. I had no use for these rooms since I chose to circulate throughout the village and make myself available to the people. I was not one to sit and wait for someone to approach me for help.

I rose early that morning to celebrate daily Mass at the Church. I showered quickly with cold water, shaved and put on a long white robe, called a "habit", over my t-shirt and khakis, and encircled by waist with a wide leather belt. This was my official dress as a priest and missionary. I descended the stairs and came into the kitchen area to exit the back door of the convento. When I entered the kitchen, the twenty Manobo children were all huddled around the breakfast table about to eat. As soon as they saw me, they broke into shouts and clapping to show their appreciation for being here. I was so surprised at this outbreak of enthusiasm and was quite embarrassed at the show of affection. All that I could mutter was..."Thank you children and have a good breakfast." None of the children understood what I said but they did understand my kindness and love for them. The teacher moms were laughing at my evident embarrassment, seeing a side of me that I rarely showed. After all, I was a take charge kind of guy…a let's get it done now, kind of person. I was not one to wear my feelings on my sleeve except for the occasional anger that flared up when faced with opposition, real or imagined. But there were moments when my softer feelings shone through…this was a moment when I let down my guard.

Six weeks had passed since the children began living and studying on the N.D. Campus. I thought it would be appropriate to hold our first Manobo Fiesta to celebrate the children's presence in Milbuk and also to give their parents an opportunity to see the home in which they lived and the school they attended. The date of the fiesta was scheduled for July 15th, a Monday.

We decorated the Church with large bouquets of Anthuriums and Hibiscus and neatly arranged the flowers in front of the altar, a marble like table of concrete centered in the sanctuary of the Church facing the congregation. The front rows of pews were reserved for the parents and family members of the 20 Manobo children who were residents in the program.

The mission extension plan of providing the Manobo children a place to live and learn was successful so far. I was overjoyed that the children were doing so well. This fiesta was an acknowledgement of the work done by the two High School teachers, Cecilia Ramos and Lisa Alcera and a tribute to the children and their families for believing in the project. This fiesta was the occasion to share in the pride and happiness of these children and to give the families the opportunity of seeing the home in which they lived and the school that they attended. But above all, it was a time to offer praise and thanksgiving to God for blessing this endeavor.

The fiesta was composed of three parts. First there was the show and tell section where the children gave their parents and family members a tour of their home and the school they attended. The second part was the celebration of the Holy Mass in the parish Church. The Mass would be conducted in Tagalog but the Gospel would be read in the language of the Manobos. The two teachers, Cecilia and Lisa had learned the language well enough from the children that they could translate the words of the Gospel into the Manobo dialect so that the children and their families would be able to understand the message of Jesus and what he meant when he said "This is my commandment. Love one another as I have loved you". The third phase of the fiesta was the banquet itself, prepared by the Catholic Women's League, an active group of women in the parish.

On the day of the fiesta, the parents of the children arrived early in the morning. By 9:00 A.M. most of them were present, wandering about the house and enjoying the social atmosphere of the occasion. The women were all dressed up in their native finery. Large round copper rings hung from their ears. Their dresses (skirt and blouse) were a harmonious blend of woven colors. Some of the men wore similar jackets of woven material. These people were poor... extremely so. The clothes they ordinarily wore were old and tattered. Even their best finery worn on this occasion showed its age. But they were happy on this day and so were the children.

The president of the C.W.L. was busy directing the other women, pointing out the place where the banquet tables of food would be placed. She was overseeing the preparation of the food and the hundred and one details for the success of this affair. 'Tita' Barrales was used to supervising and preparing banquets and special meals for the out of town visitors who frequently visited Milbuk's logging facilities and were entertained at the Company's guest house. This affair was quite different.

'Tita' approached me as I strolled slowly on the lawn bordering the home of the Manobo children. "Father, good morning" she respectfully greeted me.

"Good morning to you 'Tita'. I see that all the women's league members are busy preparing the food for the fiesta. I can't tell you how grateful I am to all of you for your help and for the donation of special foods for the occasion. I am very happy that so many of the family members of the children were able to attend this fiesta."

"Yes, Father," she replied, "I've seen the Manobo men and women walking about. But where are the children"?

"Where are the Manobo children"? I repeated. "The children are all over the place. Do you see those three children running about over there? Or look at these two children just passing by us now? Well, they are all Manobo children. Let me introduce you to a few".

"O my", she sighed, somewhat ashamed. "They don't look at all like Manobos". By that remark, 'Tita' meant that the children she was looking at did not fit the image. These children living on the Notre Dame High School campus were healthy looking and cleanly dressed so unlike the thin, wretched creatures she had seen on her way to the market place, straggling along with their parents, dressed shabbily in torn, dirty, and worn out clothing. What a change had occurred in these children over the past two months. What a difference it makes when children can eat nutritious food three times a day and are given the means to clean themselves and wear decent clothing. What a difference indeed.

All during the "show and tell" section of the fiesta, I was busy greeting the parents and taking their pictures with my camera. Then toward 11:00 A.M., I summoned everybody to the Church which was only a stone's throw away from the children's home. I accompanied the parents into the Church. This was the first time that any of these Manobos had entered any Church at all. The Manobos were animists. There were no Manobos in the vicinity of Milbuk who called themselves Christians. Definitely, they were not Muslims either. It didn't seem that the Muslims were at all active in the proselytizing of the Manobos. The two cultural groups appeared to keep their distance from one another.

The parents and the children sat together as families in the front pews. I began the Mass with hymns sung by a small choir of C.W.L women. When it came time for the reading of the Gospel, I took the single type-written sheet of paper prepared by the teachers and began to read the Gospel to the people in the language of the Manobos. I had practiced the reading with the help of Cecilia Ramos, who was chiefly responsible for the translation. The words I spoke to them were from the Holy Gospel according to Luke. This is what the Manobos heard for the first time about the teaching of Jesus Christ.

Jesus said to his disciples: *"To you who hear I say, love your enemies, do good to those who hate you, bless those who curse you, pray for those who mistreat you. To the person who strikes you on one cheek, offer the other one as well, and from the person, who takes your cloak, do not withhold even your tunic."*

*Gasps and murmurs arose from the throats of the Manobos as they listened in amazement...not disbelief.*

*"Give to everyone who asks of you, and from the one who takes what is yours do not demand it back. Do to others as you would have them do to you. For if you love those who love you, what credit is that to you? Even sinners love those who love them." "...But rather, love your enemies and do good to them, and lend expecting nothing back: then your reward will be great and you will be children of the Most High, for he himself is kind to the ungrateful and the wicked. Be merciful, just as your Father is merciful*
Luke 6:27-36

I slowly looked up from the white sheet of paper and gazed over the pews of Manobo men, women and children. Their faces were pleasantly looking back at me. There were no grins or grimaces... just peaceful, relaxed and expectant faces waiting for more words in their language that spoke of so much of what they already believed. The Manobos lived as a community, sharing everything with one another. I spoke no other words in dialect to them. I felt awkward and somewhat stupid that I hadn't attempted to learn their language when I first arrived. What might have been accomplished in that period of time? But. I resolved that I would learn their language and culture, the better to serve them and minister to them in a spiritual way. My work was cut out for me.

After the Mass ended, the whole assembly filed slowly out of the Church and across the lawn to the children's home. At the end of the house, an addition had been built. A long roof had been constructed, the length of which was about thirty feet. It was opened on both sides and covered the outdoor kitchen and dining area that the children used. The tables in the dining area were covered with all kinds of savory dishes. Fish, beef and some pork together with vegetables and rice were plentiful. Some of the C.W.L. women had made special desserts which the Manobos had never tasted. The people were instructed to form a line and plates were given to them. The Catholic Women's League members stood on the other side of the tables and served the dishes to the Manobo men, women and children as they passed along the food laden tables buffet style. Chairs were placed on the lawn just outside the eating area. After the Manobos had been served, then the women of the C.W.L., the other invited guests and I took our turns at the buffet table. Everyone ate well and enjoyed the day.

So this was my family...my community; three Oblate Sisters, the eighteen teachers at the Notre Dame High School, Rudy my secretary and the three convento boys that he supervised, the twenty Manobo children and Dodong my boatman. What a family and a large one at that. How lucky I was!

Katawang Lumad (Tribal Peoples): (Top: L to R Clockwise) Typical Manobo dwelling in the mountains. A young family resting from their labors. One of my young students smiling for the camera. And the panorama of a Manobo village hidden within the canopy of trees.

# CHAPTER 9

# *Necessary Journey*

A s missionaries, we were required by our Congregation to spend a few days with our fellow priests each month to afford us the necessary rest, camaraderie and recreation as well as the opportunity for spiritual renewal. This usually occurred on the first Monday of each month. My mode of travel was by a specially made banca or outrigger canoe quite common along the shores of Mindanao. This motorized banca or "pump boat" enabled me to make the long journey from Milbuk to Calumpang in about 5 ½ to 6 hours. The boat was built for me by my friend Dominic Lacson, a successful business man who ran a large fleet of fishing boats out of Bula, a barrio close by the City of General Santos. I had been the parish priest at this large barrio during my first tour.

I usually left Milbuk in the dark just before 5:00 A.M. for the 160 kilometer journey to Calumpang. As I stepped into the banca at the water's edge behind the convento, I stood upright in the boat and gazed out to the emptiness before me. The Celebes Sea was a magnificent watery sheet of glass. There was no wind and the movement of the sea was almost imperceptible. The coolness of the morning was refreshing, quickly removing any sleep from my eyes. I settled into my place, sitting on a small narrow plank of wood bridging the floor of the banca, toward the front, as the two boatmen pushed the out-rigger from the sandy beach into deeper water. Dodong, my boat man, started the twin Briggs and Stratton engines, first one, then the other. The silence of the morning was momentarily shattered as the boat roared to life. Then with a click of a switch, the gears were engaged, putting the revolving shafts into motion, driving the boat forward by the force of the twin propellers.

The Briggs and Stratton engines enabled the banca to be one of the fastest on the coast or so I was led to believe. The "pump-boats" were long, narrow, out-rigger canoes, 30- 35 feet in length, carved out from a single tree. The framed out, plywood sides of the boat were fastened to the shallow canoe base of the boat's bottom. Three long bamboo poles, 20-25 feet long and five inches in diameter were positioned horizontally across the canoe. These poles were fastened to the banca about six to eight feet apart. The ends of the bamboo poles on both sides were connected to a single bamboo pole, also five inches in diameter and 16-20 feet long. These bamboo poles were so accurately positioned and fastened as to create a delicate balance to the boat as it plowed through the sea or rode over large waves. The stability of the craft was amazing.

There was an art to their manufacture. Only certain people could build one of these fishing boats. The secrets were passed on from father to son and kept within the family. The engines that powered these boats were the simple Briggs and Stratton two-cycle engines that ran on a combination of oil and gasoline. The engines were affixed to the floor of the boat on low pedestals of wood about six to eight feet from the end of the boat. Two long iron shafts attached to the engines rotated through holes in the rear of the boat. Single propellers were attached to each shaft. The shafts themselves were encased within metal piping fixed securely to the floor of the boat. Two stainless steel wires ran from the throttles of the twin engines to a control board located at the middle of the banca, enabling the boat captain to regulate the speed of the boat while seated at the helm. The whole set-up was both simple and ingenious.

Early in the morning, before the sun arose and the wind began tossing up the waters of the sea, a new "pump-boat", not yet water-logged after years of use, would be able to run quick, straight and true as it sliced its way through the glass-like stillness of the sea. Tiny microscopic animal life caused a strange glow to follow the boat's wake as it knifed its way through the smooth gelatin of a sea. What a glorious sight!

Though the sun had yet to rise above the horizon, the sea was hardly dark or foreboding. A mysterious, hidden aura cast a dim, pervasive luminescence over the sea. A cool freshness filled my nostrils and a gentle breeze from the boat's passage through the water enlivened my whole being. How I loved this part of the trip. No matter that this journey would take over five hours to complete, the pleasant experience of the first hour was worth every minute. In an hour's time, the sun would rise and the heat and glare of the day would begin.

It was important that I shield myself from the sun's harmful rays by covering my face and neck with a white cloth. The front of the cloth would drop down slightly over my forehead just above my eyebrows and hang a few inches over the back of my collar. At the same time, my ears and the sides of my face were completely protected. A blue baseball cap with the red letter "B" sewn on the front, secured the cloth in place. A long sleeved white shirt protected my arms and a dark pair of sunglasses completed the ensemble.

I sat squat within the boat idly gazing out to sea or to the shore in the hope of seeing some signs of human life. The sun was beginning to become bright and hot. Dodong had rigged up a covering strung up over a frame of wire cables. This provided a bit of shade from the blistering sun. The breeze from the sea made you forget how dangerous the sun could be if you exposed yourself for any length of time. White people like this missionary priest were prone to skin cancers and sunburns that required medical attention.

The trip to Calumpang soon became tedious after an hour or so. I would gaze at the shoreline, looking for landmarks such as the main barrios that lay along the coast, villages like Kalaong, Kran, Maitum, Kiamba and Maasim. Two of these towns had resident priests, Passionists like myself. There was Fr. John Baptist Maye, who resided at Maasim and Fr Thomas Warden at Kiamba. There was nothing much to see from the boat even if the town had a large population. The ever present forests of coconut and palm trees formed a green barrier screening out any sightseeing. Besides, the banca was running along the coast, staying a kilometer or more from the shore, too far to see anyone or anything clearly.

I sat motionless in the boat for almost four to five hours, unable to conduct any kind of a conversation over the noise of the two engines. No other boat had passed us. The fishermen didn't come out into the Celebes Sea until dark. They would bring along with them a kerosene lamp (what we would call a "hurricane lamp") that they would attach to a pole from their boat, hanging only a foot or so from the water. The brightness of the lamp drew the fish close to the surface where the fisherman's lure would entice them to bite on the hidden hook. At night you could see the gentle sway of lights across the blanket of darkness up and down the coast. Sarangani Bay now came into view. Another thirty kilometers would bring us to our destination.

In the distance, stood the two story Spiritual Center of the Passionist Fathers at a place situated on the banks of Sarangani Bay. The large concrete building was in two sections: the administration section which included the dining room, kitchen and recreation room on the second floor, and the large chapel, meeting room and offices on the first floor. The second large section of the building consisted of 30 single rooms with bathroom facilities in which the retreatants were housed during the spiritual weekend. The property was about 5-6 kilometers from General Santos City and only 2 kilometers from the Makar Wharf, the city's port site for the large cargo ships that transported the logs, pineapples, bananas, rice and other grain to various parts of the Philippines and to the world.

Upon my arrival at Calumpang, I would pick out a room at the Retreat House, meet the other priests who had arrived, grab some lunch in the kitchen and head out to General Santos for some shopping. There were certain items that I needed to buy that were not available at the isolated parish of Milbuk. While in the city, I would stop by to visit the friends I had made while assigned to this parish of Dadiangas (the old name for General Santos City). By 4:30 P.M.,

I would be back at Calumpang in time to take a swim in Sarangani Bay, then return to my room, take a brisk, cold shower and change into clean clothes, ready for supper.

It was a grand gathering of about 20 or more missionaries all seated at a long table in the dining room. After the well prepared and delicious supper, we would all gather in the "recreation room" or sala where we would listen to music, read assorted magazines and tell stories to one another. There was no TV at all. Most of us would be back at our rooms by 9:00 P.M. to catch up on our sleep and to be ready for the activities of the following day.

Most of us would be up and awake by 7:00 A.M. sitting at the dining table eating breakfast. We would all gather in the Chapel downstairs at 9:00 A.M. to celebrate Holy Mass and listen to a prepared Homily by one of our group. Then we would all gather in the meeting room to discuss on-going projects, up-dates on the activities of each parish and any problems that needed immediate remedies. These activities would occupy the whole morning until lunch time. After lunch we were free to play tennis, swim at the shore or just sit around talking to one another. Some would head into the city to shop or visit friends. We would all be present at the evening meal once more to share our companionship with each other before returning to the "isolation" of our parishes.

My companions and I would usually leave Calumpang just before 7:00 A.M., after eating a good breakfast. The "pump-boat" was loaded with supplies that were evenly distributed over the front part of the boat and covered with water resistant tarpaulin to keep out the spray of salt water. We all positioned ourselves to the middle and rear of the boat. The sea was calm but not still. A breeze had begun to kick up as we ventured into Sarangani Bay. It would take us over an hour to reach the mouth of the Bay. Sarangani Bay was rather deep. It could handle vessels of all sizes. The coral reefs rimming the edges of the bay were still pristine and undamaged by man. There was little development on either side of the Bay. Only the port City of General Santos and the small fishing villages that radiated out from the area for 10 kilometers or so were the only sizeable settlements.

Only till you arrived at the mouth of Sarangani Bay did you see a sizeable community.

The town of Glan was one of the oldest settlements in this part of Mindanao and was situated on the southern shore of the Bay only three kilometers from the rushing waters of the Bay's mouth. The mouth was seven kilometers wide, though it looked much narrower as you passed through it. When the tide was coming into the Bay, the waters at the mouth would boil up like the waters of a rapid. The banca, though, had little trouble navigating the mouth of the Bay. Within a few minutes the boat was clear of the boiling cauldron and moving smartly through the waters of the Celebes Sea.

Within three hours, we had reached Kiamba. A half hour later, we were opposite the village of Maitum, the last Christian barrio along the coast to Milbuk. The villages we now passed along the way would be Muslim barrios. All in all, there were at least six of these communities nestled within the groves of coconut trees. This large area of flatland was great for growing copra. The groves of coconut trees extended for several miles into the interior running smack up against the numerous hills that formed the backbone of the mountain system in this part of the island. The Muslims that owned the various groves of coconut palm did quite well financially. But they were few in number. However, the plantations did provide jobs for many of the other inhabitants some of whom supplemented their income by fishing the deep waters of the Celebes Sea.

These Muslim villages held a population in all of about five or six thousand people. Some of these isolated communities did have a school house in their village. The school house was often empty. The government neglected these "unimportant" areas. There were few educated Muslim teachers to assign to these barrios anyway. The Muslim teachers that were available preferred to teach in the urban schools where they could live in a more active environment. Christian teachers were afraid to teach in Muslim areas because of the ancient prejudice and enmity they had toward these people and their culture.

As the banca rounded the point of land that gave sight to Milbuk, the waves were now two to three feet high. Our "pump-boat" continued traveling parallel to the shore, about two kilometers from land. We confidently passed the Muslim barrio of Kulong-Kulong and could see in the distance the smokestacks of the Weyerhaeuser Logging Company's power station. Julio drew my attention to a lone "pump-boat" with three men aboard, rapidly approaching us from behind. Within short minutes, the fast moving outrigger caught up to us and passed us on the left side, forty feet away. The eyes of the three men in the other boat were transfixed on me and my companions. The strangers stared at us unblinking. No wave, smile or any sign of greeting passed between the two vessels. Everyone's face was taut and expressionless. The other "pump-boat" never slowed down. As they moved beyond us, the mysterious strangers suddenly dropped their gaze toward us and looked straight ahead. In minutes, their boat became smaller and smaller until it was almost indistinguishable among the oncoming waves.

"Who are those men, Ricardo?" I yelled.

"Muslims!" he replied grimly.

"Are you sure?"

Ricardo paused a moment and over the loud noise of the engines yelled again,

"Yes, Father. They are Muslims from Malisbong. They're checking us out. They must have recognized you as the American priest and let us pass."

"Their banca is so fast!" I replied. "What kind of engines are they using, I wonder", as I hollered in amazement?

Now, we were about to enter the harbor of Milbuk. It was always good to be home again and to be with "my family". The banca ran along the shore where the one story homes of the logging company supervisors lived. There at the end of the line of cottages stood the two story convento (priest's house). The outrigger came to rest gently on the sandy beach in front of the priest's residence. It was just 1:15 P.M. in the afternoon.

All three of us exited over the side of the boat into knee deep water. We placed our arms under the large bamboo struts that were secured to the canoe. Together we lifted and moved the banca up onto the sand…as much out of the water as possible. Later the boat men would place log rollers under the boat and remove it completely out of the water to dry in the sun. This would prevent the wood of the canoe from becoming water-logged and heavy, a sure way to cut down the speed and efficiency of the craft. I then grabbed my bag from the boat and with shoes in hand, strode across the band of sand in front of my house. I brought my bag upstairs, grabbed some clean clothes from the closet and showered off the salt, sand and sun of the journey.

Necessary Journey: (Top) On my monthly retreat at Calumpang, General Santos City, situated on the shore of Sarangani Bay.

(Bottom) Posing on my faithful Bangka on which I depended for a safe and reliable trip back to Milbuk.

# CHAPTER 10

# *Mountain Fiesta*

K alibuhan was a mountain barrio that I visited on the occasion of their Fiesta. It was an area with lush fertile lands, ranging in elevation from 2300 to 3900 feet with a mean elevation of 2950 feet. The short rolling hills on the top of this mountain range were composed of virgin soil left bare after the logging companies had harvested all the large hardwood and mahogany trees. The small shrubs and underbrush left on the land was easy to burn off. This "kaingin" supplied nitrogen to the soil, making it more productive. The air was clean and cool, and ideal for the planting of coffee beans, maize, pineapple and other fruits that were in great demand in the lowlands of South Cotabato. Sister Elizabeth, Daisy Santos and I had just visited another mountain barrio in these hills on March the 27th called Baningo, the oldest of the settlements in these hills. We briefly stopped here for lunch since it was on the way to Barrio Kalibuhan some ten kilometers or so away.

The distance to Kalibuhan from Milbuk was considerable. The only way to reach the far barrio was to journey by sea down the coast from Milbuk for eighteen kilometers to the small village of Mabay in the municipality of Maitum. It was necessary to arrive there no later than 4:00 P.M. The Celebes Sea in the late afternoon was very rough and stormy. Any delays in travel would mean arriving at the barrio in the dark...not something you would want to do. One of the village leaders was a devout Catholic by the name of Emilio Morales.

He lived with his wife and two young children in a well-made nipa house of bamboo, situated about a hundred meters from the shore. He owned the land on which his house was built and had planted the several hectares with coconut trees. Emilio was the organizer for this trip to Baningo since some of his relatives lived there.

The area of Baningo was originally part of the rain forest. When the Ilocano settlers arrived, they cleared areas of forest for farming and what remained was removed by the Lumber Company which had been granted the concession. This logging company was owned by the family of a government senator. It is interesting to note that one of the earliest interior logging concessions just south of Baningo was operated by the American transnational company, Weyerhaeuser.

Emilio's relatives had arrived in the area shortly after independence was declared in 1946. As mentioned before, the Americans had previously encouraged the colonization of Mindanao in order to offset the Muslim dominance of the southern Philippine islands. From the 1920s, immigrants from Luzon, in particular the Ilocanos, began settling along the coastal districts of what is now Sarangani Province (formerly South Cotabato). One of these settlers was Alfredo Tanendo, an Ilocano government surveyor, who arrived in 1919 and married the daughter of a leading T'boli datu, and settled in Maitum. The T'bolis were the dominant aboriginal tribe in the area. Thus, his descendants became prominent in T'boli affairs. One person in particular, Datu Ned Tanendo became the first barrio captain of Baningo, an inland T'boli barrio that was established in 1962. During the following year, Datu Tanendo was assassinated and the people renamed the village Barrio Ned.

Mabay was now in view. The banca straightened out and headed at a right angle to the shore, coming to a complete halt as the underside of the boat slid along the sandy bottom. We all helped drag the boat up onto the sand. Emilio's wife was busy in the kitchen making the final preparations for our supper. Lourdes Morales was an extremely pleasant woman with two young children and a third on the way. We all enjoyed Emilio's hospitality and passed several hours in conversation before retiring to bed. We would need our sleep and energy for the arduous journey to Kalibuhan.

Emilio awakened me before the sun rose. The smell of freshly brewed native coffee enticed me to quickly dress, splash water on my face and head for the kitchen. We sat down to a breakfast of fried eggs, rice and small strips of pork. Emilio had arranged for a truck from the small logging company in the area to take us up the steep mountain road to a well-traveled path that led through the mountains to several small barrios. The journey from Milbuk to Kalibuhan would take the greater part of two days; eighteen kilometers by sea, eight kilometers by truck and another ten kilometers over mountain trails, sometimes riding small Filipino horses, but most times just slogging through foot deep mud. The rainy season was just coming to a close.

We arrived at Kalibuhan about 2:00 P.M. The barrio chief and his family welcomed us heartily. They led me to a large barn next to the main house to a second floor loft where a large basin of hot water had been prepared for me to clean off the mud and sweat of the journey. I washed off the grime from my legs, feet and hands, pouring the clean, hot liquid over my head and face. Having completed my ablutions, I sprinkled some talcum over my body and put on fresh, dry clothes. I ventured down the ladder from the loft, carrying my soiled clothes under my arm. I no sooner entered the kitchen when one of the young ladies of the house took the clothes from me and hurried off to the water pump in the back yard to wash and hang them. Such service!

By now I was ravished with hunger. We hadn't eaten anything since breakfast except the delicious marang fruit that was offered us as we passed by a farm house on horseback. A merienda of rice cakes and sumang was set before us and we washed down these sweets with hot, black coffee. Within two hours we were all gathered together again at the dinner table for a meal of fresh chicken, rice, gulay (vegetables) and other Filipino delicacies. We lingered at the table for another hour or so in pleasant conversation and then by 8:00 P.M., as if by signal, everyone rose from their chairs and bid each other pleasant dreams as we headed to our respective rooms to sleep. Tomorrow would be a busy day.

The Fiesta this year was a grand event and well organized. There must have been more than 400 people from the barrio and surrounding farms and communities that showed up for the Mass and Baptisms. I baptized a couple of dozen children and witnessed six or seven marriages. Services were well attended and the people were generous. On our way home, my companions and I carried sacks of fruit and 8 or 9 live chickens that were strung by their feet to the saddles of the horses. Half of the chickens died on the way. That didn't stop my comrades from cooking them up for supper when we reached the bottom of the mountain at the village of Mabay, the base camp for the journey.

We left Kalibuhan about 1:00 P.M. after a delicious fiesta meal of native delicacies and of course the lechon (roast pig). The leader of the expedition decided to return by another route that proved to be much drier and faster than the route of our arrival. The weather had improved. Fresh horses were provided for all of us. There were about eight of us in the group. When we finally emerged from the jungle fastness of the mountain onto the logging road there was no one to meet us. It was already past 4:00 P.M.

We had to surrender the horses to the men who had accompanied us. They would be returning back to Kalibuhan. We would have to walk the eight kilometers to Emilio's village but without the aid of the horses or a logging truck. The baggage of clothes, Mass equipment, chickens and fruit would be divided up among the five of us. After a kilometer or two, the shoes that I was wearing began to come apart, due, I suppose to the water and mud of the day before. I removed them. My socks were thick enough not to make my feet cut or bleed on the road. In fact, I felt much more comfortable walking barefoot than when in my shoes. Luckily, the road to Emilio's village was all downhill. When we were but a kilometer away, we could see the village in the distance and the orange sun hanging beautifully just at the horizon. We would reach Emilio's home right at the point of darkness…just in time to rest and wait for the cooking of the chickens.

Though I felt tired after two days of travel, there was a wonderful satisfaction that filled me. This is what I thought missionary work was all about…traveling to distant and isolated places to bring the Word of Jesus and His Sacraments to the people in need. I slept soundly that night and rose early in the morning to return to Milbuk by banca. We thanked Emilio and his wife for their kind hospitality and asked God's blessing on the upcoming birth of a new child. We pulled out from the shore of Mabay by 7:30 A.M., heading out to a calm sea and pleasant weather.

During the next hour and a half, I was deeply in thought concerning the element of danger that faced the people of Baningo and Kalibuhan and the other smaller communities of farmers who lived in those mountain areas. There were no security forces close at hand to assist them in times of trouble.

Rumors had been flying around for weeks now, that certain elements of the MNLF (Moro National Liberation Front) had penetrated even the mountain settlements. Muslim youths from the numerous villages and towns along the coast had been recruited to join the rebellion against the government and to establish what they called the Bangsamoro, 'Muslim (Moro Land) Country'. Stories of training camps being set up far back in the mountains were sending chills into the local Christian communities.

Thus, when the news reached me of the massacre in Baningo, four months after the Fiesta in Kalibuhan, it was truly shocking but hardly surprising. The village was attacked by Muslim rebels early in the morning of July 18th. It was a Thursday and some of the people had gathered in the small chapel to recite their prayers before their long day of work. The villagers were surprised at this uncalled for attack, since they had never been warned by anyone that their presence on the mountain was not welcomed. They wouldn't have listened anyway. These were rugged, pioneer people, individualists who depended upon themselves for survival. The men of the village fought back valiantly, making a way for their families, the women and children, to escape into the forests and down the mountain to the Christian villages below. The barrio captain and his sons were all killed as were most of the men who defended their homes and families.

The rebels had captured some of the women and forced them to prepare food for them as the rebels took up residence in the barrio. They had decided to remain in the town for another day or two, thinking that a response to their raid would take two days or more. Later on, the rebels would loot and burn down the homes and kill the hostages except for one woman who managed to hide herself from the rebels and escape down the mountain undetected.

A squad of Philippine Constabulary based in Koronadal responded the next day to the attacks. A fierce battle broke out which took the life of the commanding officer. Finally, even the P.C. soldiers too would flee the area in the face of superior numbers and fire power.

What could these farmers do with their primitive weapons even with the few P.C. soldiers fighting with them? The two dozen or so rebels were all well-armed with AK-47s. Some were battle hardened veterans who had fought the Philippine Army in Jolo and in other parts of Mindanao. Now they were establishing training camps in these mountains to supply additional troops to thwart and harass the Philippine Army in Cotabato City. The attack was very successful for the MNLF rebels. It created a. "no-man's" land throughout the whole area. Further settlement came to a complete stop for several years because of the lack of security.

# CHAPTER 11

# *The Displaced*

**Monday, July the 29th …**

I was still at my prayers in the parish Church after celebrating the daily Mass. Cecilia Ramos quietly approached me as I sat, eyes closed, in meditation.

"Father Art? I need to speak with you".

"Good morning, Cecilia. Is there a problem?"

"Yes, Father. Some of the parents of the children are at the house and they told us that they've been driven away from their village by armed men".

"Who were these people who told them to leave their village"?

"They were Muslims! The Manobos say that there were over a dozen or more men, all armed with rifles. The rebels told them to move down the mountain and don't come back to their village anymore. Father, they're frightened".

"Come on, Cecilia, let's go over to the house and talk with them".

I accompanied the teacher to the house of the Manobo children and saw half a dozen Manobo men and a few women squatting by the back end of the house near the outside kitchen close to the tables and benches where the children ate their meals

"Magandang umaga", (Good morning)! "Kumusta kayo ngayon"? (How are you all today?)

"Mabuti naman, Padre", (Very well, Father) they respectfully replied as they stood up to face me.

I then instructed Cecilia to translate for me in the Manobo dialect what I was about to say. "Tell them that I am very sorry about what happened to their people".

I paused, while Cecilia translated my words into their dialect. "Ask them if they have found a suitable location for their new village". Again I paused.

Cecilia answered, "Yes Father. The other members of the village have been clearing an area about four kilometers from Milbuk, just off the side of the logging road. They've been working now for the past three days."

"Tell them that I will visit them tomorrow to see where their village lies. The children can remain here at the school during the weekend if they want to".

The children would usually return back to their villages each weekend early on Saturday morning, taking a ride on one of the logging buses. Then on Sunday, when the logging buses would be returning back to Milbuk in the afternoon, they would board the bus, return to the school house and prepare for classes on Monday. I bid the Manobo men farewell as I headed over to the convento for breakfast.

## Tuesday, July the 30th ...

Looking out my bedroom window I could see Cecilia Ramos and Lisa Alcera waited patiently outside for me. They stood by the jeep parked in front of the convento. I quickly descended the stairs leading to the front office and burst through the screen door, bounding down the stairs with a hearty, "Good morning, ladies. Hope you weren't waiting too long." The young women smiled politely as I opened the door of the jeep to let them in. It was 9:15 A.M. as we set out from the logging camp to the main road leading to the road spur that would bring us to the Manobo village four kilometers away. It was not a long distance but the road would be hilly and circuitous as it snaked around the mountain. I brought no supplies with me since this was only a scouting mission to survey the area of the new village and observe the work that the Manobos had accomplished. I planned to return to Milbuk sometime before noon. There were appointments to keep and several issues to settle at the high school.

Luckily the jeep was behaving well today. Even the brakes worked. I dreaded traveling into the mountains with this jeep, since the memory of my experience six months ago still haunted me. Cecilia and Lisa were with me on that trip too, together with Sister Ana. It was another of my scouting forays into the hills and mountains to locate another village of Manobos who had established a large village near one of the logging sites in the northern region of the township.

The incident occurred on our way back from the logging site, about 20 kilometers from Milbuk. All during the trip through the mountains, I was constantly down clutching the jeep to avoid over using the brakes. But once in a while, I would need to pump the brakes to slow down the jeep as it picked up speed on the steep down grades, bouncing and sliding as it careened down the hills just under control. There would be no traffic on these hills till later in the afternoon when the logging trucks and buses would be returning to Milbuk or to the log depot at Wasag to deliver their cargo of logs.

As I rounded the bends of these treacherous hills, I would drive far left or right of center clinging to the mountain side, keeping as much distance from the open side of the road as possible to avoid the danger of plummeting to the valley below. Coming around one "hair-pin" turn, I was suddenly faced with a steeper than usual grade that made it necessary for me to apply the brakes rather quickly and hard. Suddenly, the brakes gave way. The jeep was now in free fall as it picked up speed and hurtled down the hill. The road was extremely rough in this section, with large stones scattered generously over the surface adding more danger to my predicament.

I had already begun to steer the jeep over to the left side of the road, hugging the mountain. Then it happened. The steering wheel no longer responded. It was loose in its action. There was no tension in the wheel, whether I turned it left or right. There was no response at all. I was now only a passenger in this jeep gone wild.

"Hold on to something. Hold tight, we are going to …" I yelled in vain to my three passengers in the rear of the jeep. They couldn't hear me and didn't know what was happening. The jeep was now half way down the hill and gradually moving left toward the side of the mountain where small trees and branches ran along the side. The jeep hit the bottom of the hill going about 40 kilometers an hour. Luckily the road leveled off and the jeep began to make contact with the heavy brush and small trees lining the road. The friction and force of the contact slowed the jeep until it came to an abrupt stop with its wheels imbedded in the rut of the canal that ran along the side. We were all safe and unharmed. The jeep was not damaged in any way, except for the malfunctioning of the brakes and the steering wheel.

I stepped out of the jeep, opened the side door and helped the three women out.

"Are you all O.K.? Did anyone get hurt"?

"No, we are fine, Father. Why? Did something happen to the jeep"?

The women all had quizzical expressions on their faces. They didn't get it. They didn't realize how close they came to catastrophe. But I knew.

"Well here we are", I muttered.

"We are going nowhere in this jeep. Before we start walking out to the main road, let's eat first. Are you hungry"?

I had brought along some sandwiches, fruit and drinks for the trip. I now opened the lunch box and offered sandwiches to each of them. Each sandwich was wrapped in a paper napkin. As I extended my arm in offering the sandwiches, my hand trembled uncontrollably. What a rush of adrenaline I had. This sensation had happened to me before when I was involved in a rescue operation of passengers in a bus that had overturned into a rice field. When I returned to the convento later that night after several hours at the accident site and at the hospital, I was still high on adrenaline.

Now we all could laugh and joke about what happened. But it was hardly a laughing matter at the moment. After lunch, we walked only a kilometer and found ourselves on the main road to Milbuk. Luckily again, a truck happened by only after a few minutes on the road. All four of us were now on our way back to Milbuk. Whatever angel was looking over us certainly had a busy day.

Later the next day, I and two of the workman at the school traveled back to the spot of the accident and helped get the jeep up and running again. The jeep needed new brakes. The malfunctioning of the steering wheel came about when the bolt holding one of the tie rods controlling the steering mechanism came loose and fell away. Once that happened the steering wheel was useless. Today, the jeep was working fine. The brakes were new but nevertheless I always check the steering mechanism to make sure that the bolts are tight.

In less than half an hour, we reached the new village. The Manobos had chosen a wooded area just off the logging road that led to the southern sector of the township. The land was along a sloping depression on the side of the mountain. You couldn't see the village from the road because of a ridge of land that ran along the side. You had to climb a steep incline of about ten to fifteen feet to reach the point where you could see the village.

During the past three days, the Manobos had cleared the small trees and bushes from the area covering about 2 to 3 hectares. After clearing an area of trees, they would burn all the vegetation from the land. This was a common practice among the natives and settlers as well. This practice was called "kaingin". Initially, this burning would help enrich the soil with nitrogen but after several plantings, the land would decrease in its fruitfulness. With the absence of any large trees to hold the soil in place, it wouldn't be long until the rain would wash away the topsoil and render this "kaingin" arid. When this happened, then the Manobos would pack up their belongings and move to another area where the practice would continue once more.

When we arrived and climbed the incline onto the site, nobody came to greet us. It surprised me that the Manobos had accomplished so much in a relatively short space of time. Their village was all laid out. Small elevated huts formed a "U" shaped configuration on the upper perimeter of the property. The area around each home was clean and swept. The people who were there simply sat inside the doorways of their huts and gazed at us. They appeared somewhat listless and tired. Several men came together and quietly spoke among themselves. The leader then approached one of the teachers and began explaining why there was no work being done on the planting. Half the men and women in the village were off scouring the hills for food. In fact, there is no word for obtaining food other than "searching" for food. Cecilia left the side of the chief and came directly to me.

"Father, they have no food to eat. They are not able to work and finish the planting because they are weak and hungry. Some of their people are still out in the forest searching for food to eat. The women were not able to find any food in the forest. They are not familiar with this area".

I shook my head, realizing that I should have brought along some sacks of bulgur at least, to help the Manobos in the building of this new village. "Tell them that I will return tomorrow morning with some food for them. I won't be able to bring them anything today. Tell them not to worry. I will return tomorrow".

Shortly thereafter, the two teachers and I returned to Milbuk and planned for the next day's trip back to the village. "This is what I want both of you to do. Go to the market early in the morning and buy some vegetables and fruit. See what kind of deal you can make with the vendors. Buy enough for several days. And the fish…see what they are selling at the dock and buy some to take with us to village. I will load up the jeep with some sacks of bulgur after Mass tomorrow. They will have enough food for at least a week. We can help them until they are able to find food for themselves."

## Wednesday, July the 31st …

Morning came early for the two Manobo teachers as they prepared the children for school and made sure that each was properly dressed and fed. They instructed them, "Be good in school today. Study and pay attention to the teachers. We won't be with you at school this morning. We will be bringing food to your families in the mountains. We will be back before noon to feed you". And with these words, Cecilia and Lisa went with my driver to the market place and fish pier to pick up the food so greatly needed by the Manobos.

After Mass and breakfast, I went to the back porch of the convento and opened the small bodega or storeroom where the 63 sacks of bulgur were stored, all that remained from a shipment of a 100 sacks sent by the Office of Catholic Charities in Manila. Nick and Mapandi grabbed hold of a sack weighing over sixty pounds and carefully carried it to the driveway on the side of the convento. The two teachers had just arrived with the vegetables and fish. Now the two sacks of bulgur were placed at the back of the jeep and all was ready for departure.

The trip was made without incident. Upon our arrival, the teachers began instructing the women how to prepare the bulgur since the coarse wheat grain was not familiar to the natives or to the Filipino population in general. The leaders among them distributed the vegetables, fish and grain to each family. These people practiced communitarian virtues. Everything was shared equally among the tribe.

On the following Monday, August the 5th, I stopped by the house of the Manobo children to find out how the families of the children were faring in their new settlement. Cecilia and Lisa were just finishing the breakfast for the children. All the kids were laughing and talking excitedly when I approached. I smiled at them and began to practice speaking with the few Manobo words I knew. They laughed some more. I sounded so funny. "Well", I moaned, "looks like I need more work on my pronunciation."

"Good morning ladies", I laughed, as I moved toward the two teachers who were hurriedly collecting the empty cereal bowls from the table. "Were you able to speak with any of the children about the conditions at their village"?

"Yes, Father," Lisa answered. "The conditions are much better now that they have food. It seems that the bulgur we sent them is going fast. They have already finished one and half sacks. It seems that other relatives of their tribe were in similar difficulties, so they helped them."

"That's good. I'm glad to see that our trip to their village was successful. As you know, I will be leaving for Davao on Thursday for a two-day seminar. I will return to Milbuk late Saturday morning. We need to bring two more sacks of bulgur to the Manobos tomorrow morning. Will you and Lisa be able to go with me to the village tomorrow morning about 9:30 A.M"?

"Yes, Father", Cecilia replied, "we will meet you at the convento."

"Great! By the way do you have any bulgur left? You know, I have never even tasted the stuff".

"Sorry, father, the children ate it all". "Darn! Alright then, have a nice day and I'll see you tomorrow morning".

## Tuesday, August the 6th…

Tuesday morning arrived quickly enough. The convento boys had already loaded the two sacks of bulgur on the jeep just before leaving for class. I was on time and was already sitting in the jeep when the two teachers arrived. Sister Ana was sitting in the passenger seat next to me. She had pleaded with me to let her come along to see how the Manobos were doing in their new village. The two women climbed into the seats in the rear of the jeep. Upon arriving at the site, we all exited the vehicle and climbed directly up the incline into the village. The people were all busy this time. Except for the few young mothers attending to their infant offspring, everyone else was busy raking and hoeing the land with their make-shift tools, planting root crops and vegetables for the coming months. Others in the village were busy scouring the forest for food or wild game. Fortunately, the natives had found a clean source of fresh water, really necessary to their very survival. It was only less than half a kilometer away…close enough not to cause inconvenience to the tribe and far enough to be free from human contamination.

We spent about a half hour at the settlement. I had instructed Lisa to have some of the Manobo men carry the two sacks of bulgur to the Chief of the village for storage and distribution to the community. The people were both happy and surprised at this unexpected gift. On the second trip to the village last Wednesday, the two teachers had gathered several of the Manobo women and taught them how to prepare and cook the bulgur. It seemed to have worked out well. The bulgur is wheat, dark brownish in color that is only slightly milled, just enough to remove the grain from the shell covering. The wheat is highly nutritious, maintaining almost all its vitamin content. The daily diet of bulgur caused dramatic improvement in the physical well-being of the Manobo children at the camp. The caloric content of this carbohydrate likewise provided the natives with the needed energy and stamina to perform work. I was glad that all was going so smoothly.

Now I could leave Milbuk with a clear mind knowing that my absence for a few days would not be missed. I did not travel to Calumpang this month, since the Bishop and Religious Superior had arranged for all the parish missionaries to attend a two-day Seminar on the Sacred Scriptures to be given by a noted Scripture Scholar Rev. Raymond E. Brown, S.S. Time magazine called him "probably the premier Catholic Scripture scholar of the U.S." The conference would be held at the Apo View Hotel in Davao beginning late Thursday afternoon, and ending on Friday evening, August the 9th. Saturday would be our travel day for returning to our respective parishes.

The Displaced: This collage starkly demonstrates the poverty and destitution that was the plight of the Manobo peoples especially during this crisis. They were convinced by the logging personnel to settle upon this hill overlooking Milbuk for the purpose of preventing the Muslim rebels from occupying this high position. Materials were provided by the Weyerhaeuser Company to build these shelters and food was provided as an incentive for their services.

# CHAPTER 12

## *Terror in the Mountains*

**Thursday, August the 8th...**

"It must be 4:30", I muttered to myself as I rolled over in bed to glance at the clock on the desk beside me. The rhythmic rattle of metal awoke me as the sound floated through the openings of the louvered windows of my room. Lunch pails banged in cadence as they struck the legs of loggers marching slowly toward the waiting bus that would take them to their work in the mountains. I groaned as I swung my legs over the side of the bed and began to brush away the cobwebs of sleep in my eyes. Slowly, standing erect, I raised my arms straight over my head, stretching as high as I could. Then, slowly again, I began to rotate my outstretched arms like windmills in circular motions, up and around...one, two, three...ten times around. Then, standing with arms straight by my side, I turned my head from center to left to center to right and back again to center, repeating the motions nine or ten times to limber up my neck... all part of my daily routine in rising. I quickly dressed and threw some clean clothes in an overnight bag.

This was an early rise this morning. I would be leaving Milbuk for a few days to attend a seminar in Davao. The Logging Company's Cessna would be leaving for Davao at 6:00 A.M. for the daily mail and supply pick-up. I had booked the flight with the management over a week ago. The Company readily complied out of courtesy to me as the parish priest and out of gratitude for the work I was doing for the people of the logging camp and for the children in the school. I was to be the only passenger. I was excited to attend the seminar since it would be bringing together a large group of missionaries working in Mindanao, many of them from my own congregation. Rev. Raymond Brown, a noted author, theologian and Scripture scholar would be conducting the seminar and giving talks on the Johannine Epistles. This was an opportunity not to be missed.

It was a different scene at the camp security check point. The loggers greeted one another as they congregated at the main gate of the housing compound. They milled around in small knots of familiar faces, sharing smokes and laughing at one another's jokes. The logging buses stood parked just inside the main gate of the compound, their diesel engines running steadily, providing background noise for the whole scene. The buses were specially made to accommodate the loggers who would be riding them. Looking at a typical logging bus from the front, you could see that the entire left hand side of the bus was open. There were no doors and no center aisle. Strong, sturdy wooden benches (with backs) were bolted to the floor of the bus. Each bench could accommodate at least five men. Even the seat that the bus driver occupied was bench-like and afforded space to three other workers. All in all, there were nine benches, including the driver's seat, with a seating capacity for about 44 persons.

As the hour for departure approached, the field supervisor, clipboard in hand, went over the roster of men who would be working the southern section of the mountain that day. Carefully he moved among the groups of men, checking off the names of those present. Within five minutes of departure, all the men assigned to work that day had arrived. The supervisor gave the order to board the buses. They clambered aboard the logging bus, occupying the front benches first and then filling in the remainder, as all the crew got seated.

Out of the shadows near the guard post, a group of ten native Manobos hurried across the road toward the rear of the bus and boarded as quickly as possible. The field supervisor had promised them that if there was room on the bus, they could take a ride to their village in the mountains close by the logging site. There were five men, four women and a young boy. They occupied the two last benches of the bus. The best ride on the bus was always toward the front end. The road in this part of the county was not paved with cement or macadam. Dirt roads did not hold up very well, especially when it rained. Parts of the road were like washboards and other parts were nothing but a series of potholes. Only newly graded roads offered the luxury of a smooth ride. As a result, passengers could expect the bus to buck and shake even at slow speeds. Those seated at the rear of the bus would feel every bump and jolt, some so severe that the passengers would literally bounce off their seats, be suspended in air for a moment, and come crashing painfully on their butts. Riding toward the front of the bus was not a racial issue. It was a matter of survival.

All the buses pulled out of the camp at exactly 5:00 A.M. Two headed north toward Palimbang. A lone bus took the south fork for half a mile, taking a sharp left up the logging road that would take them far into the mountains. It was Thursday, August the 8th, 1974.

At 5:30 A.M., I brought my motorcycle out of the garage, mounted it, turned the key and hit the starter with a downward thrust of my right foot. The roar of the engine quickly quieted to a purr as I engaged the clutch and headed toward the air strip. Buddy Capacite already had the plane fueled up and ready to go. I boarded the Cessna at 5:45 A.M. The plane slowly taxied to the far end of the runway that backed up against the forest of coconut trees. I sat in the co-pilot's seat, careful not to touch any of the instruments. I made sure that my feet were not anywhere near the foot controls. Folding my hands in my lap, I watched as the stick control in front of me moved in concert with the pilot's control stick. Oh, how I wished that I had learned how to fly. What excitement!

Buddy carefully and meticulously checked all the instruments and made sure that the fuel mixture was set correctly. He raced the engine, once, twice, three times, making sure that it promptly responded to his command. And then with feet on the brakes, he "revved up" the engine once again. Releasing the brakes, the plane lunged forward at full throttle, running quickly down the gravel paved runway toward the waters of the Celebes Sea. The plane lifted gently off the airstrip and effortlessly climbed high over the sea for about a mile or so before sharply banking to the right and coming back over the logging camp, still climbing steeply toward the on-coming hills and mountains. We would be flying over these tree lined mountains for about half an hour before reaching the Allah Valley, then travel the remainder of the way over more mountains until reaching Davao Gulf, a large body of water surrounded on three sides by land.

From Milbuk to Davao, as the crow flies, the distance is 115 miles or 185 kilometers. However, Buddy preferred to go almost directly due west until he reached the shoreline of Davao Gulf and then head directly north to Davao City and shortly beyond to the International Airport. Area wise, the Davao City limits is one of the largest in the world. However, Davao City proper is not that large nor densely populated. It is ideally located in the southern part of Mindanao, central to the bread basket of the island. Rice, copra, bananas and various minerals can be conveniently transported overland to this port city and shipped to other parts of the Philippines and to other countries. Davao is a protected port, nestled within a large cove, boarded on the west by Samal Island and to the South by Talikud Island. A deep water port, Davao lies safely within the protection of Davao Gulf, thus protecting it from the ravages of the Pacific Ocean.

Having reached the shoreline of Davao Gulf, Buddy headed the plane north to the airport. Over to the left, I could see the famous Mount Apo, a dormant volcano, which, on occasion, spews light wisps of smoke from its crater. Mount Apo lies about 40 kilometers from the City of Davao, its coned peak rising 9,691 feet in the air, dominating the fertile plains below for hundreds of kilometers. Up ahead, the tall buildings of the city made their appearance. To the north, lay the cement runways of the International Airport. Buddy was now speaking with the control tower receiving instructions for his landing. It was 7:06 A.M. when the wheels of the Cessna touched down. Within the hour, I would be having a real great breakfast at the Apo View Hotel and lively conversations with my friends.

Back at Milbuk, the lone logging bus that took the south fork into the hills had slowly navigated its way up the serpentine roads going ever deeper into the mountains. Forty five minutes had passed since the loggers boarded the bus at Milbuk. Their destination was less than ten minutes away. The inside of the bus was noisy with the loud, pulsating sound of the diesel engine and the raised voices of the loggers attempting to talk with their companions. All that the loggers wanted to do now was to get off this uncomfortable and cramped bus and move around freely in the forest.

The bus was nearing the top of a winding grade in the road, bearing left along the mountain. To the right side, you could view the luscious green of the valley below. The driver was just about to reach the level part of the road when the first shots echoed through the valleys. A concerted barrage of gunfire from automatic weapons ripped through the thin metal skin of the bus starting from the front and proceeding along the driver's side. Some of the passengers never knew what happened. They died instantly. Bullets struck the driver in the upper part of both shoulders and one grazed him on the left side of his head sending him slumping into unconsciousness like a rag doll onto the floor of the bus. The vehicle jerked to a halt as the "dead-man's switch" brought the vehicle to a shuddering stop. Some loggers and natives tried crawling over one another to escape out the open side of the bus but were gunned down by rebels coming from the front of the bus. Silence came after less than a minute of ear shattering, death dealing chaos. It all seemed like a lifetime of agony to those within the bus who were still alive but wounded.

The benches were bathed in the blood of the loggers. Some loggers sat where they died, others lay sprawled across the laps of their companions or draped over the backs of the benches. The rebels came along the left side of the bus that was completely open. They pulled themselves up onto the bus and checked the passengers for signs of life. Those still alive, they pulled outside and lined up against the bus. Most of the wounded could not stand. Some slumped to their knees and other just lay cowering on the ground, anguish and fear reflected on their faces. Only three of the Manobos survived the initial onslaught. All were wounded. Their frightened eyes filled with pain and tears. They shouldn't have been on the bus. However, no one was to be spared.

The two dozen rebels were excitedly happy over their handiwork. Some brandished their weapons menacingly toward the ten or so survivors. Some of the rebels began searching the loggers for any kind of weapon they might have on them. Only Harry, the husband of my cook, was found to have a small revolver which he had carried for his protection for the past two weeks. He had shown off his weapon to me only a few days before when he first told me about the story of being approached by a lone Muslim rebel as he was bulldozing a section of new road. The stranger related a message to Harry from the rebel commander that no one was to log this area again. Otherwise, there would be trouble. The news fell upon deaf ears. The management of the logging company had no past experience of such threats, at least not here in Mindanao, so why should they take such threats seriously. What happened on the island of Basilan is another story. Harry never had a chance to use the gun. The attack had been so quick and surprising that there was no time to fight back even if all the men had been armed. This was a professional ambush. These rebels had done this before.

One of the rebels handed over Harry's gun to a certain Dimalub, commander of the Muslim terror group. He looked it over carefully and gave it to one of his men. Slowly he walked up to Harry, cursed him for being armed and announced his sentence. The commander stepped back a few paces, raised his AK-47 and emptied the remainder of the clip into the frightened man. The bullets ripped into his body with such force that it held him suspended and pinned momentarily against the side of the bus. Then as quickly as it happened, Harry crumpled to the ground, blood gushing from every wound, forming an ever growing puddle beneath his body. The commander then ordered his men to kill the rest of the survivors. The slaughter was over in seconds. Blood drenched the ground and ran in long rivulets toward the side of the road under the feet of the executioners. The rebels looked around at the dead bodies lying within the bus and littered along the side of the road. There was no sign of life...no movement at all among the passengers. The rebel group moved on up the road to their camp hidden somewhere in these hills.

Minutes passed. Only silence could be heard screaming out the horror and evil of such an act. Not even the chirping of birds was heard. The wind had vanished from among the trees. All of nature fled this atrocity. Then, the faint sound of a rustle could be heard. A slight movement appeared from within the bus. The body of a logger, lifeless and torn by the fragments of bullets appeared to rise up from the bench in a vain mockery of death. But no, it is the man who lies beneath him on the bench who is alive. How did he ever escape the scrutiny of these killers?

Joe Vargas lives. He was wounded in the upper part of his leg and had lost some blood but he was still alive. Pulling himself from beneath the body of his good friend, Ben Soriano, Jose peered warily out the side of the bus to see if his tormentors were still present. Slowly, deliberately, he lowered himself to the ground. He ripped off a piece of cloth from his shirt and tied it over the wound in his leg. Painfully he hobbled to the side of the road and headed down the hill toward Milbuk. Joe stopped and removed a pocket knife from his pants. He dragged himself toward a stand of young trees and cut a long straight shoot and fashioned it into a cane. He had lost some blood and was very thirsty. But he dare not return to the bus. The scene was too awful and horrific. Besides, the rebels just might return again and he didn't want to be anywhere in the area. It took the bus forty five minutes to travel this distance. Joe Vargas knew that his journey to Milbuk would take much longer, if he was able to make it at all.

Ramon Tesoro had one hour left on his guard duty at the main gate of the logging camp. The streets were empty at this time of the day. At 11:30 A.M., most people are at home taking a siesta and avoiding the hottest time of the day. There's wasn't much of a breeze blowing off the sea. Ramon reached for his thermos of cold water and poured a cup for one last drink. Looking up from his place at the covered guard post, he saw the hazy figure of a man swaying to and fro. He thought to himself, "It's much too early to be drunk". He looked again and recognized Joe Vargas. What is he doing here? Didn't he leave on the bus for the mountains early this morning?"

Ramon left the shade of his post and ran quickly toward the staggering man. "Joe what happened?" Jose was speechless. His mouth felt like cotton.

"Water, I need water".

Ramon helped Joe to walk the fifty meters to the guard post and sat him down on his chair.

"Here, take this water". Joe drank the cup of water with a mighty gulp. Then with a loud cough he spit half of what he drank.

"Drink slowly, Joe", Ramon cautioned. "Rest here now, while I get help for you".

Ramon quickly called the Chief of Security and told him that Joe Vargas had returned from the mountains alone and wounded.

"We need to take him to the clinic, Chief Dorotheo. Joe Vargas is wounded in the leg. Something must have happened to the other loggers on the bus."

A jeep was quickly sent to the guard post. The wounded man was carefully placed inside for the short trip to the medical clinic.

Doctor Domingo ripped open the pant leg to get a better look at the wound on Joe Vargas' leg.

"Joe, I'm going to remove your pants before I start working on the gunshot wound in your leg. The bullet is still inside".

Painfully, Joe lifted his butt off the hospital gurney as the nurse's aide unfastened his belt and pulled the pants slowly off his body.

"Joe, I will be cutting into your leg to remove the bullet so that you won't become infected. I will be giving you some anesthetic. You will not feel much pain."

"O.K. Doc, that's good".

Suddenly, the door to the operating room swung open and Security Chief Dorotheo marched in with two of his guards, all heavily armed and trailing behind him.

"Wait a minute Doctor. I need to speak with Joe here about what happened on the bus this morning. You'll have to wait until I get his whole story".

"But he needs to be treated now or the bullet inside will infect his whole leg and it might become gangrenous".

"This won't take too long, doc, I promise. Joe, tell me everything that you can remember...what happened up there in the mountains"?

Joe Vargas shifted to his side in pain and began his narration.

"It all happened so quickly. The noise of the gunfire, the screams of the men and the sharp pain of the bullet striking my leg...it was all so sudden. I tried to get off the bus but my leg hurt so badly... then Ben Soriano came crashing down on me and I was pinned to the bench. The rebels came running up to the bus shouting and firing their guns. They climbed up the open side of the bus and began to search out those who were still alive".

Painfully, Joe continued, grimacing as he spoke,

"They must have thought I was dead because of the blood that poured on me from Ben's wounds. They brought the wounded outside the bus and I could hear someone shouting at one of the men for having a gun. Then one of the rebels fired off his AK-47. Their leader ordered the other rebels to kill all the wounded and leave no one alive. The sound of the guns frightened me so much. I thought surely they would be shooting inside the bus again. Then they left as quickly as they came. I waited for about 15 or 20 minutes before I even dared to peek outside the bus. It was very quiet outside. I decided to leave the bus. My leg was hurting so much but I couldn't stay in the bus. I was able to move Ben's body off me. I started down the road but it was so hard to walk. I cut myself a walking stick from one of the small trees by the side of the road. I was so thirsty..."

"O.K., that's enough", the doctor interrupted.

But the Chief continued,

"Let me ask you, how many men do you think there were"?

"I don't know. There must have been at least a dozen or more. It sounded like it. I didn't see any of them. My eyes were closed. I was supposed to be dead".

"Thanks, Joe! He's all yours doctor".

The Chief exited the room as abruptly as he entered. Now was the time to gather the men together and bring their bothers home from the mountains.

The Security Chief met with the P.C. Sergeant, the Logging Company Manager, the Chief of Field Operations and other relevant supervisors to quickly plan a strategy to bring back the bodies of the loggers and to begin to set up security plans for the camp itself. It was agreed upon that a force of men would be needed to travel to the ambush site and retrieve the thirty or more bodies of those who perished in the ambush. A large, flat-bed truck would be used to transport the bodies back to Milbuk. The bodies would be taken directly to the medical clinic and placed in a temporary morgue until the bodies could be prepared and embalmed for burial. The combined force of six P.C. soldiers, ten company security guards and a rag tag band of twenty armed volunteers would ride up to the ambush site in a couple of heavy-duty dump trucks with steel sides. A Toyota Land Cruiser would bring up the rear. It would carry the emergency medical supplies and a radio for contacting the main base at the logging camp.

It was almost 2:00 P.M. by the time the armed force was ready to leave Milbuk for the ambush site. There was no loud shout or noise of any kind. These men were aware that they could be pulled into an ambush themselves. They needed to proceed with caution and not rush headlong into a situation that could be catastrophic for them. The convoy of three trucks and the Toyota moved slowly up the logging road. If it took the bus forty five minutes to reach the ambush site, it would take this force of men a bit longer as they scouted the terrain and searched the darkness of the forests for any strange movements. No one spoke. Only the sound of the heavy trucks echoed through the mountains ever nearing the scene of horror. Every eye was sharply peeled, every gun at the ready to respond to an enemy as yet unseen.

Then as they proceeded up the steep incline, they could see the back of the yellow painted bus, high at the crest of the hill. The trucks stopped as two groups of scouts ran up along the road past the bullet ridden bus and around the curve in the road. The area appeared to be clear of any rebel troops. The scouts remained in place to guard against any hidden assault. The lead scout waved the rest of the armed men forward. The men approached the bus and with one chorus let out a groan of disbelief at the horror set before them. Some fell into a squat, covering their eyes as tears poured down their faces.

The Security Chief, anger in his gait, began to issue orders.

"Come on men, we need to remove these bodies quickly. We don't want to be returning in the dark. Bring the flatbed truck closer here so we can load the bodies. Start with the people on the outside of the bus".

The dump trucks pulled to one side to permit the flatbed truck to move closer. The loggers and security guards moved quickly to retrieve the bodies. Removing the bodies from the bus was made difficult because the bodies needed to be first disentangled from the benches. The men inside the bus would pass the bodies to loggers on the ground. They, in turn, would pass the bodies up to the loggers standing on the flatbed truck. Gently and with reverence, they lifted the bodies to the bed of the truck, while two other loggers positioned the bodies in rows, so that all of the dead would be accommodated. They would be making only one trip.

The sorrow of the men on this gruesome detail quickly turned to anger. Loud cursing and words of revenge echoed within and around the bus. Two of the loggers within the bus began to remove the bodies of the men sitting on the front seat with the driver. As they lifted up the first body, a moan came from beneath the bench. They looked at each other in surprise and placed the body they were holding on the bench behind them. There, half hidden on the floor of the bus lay the driver. His face and chest area was soaked in blood. His lips moved but no words came out only a low painful groan. "Someone's alive...We have a live one here!" shouted the loggers. They first removed the dead body of the second logger and passed him down to the men below in order to retrieve the wounded driver.

Gently, they lifted him up from the floor of the bus and handed him to two waiting loggers below.

The Security Chief came over and ordered his men to carry the seriously wounded driver to the Toyota.

"Take him back immediately to Milbuk", the Chief bellowed.

The bus driver was placed on the bench seat behind the driver. First aid was applied to the wounded man. Slowly he opened his eyes. One of the men gave him a small sip of water, encouraging him to hold on till they reached the clinic. The Toyota had a radio and could communicate with the main camp. It was difficult to radio the main office while deep within the mountains. But the closer they came to Milbuk, the reception became clearer.

"Tell the clinic to be prepared. We have a seriously wounded man on the way. It's the bus driver!" What a miracle! Two had survived the ambush. What stories they would tell.

All the bodies were finally loaded onto the flatbed truck. Yes, all the bodies were placed there...the twenty eight loggers and the ten Manobos. All were riding back to Milbuk together as they had ridden all together that morning. What a bizarre and gruesome site this was. Bloodied, broken bodies placed like cords of wood, being carried into a village of immense sorrow and grief.

Chief Dorotheo gave the order to return to Milbuk but first there was one other thing to do.

"See if you can get the bus started again", the Chief yelled to one of the loggers still standing within the bus.

"Alright, Chief, I'll give it a try".

The logger jumped into the driver's seat and turned the key...it wouldn't start.

"Try it again!" A second attempt was made. The driver pulled out the throttle and feathered the engine with gas, finally chocking the engine into life.

"Now what do you want me to do?" the driver yelled.

"Bring the bus close by the edge of this ravine. We are going to push the bus over the hill".

Making sure that nobody was left within the bus, living or dead, one of the dump trucks drove up and positioned itself behind the bus. Slowly, the bus began to inch forward as the force of the truck was gently applied. Eight feet, five feet, one foot to the edge, then gravity took over. The bus gradually separated itself from the truck behind it and rolled down the deepening incline, lurching forward, rolling head first down the steep, slopping hill. The floor of the ravine lay some 150 feet from the top. The noise of the bus, crashing and annihilating the small trees and bushes in its path created a mighty sound that rushed back up the hill. The bus became airborne during the last thirty feet, landing on the ravine floor throwing up a cloud of dust and debris. In a short while, the vegetation would cover over any trace of what happened here. There would be no memorial on this hill, nor any reminder to passersby of the lives that were unnecessarily taken on this day.

The convoy of trucks headed down the hill toward Milbuk. The flatbed truck was in the lead with the two dump trucks filled with men following close behind. This funeral procession made the return trip in just under an hour. It was about 4:30 P.M., when the convoy reached the main road, only half a kilometer from the main gate of the camp.

A cry went up from the main road. At the entrance to the camp, hundreds of people waited… crying, swearing, and praying. The people strained forward, spilling out of the gate onto the main road as the flatbed truck came into view.

"Clear the way, clear the way!" shouted the three security guards as they vainly attempted to open a path for the truck. The driver of the flatbed was being coached by the Security Chief who was riding with him,

"Do not stop! Go directly to the clinic. Don't let the people stop you. It will be madness!"

The truck turned off the main road and without hesitation headed toward the main gate, slowing only enough so as not to hit or hurt the people. Like the parting of the Red Sea, the crowd split in two, encircling the bus like churning, rushing water rapids. The noise was bedlam. Screams, cries, pleas to God…all lifted high in a chaotic chorus of grief. Women were fainting to the left and to the right, falling into the arms of their family and friends…so overcome by the horror of such a sight. The flatbed truck swung right to the road leading to the medical clinic. Here too, scores of people lined the way to the clinic's entrance, the dump trucks following close behind with the armed force of men.

Once at the entrance to the clinic, Dr. Domingo gave directions to the Security Chief and his men on where the bodies were to be placed. A large room was set aside for the bodies of the loggers to be laid out for identification. Nobody was allowed inside the clinic until all the bodies had been removed from the flatbed truck. No sooner had this been done, that the relatives of the dead loggers poured through the doors of the hospital toward the temporary morgue. The hospital workers and security guards tried in vain to stem the crushing flow of grieving people. The doctor pleaded with the Security Chief to help provide some order. Gradually, some of the people began to see the futility in all this madness and began to follow the instructions of the guards and hospital workers. Lines began forming to allow the wives, children and relatives of the fallen men to identify the bodies and make plans for preparing the bodies for burial.

Doctor Domingo approached the camp manager and let him know how many cases of formaldehyde he would need to embalm the bodies. It would be several days before funeral services would be conducted and in this hot climate, the bodies would deteriorate quickly if not embalmed soon.

# CHAPTER 13

## *Torment in the Camp*

Emilio Tesoro, the driver of the ill-fated bus, lay on the operating room table as Doctor Domingo finished placing the shunt into the vein of the man's arm. On the adjoining table lay one of his fellow loggers. He was waiting to transfer some of his blood to this wounded man. Emilio's other arm was already hooked into a bottle of glucose that was steadily dripping into his veins. This man must be stabilized first before there was any attempt to remove the bullets in his chest. The doctor was able to stop the bleeding of the wounds in his upper chest area, but the two bullets lay deeply embedded in both pectoral muscles. He was lucky. If the bullets had entered an inch lower, he would have surely died. His sturdy build and musculature were deciding factors in his survival. His head wound, though painful, was not serious. The bullet had grazed the left side of his skull, but had not penetrated the bone nor hit any vital veins or arteries. Emilio had lost a lot of blood. Doctor Domingo was not going to attempt to remove the bullets but only to stabilize him for the flight to Davao. Emilio needed the medical support that only a large city hospital could provide if he were to survive the operation. The larger plane, a Beechcraft, was due to depart from Milbuk at about 5:30 P.M. Emilio needed to be operated on immediately if he were to live.

An ambulance was waiting for them at the airplane hangar in Davao. Carefully, the pilot and his companion helped the wounded driver off the plane to a waiting stretcher. He was immediately placed in the ambulance and driven directly to the main Regional Hospital in Davao. The logging manager made all the arrangements by radio through the Company's office in Davao.

Sister Helen had been at the Milbuk clinic consoling the families of the murdered loggers. When she heard that there would be another plane traveling to Davao to pick up medical supplies for Dr. Domingo, Sister Helen approached the logging manager, Mr. Robinson and urged him, "Mr. Robinson, sir, the people need to have Father Art return to Milbuk as soon as possible. If he is here, he can help bring calm among the people. Fr. Art is attending a conference at the Apo View Hotel. May I suggest that Sister Ana accompany the pilot to Davao and break the news to Father Art so that he may return immediately?" The manager approved Sister Ana to accompany Buddy Capacite to Davao. The Cessna left Milbuk as the sun set over the Celebes Sea. The plane would arrive at Davao in darkness. Buddy never liked to fly over these mountains at night. He hoped that his instruments were working accurately. He would be flying blind almost all the way until he reached the coast and the Gulf of Davao. There he could follow the stream of lights right up to the airport.

The trip to Davao took about an hour and fifteen minutes. Buddy had a good tail wind as he crossed the mountains. The clouds were high and patchy. Once he reached the coast, he had good visibility all the way to the airport. The plane touched down at about 7:15 P.M.

Buddy and Sister Ana were met by one of the Company's employees and driven to Davao. Buddy directed the driver to stop first at the Apo View Hotel so that he could contact Fr. Art and relate all that happened. Buddy and Sister Ana arrived at the hotel at 7:45 P.M. They entered the hotel and approached the concierge. "Can you tell us where we can find Father Art Amaral? He is supposed to be here at a seminar"?

"Ah, yes," the concierge answered, "He is probably with the other priests in our banquet hall. They are just about to take their dinner. Let me show you the way".

Buddy and Sister Ana were ushered into a large hall where thirty or forty priests were present, milling around with drinks in their hands, waiting to be called to supper. Buddy approached one of the priests and asked, "I'm looking for Father Art Amaral."

"Yes, he's here. Hey, Art, There's someone here to see you".

I walked across the room and saw Buddy and Sister Ana standing dejectedly in the entrance to the banquet hall.

"Buddy, Sister Ana, what are you doing here," I asked with great surprise? "Would you like something to drink?"

"No thank you, Father," Sister Ana replied. "Something horrible has happened in Milbuk. There was an ambush in the mountains. Muslim rebels attacked one of our logging buses and killed 28 of our men. They also killed the ten Manobos who were riding the bus. The Security Chief and an armed force of men from the camp were able to retrieve all the bodies. The logging camp is in chaos. They're afraid of another attack. They want you to return back to Milbuk."

I was shocked, to say the least. All I could mumble was, "Yes, of course I will. Can I come with you, Buddy, when you return to Milbuk?"

"Yes, Father. I will be leaving Davao tomorrow morning at 6:00 A.M. Tonight, we will be gathering together some supplies for the hospital."

"I'll be there, Buddy. I want to thank both of you for coming here to tell me the news." Turning to Sister Ana I inquired, "Where will you be staying tonight, Sister?"

"I'll be staying overnight with the Oblate Sisters. Can I return with you tomorrow morning, Father?

Yes, of course. Give me the address of the convent so that I can have the taxi driver pick you up early at 5:00 A.M.

I accompanied my Milbuk friends to the hotel entrance and bid them goodnight. I entered the banquet hall and immediately went over to my religious superior, Father Edward Deviney.

"Ed, there was a massacre at Milbuk today. A logging bus was ambushed. Twenty-eight loggers and an unknown number of Manobos were killed. The pilot tells me that the people suspect that a roving band of Muslim rebels did this. It seems that the rebels are driving away anyone living or working in the mountains. The people are afraid that the rebels will attack Milbuk next. I'll be leaving here early in the morning for a flight back to Milbuk on the company plane."

Father Edward stood there dumbfounded. "I'm so sorry to hear about this. Of course, you need to return to the people. If there is anything I can do to help you, please let me know. Come on. Let's tell this news to the Bishop. He's over at the other side of the hall speaking with Father Ray Brown".

Bishop Reginald Arliss was the second bishop to be appointed to the new diocese of South Cotabato in the last five years. He was a good man with the people, genuinely interested in the welfare of the people and very supportive of his priests. The Bishop was a Passionist like me. Bishop Reginald had previously served with distinction in Rome as the Rector of the American College for over six years. He was visibly saddened at the news that I related to him.

"Bishop, I don't know where all this will lead to, but I will keep you well informed about any further developments. Please keep the people and me in your prayers." I retired to my room shortly after supper. I had arranged that evening for a taxi to pick me up at the hotel early the next morning.

In Milbuk, the relatives of the slain loggers were busy preparing the bodies for burial. The families were reverently removing the blood caked and stained clothing of their loved ones and washing away the crimson colored stain from their skin. Now they could view the many wounds that cut these men down in their prime, leaving behind only the shadow of their once vibrant lives. And they cried, mixing their tears with the bath of water. The bodies lay modestly naked on the floor, prepared now for the service of embalming. It would be a day or more before the bodies could be taken home for the family prayers and rituals. The church services would come next, the final commendation of their souls to a merciful Savior who underwent his own suffering, death and burial but who now lives through Resurrection to a new life. This is the hope that prevents the people from drowning in the dismal despair of this great loss. Jesus had once said, "If you believe in me, even if you die, you will live forever...and I will raise you up on the last day".

In a room at the back of the hospital, used as a service entrance for supplies and equipment, ten bodies lay on the floor. These were not the bodies of the loggers. The Manobos who were slain on the bus had lain there for several hours now. There were no relatives in attendance to cry over them or close friends to grieve their passing. Word of the massacre had yet to reach the far flung villages in the mountains where these men and women live. It was not safe to send anyone back into the hills with the sad news. Who will minister to them?

The double doors to the service entrance room opened gently and two women passed through, each carrying a bucket of warm water, soap and toweling. Sister Helen and Daisy Santos, (my former Director of Catechetics for the parish of General Santos City), devoutly knelt next to the bodies and silently prayed before beginning their service of preparing the bodies for embalming and burial. Then, one by one, they removed the blood drenched clothes of the men and women. The clothes were placed in a heap upon the floor to be washed later. Taking one pail, they soaked the wash cloths in water, applying a little soap. They remove the caked on dirt and blood from the bodies, revealing the many unnecessary wounds inflicted on such gentle people. The Manobos also needed to be prepared for burial and the subsequent funeral services, for these people were also children of God. All night long, the two women lovingly cleansed the wounded bodies. The clothes were soaked in soapy water and washed of every stain. Rinsed clean, wrung out but still damp with water, the clothes were placed back on the bodies of the Manobos. There was no time for drying clothes on a line in the sun and no time to obtain other clothes to cover them with honor. The women tidied up the room. They placed the bodies of the slain Manobos side by side on the concrete floor. Having finished their "work of mercy", they picked up the buckets and toweling and returned to their homes where they tried to sleep with the memory of what they had seen this day.

## Friday, August 9th…

It was still dark at 5:00 A.M. The streets were deserted as we sped to the airport in the taxi. The news of last evening was grim. Twenty eight loggers had been killed, together with ten Manobos who were riding back to their village in the mountains, all victims of an ambush by the Muslim rebels, members of a secessionist group called the MNLF. I had just left the town of Milbuk that very morning of the ambush for this important conference here in Davao. Now 24 hours later, I was at the airport ready to return to the aftermath of the massacre.

The taxi pulled up at the airfield and I handed the driver twenty pesos, grabbed my small bag of clothes and headed toward the hangars. The Weyerhaeuser plane was a Cessna, a single engine, four-seater. The pilot was just returning from the plane when I greeted him, "Good morning, Buddy. Hope, I'm not late."

"No, you're right on time, Father", Buddy said with respect.

"Need any help loading the plane?" I replied.

"No", he answered, "Pedro and I finished a few minutes ago. There's just one problem. I had to remove the two back seats to make room for some extra cargo. I hope that Sister Ana and you don't mind sitting on some crates?"

I thought to myself, "We don't have any choice in the matter. I really need to get back to Milbuk. There so much to be done".

So I answered, "No, not at all." The flight to Milbuk would take about an hour and a quarter, hardly time to get uncomfortable. We all walked toward the plane, Buddy, Pedro, Ana and I.

Climbing into the plane behind the co-pilot, I sat on one of the crates. There was nothing to secure me in place like a seat belt so I just reached up and held onto the leather hand strap above the door. I started to wonder what was in the crate on which I was sitting. The words printed on the box in bold lettering read:

FORMALDEHYDE! "O my God. I'm sitting on embalming fluid", I gasped to myself. There must have been at least four crates of the stuff surrounding me. I said to Buddy and the co-pilot, "God forbid we should crash. We would be instantly embalmed for burial." There was no response from either of them, just a mild grunt to acknowledge that I was heard. Sick humor, they probably thought.

The plane ran smoothly along the runway and rose quickly into the cool morning air. The plane banked sharply west toward the mountains of Southern Mindanao. Off to the left you could see Mt. Apo, standing sentinel-like over this principal city of Davao. The base of this fertile mountain rose majestically into the still air, forming an almost perfect cone. Thousands of people climbed this volcano every year, many coming from foreign countries to view the splendor of its sights.

The sun was just rising behind us casting long shadows across the carpet of green canopy that covered the mountains. The carpet was not seamless. Here and there, brown, snaking roads like rips in a garment, ran over the hills and through the valleys, some ending in large swatches of downed trees and empty land that had been raped of its beauty.

Usually this trip was made flying blind through low flying clouds. Today the skies were clear, the visibility excellent. The pilot and Pedro were silent except for some small talk about the plane, weather and terrain. Nobody wanted to discuss the matter of the massacre. In less than an hour, they would all be deeply involved in the consequences of the incident. It occurred to me as I sat silently on the embalming fluid that it was at the exact moment that we boarded the Cessna, the morning before to travel to Davao, that the busload of loggers and Manobos were being systematically killed ten kilometers away in the hills. We probably flew over them as the plane headed over the mountains for Davao.

As we neared Milbuk, Buddy dropped the plane down into the winding valleys that led to the airstrip. What a sight it was, as the plane threaded its way through the steep, towering hills, lush with green. The wings of the plane seemed so close to the on-rushing hills, so close you could touch them. A cascading water fall to my right surprised me with its very presence and beauty. I never thought that there was anything like this back in these hills. The suddenness of such splendor filled me with exhilaration. Down below a small river inched its way through the heavy jungle vegetation. Coconut trees were everywhere, haphazardly growing without rhyme or reason. No human hands seemed responsible for their planting.

Then in the distance, the thin ribbon-like landing strip appeared. A small rounded hill blocked clear access to the runway. So Buddy ran his plane up and over the hill. The plane then dropped suddenly onto the runway and touched down so smoothly that there was nary a quiver. Buddy taxied the plane to a small building that served as an office and maintenance shack.

So silently did we land that there was nobody to meet us at the airstrip. A few soldiers, members of the Philippine Constabulary (P.C. Troopers), were walking about aimlessly, smoking the local brand of cigarette. Their presence here was to guard the airport and warn the community of any incursions by the Muslim rebels.

Buddy reached for the plane's radio and pressed the channel button that accessed the receiver at the main office of the logging camp. He requested a pick-up truck to carry him, his passengers and the medical supplies, including the formaldehyde, to the clinic. The truck arrived almost immediately as if they were waiting for his call. The supplies were quickly loaded into the back of the pick-up. Sister Ana and I climbed into the front seat with the driver, while Buddy and Pedro rode with the cargo.

We drove through the large barrio of San Roque, the village bordering the north-western side of the airport. All along the road there were these ramshackle type houses made of cast off lumber. Some homes were of bamboo construction with thatched roofs, others had sides covered with veneer, pieces of unfinished plywood, cast-offs from the plant, veneer so poorly made that they were worthless for export. Some of the roofs were topped off with thin, rusty corrugated iron panels. These houses were nothing like the homes you would find in Home and Garden magazines. The houses were strung along on both sides of the main road, all the way up to the very gate of the logging camp itself.

The people gaped at the passengers in the pick-up. I held nervously onto the handle of the door as the driver drove quickly over the bumpy road, heedless of anyone's presence, throwing up clouds of dust as the truck passed. Mothers hastily ran after their children, herding them close to the houses and away from the dangers of the road.

This road ran parallel to the sea. There was a small boat landing half a kilometer from the airstrip itself, a docking area that served as a "small port" for the various launches and "pump" boats that carried supplies up and down the coast. This was a busy place during the morning with fish for sale, freshly caught during the dark of the evening, but not today. The landing was empty of both people and boats.

The distance from the airfield to the main camp was a little more than a kilometer. As we entered the main gate, the camp was like a ghost town. The streets were empty at 7:00 A.M. in the morning. This was quite unusual. There was no work this morning for the loggers. The veneer mill was silent for the day. The people had been awake all night long preparing the bodies of the slain. Sleep did not come easy even when they had finished.

The pickup pulled up to the hospital. Just as I was about to get out, I turned to the pilot and said gratefully, "Buddy, I want to thank you for getting me back to Milbuk so quickly. I don't know what I would have done without your help. I am in your debt." And I added in Tagalog, "Maraming salamat!"

Buddy replied, "Walang anuman!" And he continued in English, "It was my pleasure, Father. Please think nothing of it. The people really need you to be here with them."

I grabbed my bag from the back of the pickup and headed toward the convento across the street. Workers from the clinic began to unload the cargo from the back of the pickup.

My plans for the day raced through my mind as I approached the side door of the convento. What would I do first? I would need to inform the Sisters and the principal of the Notre Dame, Mrs. Gaviola that I was back.

I was greeted by a surprised Rudy in the kitchen with a, "Good morning, Father! You're back already."

"Yes, thanks to Buddy. How are the boys doing?"

"Just fine! They will be cleaning up around here today, since all classes have been cancelled."

"And Mapandi... how is he? Did he say anything to you?"

"...About what, Father?"

"...About the fact that he is the only Muslim still remaining in Milbuk. He will need to stay close by the convento until this whole affair settles down. You know how some of these people are. You know how they talk. I would hate to send him back to Surallah. He is doing so well here and he is such a help around the house. Tell Mapandi that I will speak with him later this afternoon. Keep me informed. ...By the way, is Mrs. Gaviola over at the school?"

"No, Father. Since classes have been cancelled for the meantime, she chose to remain home and look in on some of her friends who lost their husbands during the ambush. She's waiting for you to return and give some directions concerning the evacuees who now occupy most of the classrooms."

"That's what I need to know. Rudy, what I want you to do is to find Mrs. Gaviola and tell her to meet me in her office at 1:00 P.M. We need to discuss many things. And contact the other teachers. There will be a general meeting of the whole staff at 1:30 P.M. this afternoon. This meeting is mandatory!"

"Yes, Father...I'll contact Mrs. Gaviola immediately and give her your message."

There was stillness in the house as I walked up the stairs to the second floor living area. I paused briefly in the parlor to gaze out the screened porch area to the wide expanse of sea. Over to my right I admired once again the forest-like mangrove swamp that buffered the shoreline bordering the High School. Birds flocked to its branches early in the morning and late in the afternoon. The loud sound of their chirping would fill the air and then with an explosion of feathers, they would burst forth in a dark, noisy cloud, rushing over the homes of the camp in a ragged formation toward the neighboring hills.

I slowly walked the few steps to my bedroom, opened the door and dropped the bag of clothes on the bed. I turned and headed out of the room to the refrigerator stuck in a small alcove between the bathroom and the guest room. Opening the frig door, I saw very little that appealed to me. There was a half-gallon jug of Mass wine, a quarter piece of Gouda cheese and some saltine crackers still in cellophane. I closed the refrigerator, went down the stairs and outside to the Sister's convento next door. I knocked at the kitchen door and Sister Ana opened almost immediately.

"We've been expecting you," she said with her 'Cheshire' cat-like smile. "Did you eat breakfast yet?"

"No. That's why I'm here. Feed me."

The other two Sisters laughed at our interchange. They were already seated at table eating rice and some left over dried fish from the night before.

"Do you have any eggs?" I pleaded.

"Yes, we have a couple left."

"Could you please fry me up two eggs...turn them over lightly, thank you. What I really need now is a cup of coffee."

"We have some tea", Sister Helen, the religious superior of the Sisters, disclosed.

"O.K....that will be fine," I said as I sat down and exchanged pleasantries with the Sisters.

Half way through the breakfast, I became serious, "I'm going to need your help during this critical time. First, I need to know all that has happened during the last twenty four hours. Secondly, it will be important for all of you to be out in the community with the people. Speak with them...listen to them...counsel them. It's necessary to offer the people all the spiritual support you can and to help them deal with this terrible event. They must mourn and grieve but this cannot be dragged on forever. You have to make them understand that they will need to plan for the living...for themselves and their children. All of you will keep me updated on what the people are thinking and saying. Unfortunately, I cannot be everywhere at the same time. You will have to be my eyes, ears and tongue. Encourage the people not to spread rumors. Find out the facts. We need to bring calm to the community. Are there any questions?"

"Yes, Father...I need to know how you plan to handle the funerals of the deceased loggers," Sister Helen inquired.

"We cannot schedule individual Funeral Masses for everyone. Tell the families of the deceased that there will be only one Funeral Mass for all the loggers. They died together; they will be buried from the Church together. Sister Helen, you and I will plan the Funeral arrangements. We want the ceremony to go as smoothly as possible. Also, there will be a general meeting for all the teachers in the Notre Dame High School meeting room at 1:30 P.M. Sister Ana, I want you to attend the meeting and to stay with the teachers. Give them your support. I'm sure that some of them are quite anxious about the situation here in Milbuk. Are there any more questions?"

I paused and looked around at the Sisters. There was only silence. Then, I continued, "Sister Helen, could you be ready in fifteen minutes to accompany me to the hospital? I haven't seen the bodies yet nor spoken to any of the families of the deceased."

"Yes, Father...I will meet you outside in fifteen minutes."

"Thank you...and thanks for the breakfast."

Exactly fifteen minutes later, Sister Helen and I went to the hospital to view the bodies and speak with the families of the slain loggers. As we approached the hospital, there was a strong smell of formaldehyde permeating the air of the hospital lobby. It was apparent that Dr. Domingo had started the embalming process. In fact, he had just completed embalming one of the loggers and the family was carefully wrapping the body in a white sheet, gently carrying their loved one to a jeep waiting for them on the outside. The slain logger would be dressed in his best clothes for the viewing and family prayer rituals.

We went first to the temporary morgue where the bodies of the loggers had been laid. The lifeless forms lay in rows along one side of the large room in modest nakedness, covered over by a white sheet, waiting their turn for embalming. The relatives of the deceased sat in chairs along the opposite wall. There weren't as many as the previous night. I went from person to person extending my condolences and assuring them that even at this time God's love for them was present.

"Keep the cross of Jesus before your mind's eye in all of this. Unite your sufferings with those of Mary, His mother, as she stood in sorrow beneath the cross of her beloved Son." With these words, I hoped to stir up their faith in a God who so loved them that "…He sent his only Son into the world, so that through Him…all who believed would live forever. …even if you die, if you believe in me, you will live forever."

I then turned to Sister Helen and whispered, "Where have they laid the bodies of the Manobos?"

"Follow me, Father."

Sister Helen led me to the service room at the back of the hospital. She swung open the double doors and we entered. There in a neat row lay the ten Manobos, a combination of men, women and a few children, who had taken the logging bus to return to their village. The bodies had been washed clean. Even their poor clothes had been washed of the dirt and blood. I stared in sorrow and disbelief.

"How small and fragile they look."

I gazed dejectedly on these gentle people and continued, "See here how this young girl has been wounded. Why she's the sister of two of our students. I tried to convince her to stay and assist the teachers in caring for the other children. But she told me that she needed to return to her village. She was close to marrying age… maybe 13 or 14 years of age."

I felt very sad as I mentioned all this to Sister Helen. Then turning to Sister Helen, I inquired, "Who bathed and cleaned the Manobos?"

"Daisy Santos and I took care of them, Father," she replied.

"Well, you did such a remarkable job. God bless both of you. We will bury the Manobos after the ceremonies with the loggers.

We need to inform the person in charge of the Company's funeral arrangements to set aside a site for the Manobos."

Sister Helen and I opened the back door of the service entrance and heard the sawing of wood and the hammering of nails. The Company had set up a make shift carpentry shop for the manufacture of coffins. The carpenters were all busy building coffins for the deceased loggers. A truckload of lumber and sheets of veneer plywood were piled along the side of the shed. The carpenters framed out the coffins and covered the sides with the plywood. The coffins were sturdy enough for encasing the bodies of the loggers and for transporting them to the church and finally to the cemetery.

As I strolled along the assembly line of carpenters, I noticed one carpenter who was framing out a rather super large coffin and I inquired, "What are you doing? Whose coffin will this be?"

"Oh, this coffin is for the bodies of the Manobos."

In disbelief, I blurted out, "And who gave you the order to make only two coffins for the Manobos?"

"My supervisor, Father," he answered ashamedly.

"Well, let me speak with your supervisor then. I'm telling you now; you will not put all the bodies of the Manobos into one or two coffins. They will all have their own coffin, just like the loggers."

By now, my face had turned red. I was angry. I tried not to take it out on this carpenter, but I couldn't hide my disgust at this apparent prejudice and disregard for the dignity of the Manobo natives. As it turned out, the carpenters did make only two coffins for the bodies of the slain Manobos. These people were small in stature, the adults weighing no more than 90 lbs. *(As I look over the past 40 years, I regret my reaction to this event. I don't know what I was thinking.)*

At exactly 1:30 P.M., Principal Lourdes Gaviola and I entered the teachers' meeting room. The twenty-two teachers and support staff were all assembled around the large table. Sister Ana was sitting there among them. I sat at the head of the table and began the meeting with a brief prayer for God's guidance in the decisions that we would be making that day.

I began the meeting by observing, "I know that all of you are anxious concerning the recent events. We all have suffered loss. We must support one another. The school will be closed to all students until some stability comes into our community. Already there are evacuees living in most of the classrooms because of the danger that lies within their villages. Each teacher will be responsible for monitoring the hygiene and cleanliness of his/her classroom. You will instruct the evacuees concerning the use of the bathroom facilities. Their children must not be allowed to use the grounds of the school as a bathroom. All of us must prevent the spread of disease coming from unsanitary classrooms, bathrooms and grounds. The people must be encouraged to use water for bathing. They may use the picnic area over in front of the mangrove swamp for cooking their food. Sufficient barrels will be placed along each corridor and at the picnic area for any garbage. Encourage the people to use the barrels and to pick up any litter they see on the grounds of the school. I will arrange for the Company to pick up the trash from the school on a daily basis during the crisis. Right now we have about two dozen families living in the school. If this conflict continues, we may have all the classrooms filled with people. Let's pray that it doesn't come to that. Are there any questions?"

One of the older teachers timidly raised her hand and asked, "Will the teachers be paid even though there are no classes being held?"

"Yes. You will be paid but you must make yourselves available for special assignment when called upon. Right now I want all of you to assist the evacuees, maintain the cleanliness and hygiene of the school and prevent any unnecessary damage to the building. I am hoping that we can open the school for classes within a week or two. Please direct all your questions and problems to Mrs. Gaviola. She will be in complete charge of the school. Mrs. Gaviola, is there anything you care to mention to the teachers at this time?"

"No, Father. You've said everything. I just want to commend all the teachers for arriving on time for the meeting and thank them in advance for their continued help and cooperation."

I then stood up from the table and was about to depart when I turned and said, "One more thing...I imagine that some of you teachers may be having second thoughts in working here at Milbuk. I know that it's much more peaceful in the places from which you came. I only ask that you stay with us for a while. If the situation worsens, it may not be safe for any of us to remain. But we haven't come to that stage yet. Let's just pray to Mother Mary, our Lady of Perpetual Help, to bring an end to this conflict. God bless all of you." And with these parting words, I exited the room, leaving the teachers to discuss plans for implementing my directives.

After my meeting with the teachers, I returned to the hospital to meet with other members of the slain loggers' families whom I hadn't seen earlier in the morning, to console them. They were all waiting to receive the embalmed bodies of their loved ones. Dr. Domingo had been working tirelessly for the last six hours, trying to complete the embalming of the more than 30 bodies. As soon as he would remove the blood from the veins and arteries of the deceased, he would pump in the chemical substance, formaldehyde. This chemical delays the quick and unpleasant decay and decomposition of the human body.

Dr. Domingo was standing outside the main entrance as I approached, leaning up against the side of the building, smoking a cigarette. Seeing me, he exclaimed, "Twenty more bodies to embalm and then I'm finished. I never thought I would be running a funeral home."

"How can you stand breathing in that formaldehyde all day long," I replied.

"I think my sense of smell has ceased to function. I can't smell anything now."

I know, I replied, "The smell is so bad. The scent has filled every room in my house. When I go to sleep tonight, I imagine that the smell will fill my nostrils. And when I wake up, the aroma will still be there. I can smell it on my clothes even when I'm outside the camp."

"Let me tell you the trouble I've had in embalming Harry Martinez", Dr. Domingo exclaimed.

(Harry, of course, was the husband of my cook, and the logger who had shown me his revolver several days before.)

"The rebels shot him up so badly that I can't keep the formaldehyde in him. I've sewn up hole after hole in his body and still the fluid leaks out. His wife wants to ship his body back to his home town in the Visayas. The body has to be preserved...I don't know what to do. I just have to keep on sealing him up."

"I'm glad that I don't have your profession", I said gratefully. "You're doing such a fantastic job here. In case nobody has told you... thanks, thanks a lot."

"You're welcome, Father...and thank you for your support."

Then, I added, "Look, if you ever need my help, don't hesitate to ask me...I mean anything."

# CHAPTER 14

## *The Defense of Milbuk*

**Saturday, August 10th...**

There was no logging being done anywhere in the township. Even the veneer mill which ran almost twenty-four hours a day was shut down. The schools had cancelled classes until further notice, due to the emergency nature of the recent events. There were evacuees from the outlying barrios who now occupied most of the classrooms in both schools and even the pews of the Catholic Church. The whole town was on edge.

Almost immediately after the ambush, the Company authorities organized the loggers into paramilitary groups patterned after the barrio self-defense units so popular among Christian settlers who lived in Muslim dominated regions. Each armed group was responsible for patrolling a designated area or post. Some groups were assigned the night watch. They patrolled the perimeter of the logging camp and airport. The patrols were stationed at key points on the main road, along the shoreline of the camp and veneer mill as well as protecting the airstrip itself from any attempts at sabotage. This activity was called among the people, the "ronda".

On the second day after the ambush, I had just returned from the Church where I had celebrated Mass. This morning, the Church had many more attendees than the regular dozen who showed up daily. The people found themselves between "a rock and a hard place" and they knew to turn to God for help. I was just about to enter the kitchen through the screen door when the first loud, harsh sounds of the chain saws broke the peaceful cool of the morning. I stopped dead in my tracks, closed the screen door to the kitchen, turned around and headed toward the beach at the back of the convento and walked close to the gently lapping water. It was low tide. There to my right, about sixty meters away, were perhaps two dozen men, half of them with chain saws. They were wading knee deep in the water within the small forest of mangrove trees that guarded the high school from the waves of stormy seas. These tough, strongly rooted trees had borne the brunt of heavy waves over the years, providing a natural barrier and protection for both the school and convento. It was a beautiful mangrove swamp that hosted myriad types of tropical fish and provided a scenic backdrop for the regular picnics held under its shade. However, these trees could easily shield oncoming bancas of MNLF rebel soldiers who would be able to penetrate the perimeter of the camp unseen and create havoc and death to the residents of Milbuk.

The loggers moved quickly from tree to tree, deftly amputating branches, limbs and trunks right down to water level. And as swiftly as they tore up this small forest, other loggers dragged the mutilated remains to the shore where the wood was loaded onto trucks to be used as fuel for the night watch, illuminating those areas of darkness and shadow. Within two hours, only the stumps of mangrove trees could be seen. The waters of the Celebes Sea would soon cover even this evidence of a once picturesque scene.

Later in the morning, I again went outside my house and stood before the expanse of sea before me to gaze again at the emptiness of what was once an exquisite mangrove forest. "What a waste this war is making," I mumbled to myself. Then, from behind me, I heard my name being called, "Father, can I speak with you, please?"

It was Security Chief, Dorotheo with two of his men. I turned and greeted them, "Good morning, Chief. Good morning, men. What can I do for you?"

"Well, we were thinking ...could we use your banca for patrolling the harbor. Our plan is to fit out the boat by installing an iron plate around the pilot's seat to protect the boatmen from bullets. What do you think?" Can we use your banca?"

I was somewhat attached to my boat. I depended on it for transportation. It was reliable. I didn't need to wait on anyone if I wanted to leave Milbuk and travel to Kiamba or General Santos City. I was in control. But the circumstances had changed. What use was my banca now with this on-going conflict?

After a moment of silence and deliberation, I consented, "Yes, of course you can use the banca for patrolling. I want to do everything possible to help with the security of the camp. Yes, use the banca. Maybe my boatman will volunteer to assist you with the patrols. In any event, he will keep the boat and engine in good condition for you."

"Thank you, Father. I'll have some of the men from the mill come and measure the boat for the armor plating."

"That's great, Chief", I said encouragingly. With that, I left the men alone to plane the defense of Milbuk.

Overlooking Milbuk was a steep slopping hill, rising 250-300 feet above sea level, which ran the full length of the camp and then some. From the base of the steep hill to the shore was a distance of less than half a kilometer. Any enemy commanding the top of this hill could easily snipe at anyone within the camp housing or logging mill area. Troops and lookouts needed to be positioned on this important vantage point to offset any surprise attack by the rebels. The hill was likewise steep on the back side and would prove difficult to ascend especially under fire. This back side of the hill was heavily wooded and choked with thick, green vegetation. It looked down upon a deep green valley. The logging company engineers carved out a narrow graded road on the front side of this hill reaching to the very top from the main road. The loggers cleared all the trees from this side of the hill and hacked out a clearing on the top.

The Company couldn't station too many of their men at this site since they were already stretched thin at other critical positions.

Someone came up with the idea of having the local tribe of Manobos set up a new village on the crest of the hill. This indigenous tribe had been driven from their village in the mountains twice already by the Muslim rebels during the past two weeks. The rebels didn't kill any of the Manobos since they did not pose a threat to them and besides, if they did kill a dozen or more who was going to complain or take note? The Manobos had moved their settlement closer to Milbuk in the hope that they would be undisturbed. However, when the natives heard news of the massacre and that ten of their own tribe had been horribly killed; they abandoned the new village and were now squatting on the outskirts of Milbuk near the camp. When the plan was explained to the Manobo chief and his community, they agreed to cooperate. Yes, they would build their new village on the crest of the hill overlooking Milbuk. And so it came to be. This would be a sight so strange and unusual that the memory baffles my mind to this day.

The trees that had been cut down on the front side of the hill now became the building material for the huts of the Manobos. The natives harvested the long straight trunks of the young trees and used them to construct their homes. The larger remnants of trunks and tree branches measuring 6 to 8 inches in diameter were used as posts for the four corners of the huts with other posts placed midway to hold up the roof. All of the roofs were flat, slanted at a 40 degree angle. Each hut was elevated at least a foot off the ground. The flooring was a series of straight branches covered by overlapping pieces of veneer. The sides of the huts were covered by overlapping pieces of veneer. The roofs were tiled with overlapping pieces of veneer. It didn't look pretty, but it kept out the sun and rain.

The logging company provided all the veneer that the natives needed plus the hammers and nails to secure the trunks, branches, and veneer covering. Some of the huts were well constructed. Most of the huts were relatively small, measuring 8 by 10 feet. There was just one room. A few of the "huts" were larger still, elevated over 2 to 3 feet off the ground. The huts ran along almost all the whole length of the hill's crest like a series of row homes.

Within the short period of only a day or two, the whole crest of the hill was decorated with the ramshackle veneer wrapped huts of these mountain peoples. The Manobos didn't seem to mind since there was a promise of food for their services. There must have been at least 70 Manobos living on the top of this hill, men women and children, seventeen families in all.

The Manobos didn't have modern weapons like pistols or rifles. Each man carried his bolo by his side…a long wide knife, whose blade measured fifteen to eighteen inches long, much like our machete. This was more a tool than a weapon. Nevertheless, these natives would be the eyes and ears that would protect Milbuk from a surprise attack.

When elements of the regular army arrived at Milbuk, the commander did assign troopers to guard and patrol the crest of the hill. Half were regular army, the other half, men from the local Barrio Self Defense Unit. Any rebels looking for a way up this hill to snipe on the logging camp would think twice, seeing the long row of shacks set on the top of this hill. They too would marvel at such a strange sight.

While all this activity was occurring on the hill overlooking Milbuk, the camp security chief and carpenters from the Company were huddled in conversation on the road in front of the High School. Security Chief Dorotheo was pointing here and there giving instructions to this motley crew. I was watching from the window of the convento, curious as to what they were up to. I came down from my house next to the school and approached the Chief.

"Good afternoon, Chief", I said, as I neared the group. "Good afternoon, men! What's going on…?"

"Hello Father", the Chief replied. And a chorus of greetings followed.

"We're planning the last defensive positions of the camp in case the rebels are able to penetrate and over-run our present defenses at the airport and elsewhere," the Chief informed me. "My plan is to construct wooden barricades, four feet square and four feet high, then fill each wooden box with dirt and stone. These barriers will run the perimeter of the road from the Elementary School to the Church and right here along the front of the High School. Each fortification will be placed four feet from the next one. We need to erect these barriers in this open space so that we may safely retreat to the Church, which will be our last outpost of defense. We figure that we will need to construct at least 100 of these protective barricades along the whole perimeter of the school area."

I thought silently to myself, "What is he thinking…he wants to make the Church the last defensive outpost? If we don't prevent the rebels from entering camp, then it's all over anyway. What will happen to the several thousand civilians…the men, women and children who are hiding in their homes, in the schools and in the Church?"

Diplomatically, I replied, "Oh! That's interesting. Well I wish you all luck on your plans. We should all pray that help comes before anything like that happens. I have to leave now and visit some of the wounded at the Clinic."

The men were right. The large open field between the two schools had neither trees nor any barriers to hide behind. Just a large, wide open space. I left the men to their planning and walked across the street to the hospital to visit the wounded.

Sunday, August 11th…The whole camp was tense and anxious. Any disturbance set people running here and there, worriedly asking questions. On this day, early in the afternoon, there was a report of gunfire coming from the neighboring Muslim village of Sinangkangan, about a kilometer away. Such news spread like wildfire throughout the camp. I happened to be near the garage at the time working on my jeep. When I heard the news, I quickly mounted the trail bike and sped out of the camp in the direction of the reported disturbance.

I took a hard left out the camp's main gate and headed north along the road to Palimbang. There was a sharp bend in the road about ½ a kilometer from the main gate. This road was elevated about 30 feet above sea level, cut out of the mountain hill that overlooked Milbuk. As I rounded the bend, the road began to descend down to a level stretch that led to the nearby Muslim village. I turned off the main road onto a narrow lane that led to a group of houses, adjacent to two "Marcos" type school rooms. There in a clearing stood about sixteen villagers, mostly women. They all looked surprised at my sudden presence in the barrio. These Muslim men and women listened carefully as I spoke to them in Tagalog, first greeting them with the Arabic words of peace ..."As Salaam Alaikum". A few responded, "Alaikum Assalam." I continued, "Anong nangyari dito?" "What happened here? Some people in the logging camp thought they heard gunfire coming from your village." "Wala nangyari dito, Padre," one of men replied. (Nothing happened here, Father.)

Nothing appeared to have taken place in the village...so I observed...but who knows. The people did seem a bit nervous. "What was I doing here"? The thought of the danger of being in a Muslim village alone, after 38 people had been killed in the mountains three days earlier by alleged Muslim rebels, suddenly came over me and a chill ran through my body. "Fools enter in where angels fear to tread."

I thanked the people and spun around on my trail bike to return back to the camp. As I approached the hilly part of the road leading back to the camp, there up ahead of me was a phalanx of Milbuk men, thirty in number, led by the security chief of the camp. Their rifles were drawn and they were staring at me grim faced and deadly serious. "Hi everybody" I bellowed.

"Father, where did you come from?" the security chief said incredulously.

I felt so embarrassed at the question since my action could be judged as foolhardy. "I just returned from the Muslim village after speaking with the people. They told me that nothing was happening there. You can see for yourself."

I pulled my bike to the side of the road and let the 30 armed men pass by. I followed them to the barrio. The chief was speaking with the people now, his eyes darting back and forth, searching the doors and windows of the houses and looking off into the distance at the coconut trees, bamboo groves and palm fronds...any place that could hide a man with a gun. After five minutes or so, the armed group turned toward Milbuk and left the area, cautiously looking behind them and to the sides. Sheepishly I followed them for a few minutes and being somewhat ashamed, I went ahead of the group and sped on into the camp to seek refuge in the quiet and safety of my room.

## Sunday, August 11th...

During the weekend, some of the loggers' families approached Sister Helen and inquired whether or not it would be possible to have a separate ceremony for their deceased loved ones. I had made it clear to Sister Helen that there would be one Funeral Mass celebrated for all the slain loggers. This was the right thing to do. Since all the slain men suffered death together, it was fitting that their final commendation to God by the Church should likewise be together, to signify their unity to a new life. When Sister Helen brought up the subject of separate funerals, I became agitated and angrily repeated my decision that there would be only one Funeral Mass. My outburst of anger surprised Sister Helen. My anger surprised me as well. I wanted to control the situation and not become a victim of the events. Later, I apologized to Sister Helen for my outburst but remained steadfast in my decision.

## Monday, August 12th...

There was no early Mass this morning, but I still rose at the regular time to make final preparations for the Funeral Mass to be celebrated at 9:00 A.M. The coffins were laid in rows on several flatbed trucks, parked in front of the church. It was impossible to bring all the coffins inside the building since it was not large enough to accommodate so many. Hundreds of people milled around the front entrance to the Church. Most of the people squeezed into the pews and stood along the side aisles. The church was packed with the families and friends of the deceased. The ceremony would be solemn but not prolonged due to the onset of heat as the sun rose higher in the sky. The bodies in the coffins would bake in this oppressive heat. Time was of the essence.

After celebrating the Funeral Mass, I went to the front entrance of the church and prayed the final blessing over the coffins. I walked along with the bereaved families, who trailed behind the coffin laden trucks, all the way to the cemetery, a distance of about two kilometers. The cemetery was hidden beneath a grove of trees lying about 40 meters on the other side of the airstrip, only a hundred meters from the beach. Armed guards had preceded the funeral procession to insure that no rebels were in the vicinity ready to ambush. I went from grave site to grave site reciting the final prayers of farewell and hope, blessing both the coffins and burial plots with holy water.

Upon completing the ceremonies for the deceased loggers, I was led by one of the parishioners, to a large hole dug deep in the sand just outside the boundaries of the cemetery on a small plot of land that lay only 20 meters or so from the edge of the shore. Here the bodies of the Manobos would be laid to rest...but not in the cemetery of the Milbuk residents! I was a bit upset over this course of events but could hardly object under the circumstances. Besides, it was dangerous to linger in the area too long. I repeated the self-same prayers of petition and hope for the souls of these gentle people who truly belonged to God. And then, one by one, the coffins were carefully passed down to one of the men in the hole. The coffins were laid one on top of the other, until all two coffins filled the empty space.

There was sadness among the few people gathered at this grave site. The teachers of the Manobo children, the O.N.D. Sisters, the convento personnel and I, all raised our voices in prayer to God... "Our Father, Who art in heaven, hallowed be thy name..." and we ended with "Eternal rest grant unto them, O, Lord and let perpetual light shine upon them." No one remained in this isolated spot very long. All the mourners quickly placed the flowers and mementos on the graves and hurriedly retraced their steps across the airstrip, through the village of San Roque and into the safety of the logging camp. The living now needed to care for the living and insure their well-being.

# CHAPTER 15

## *Seeking Relief*

### Tuesday, August the 13ᵗʰ...

It was the day after the funeral. I had arranged with the Company's manager to be flown to General Santos City. I explained to Mr. Roberts that there was a need to purchase food for the evacuees. There was no telling how long this conflict would continue. In the meantime, there were about 600 people, evacuees living in the school classrooms and church, who needed to be fed.

General Santos City was a growing town of over 60,000 people. It was the port city of the Province of South Cotabato, situated one hundred and forty kilometers (87 miles), South-east from Milbuk by land. I began my missionary work in this city when it was named Dadiangas. President Marcos inaugurated the new city in 1967. I felt that I could obtain any help I needed from the many people I knew in the city.

The plane circled the Lagao airport at 6:40 A.M. in the morning, having taken only thirty-five minutes to reach. This airport serviced the region around General Santos City and was guest to many dignitaries and business men associated with the Dole Corporation, whose huge pineapple plantation was only forty minutes away by car. The airport was only six kilometers from the city. It was a one-runway airport, not much changed since the Japanese last used it some thirty years ago. The Japanese built the airstrip for their fighter planes and bombers. They did such a good job that very little had to be done to maintain it. It was a dirt runway but tightly packed with gravel. The only problem that a pilot faced was the presence of animals on the runway. It was highly recommended to pilots to first check the runway for the presence of cows, sheep, goats or carabao before landing or taking off. The runway was flat and dry. Confident that it was safe to land, Buddy brought the plane down over Sarangani Bay and headed straight toward the airstrip, making a smooth three point landing. I was dropped by the terminal and waved to Buddy as he started up the plane again and immediately headed toward the end of the runway for take-off. The plane quickly reached air speed and darted into the sky for Davao.

I walked over to the main road with bag in hand and only had to wait about fifteen minutes for a jeepney that was headed to General Santos City. I flagged down the driver and was able to squeeze into the back of the crowded vehicle. The other passengers willingly made room out of deference to the priest.

Fifteen minutes later, I paid two pesos to the driver and exited the jeepney near the City Hall, walking the two hundred meters across the plaza to the main boulevard. The Catholic Church lay directly across the City Plaza facing the Town Hall. This was typical town planning as envisioned by the Spaniards whose influence strongly remains in most towns throughout the Philippines. Crossing the street, I approached the main entrance to the priest's convento located right next to the church. The front door was locked. It was too early for the secretary to be at work, so I strolled around the building to the back entrance and went upstairs to the living quarters. Fr. Albinus, the pastor, was just preparing to leave for the church to celebrate Mass. I joined him and the two of us concelebrated the Mass.

After a brief meditation, we returned to the convento for breakfast. I explained to Albinus all that had transpired at Milbuk during the last two weeks. Albinus listened in rapt attention, cigarette in hand, his eyes blinking nervously as I narrated all the gory details. Albinus and I had lived and worked together in this parish for over three years. The older priest and I had got along quite well. Albinus was a workaholic….an untiring servant to his people…available to attend to their needs no matter what the inconvenience or hour. Albinus became somewhat of a hero and celebrity some eight years ago when he challenged a certain Adan de las Marias and his gang of cut-throats from the pulpit.

This man, Adan, led an armed gang of hoodlums that threatened and intimidated the business owners of the town. He ran a protection racket and controlled the docks in a style reminiscent of the "American Mafia". One night, several of his men confronted a Philippine Constabulary trooper who was patrolling the streets of the town. They subdued the trooper and began to beat him. Finally, they had him kneel in the dusty street in the middle of town begging for his life. They laughed and mocked him. Raising their guns they executed him in cold blood. There were witnesses who saw this brazen killing from behind their locked stores and homes. Nobody came forward in fear for their lives. Fr. Albinus made such a disturbance with his sermon that journalists from Manila came down to General Santos to cover the story. It was at this time that this criminal, Adan de las Marias was dubbed the "Octopus" in reference to his influence throughout the town and throughout the Province as well. This led to a serious investigation by government officials into the allegations of corruption, murder, robbery and intimidation by this gang of terrorists. The "powers to be" had plans for this town and they didn't want this man to be part of it. The investigations led to Adan's imprisonment in the Provincial Jail several years later. The prison happened to be located no more than two hundred meters from the City Hall and equidistant to the church. Adan was let out on bail for some months, but his influence and power had greatly diminished. Other would-be gangsters were only too willing to take his place.

Late one night, a call came in for a priest to attend a dying man at one of the clinics in Dadiangas. Albinus took the call since it was his turn this night to be available for such emergencies. When Albinus returned to the convento at about 1:00 A.M., I called out from my bed, "How did it go at the hospital…were there any problems?"

Albinus answered in a matter of fact manner, "Adan de las Marias was shot by the bodyguard of the son of the Mayor of Lagao".

This young hoodlum had confronted Adan in one of the town's nightclubs along the waterfront. Adan tried to ignore the young man. However, the Mayor's son, in a drunken stupor pulled out his gun and threatened Adan. With that, the young man's body guard shot the "Octopus" Adan and then all fled the nightclub.

Albinus continued, "Adan was still alive when I arrived at the hospital. He seemed glad to see me. I ministered to him and he died shortly after."

"Wow! What poetic justice is that?" I exclaimed. "Could you imagine this in a million years?"

Albinus never mentioned this incident again. He would speak of it only if someone asked him…but he never gloated over the event. I believe that he honestly hoped that the sins of this man were forgiven.

After breakfast, Albinus showed me to the room where I would stay for the next couple of days while taking care of business. Albinus suggested that I purchase the rice at Johnny Ang's rice mill just outside town. "Don't forget to visit Major Bautista at the P.C. Barracks," Albinus suggested. "He can provide you with armed military escort to Milbuk,"

Chinese-Filipino traders had long since captured the buying and selling of rice in this province. They were very adept at cornering the market on this most precious of commodities. As someone once said, "If you want to get money, go to a bank." So, if you want to buy rice, go to a Chinese-Filipino trader. I borrowed the parish jeep and traveled just outside the city to one of the largest rice mills in the province, owned by a certain Johnny Ang. He was an astute business man and an avid gambler, luckier than most. He had amassed his fortune through clever business transactions, but most of all through even more clever gambling techniques. Mahjong was his game. He excelled in this pastime which when played would last for two or three days at a session until fatigue or loss of revenue would bring the game to a screeching halt.

I went to the rice mill of Johnny Ang unannounced. I knew these people in General Santos well. I knew the good and the bad. The people liked and trusted me for I maintained silence in all that I came to know about them. I treated all people with deference and respect, avoiding embarrassing situations at all costs.

Johnny was not one of my favorite people, but I was going to give him a chance to do something good for the benefit of others. When I was announced to Mr. Ang, he immediately left his office to greet me. I related the story of the last two weeks and asked him straight out if he could donate rice for the evacuees. Johnny looked straight at me. His face was expressionless as he replied, "I'm running a business here. I don't give away rice to anyone. What I can do is to offer you my lowest price for a sack of rice. How many sacks will you need?"

I answered unblinking, "I will need one hundred sacks of rice. I will need your help in transporting this rice. Tomorrow morning, I will return with the money and at that time I will tell you when and where you may deliver the rice." Johnny agreed. "Thank you very much, Mr. Ang. I appreciate your help."

Leaving the rice mill, I headed back into town, down the main street of the city and drove along the road that ran parallel to the shore. There outside the city, about two kilometers away, was the large barrio of Bula. This village was special to me. I had spent countless hours ministering to these people. This place was like my very own parish. I had united the people spiritually as a community. Out of this union, the people were able to work together in trust. The villagers realized early on that the small chapel that was used for weekly Sunday Mass was far too small for the growing number of parishioners. A plan was brought forth to build a large, airy church right on the shore facing Sarangani Bay. It would be elevated above sea level by about two to three feet and built on a slab of concrete. The walls of the church would be built with decorative concrete blocks, through which air could freely flow to cool off the members during services.

One of the chief contributors to the church construction project was the Congson family. The patriarch of the family and his wife had raised a large family of eight children, five of whom were boys. These sons followed the profession of their father. As skilled fishermen, they expanded their business well beyond anyone's expectations. They built their own bancas and placed engines in them. They organized their employees into what they called "nets" of fishermen. These groups would work together to catch as many fish as possible. These fishermen used the Congson bancas and equipment. All the fish they caught would be given over to the company run by the family. They would be paid a certain amount for the fish they caught. The Congson family would then sell the fish to people in the city and provide fish for most of the province. They were so successful that they bought regular commercial fishing boats and nets to fish the deep waters of the Celebes Sea.

The family had a high regard for me. When I visited the family late in the morning of Tuesday, the family was delighted. I related what had happened in Milbuk and they were saddened at the events but only too happy to help.

"I don't need any contribution from your family by way of money. What I do need is a way to transport four tons of rice to Milbuk." I explained the dangers and told them that I would be speaking with the P.C. Commandant later that afternoon. I would be requesting an armed escort of P.C. troopers.

The oldest brother, Dominic, was now the patriarch of the family since the death of his father several years ago. He offered to provide an iron-hulled fishing boat that was about 60 feet long with a span of almost 20 feet across. There was ample room for storing the one hundred sacks of rice in one of the dry areas of the boat. I told Mr. Congson that I would like to leave for Milbuk early on Thursday morning, as early as 5:00 A.M. A truck from Johnny Ang's rice mill would be arriving at the dock area with the cargo of rice on Wednesday afternoon between 2:00 P.M. and 3:00 P.M.

Dominic grimaced and said, "There's only one problem. The boat that I have available is presently under repair. They tell me that the repairs should be complete by late tomorrow afternoon. When you bring the rice, we will have a better idea how the repairs are going."

I was then invited to stay on for lunch and visit with the rest of the family. I left Bula about 1:30 P.M. for the P.C. camp.

When I arrived at the P.C. Barracks, I noticed an Army weapons carrier filled with long dark green cases. One of the soldiers was just opening a case. He removed a long narrow object wrapped in a green, plastic-coated, heavy duty paper. Inside was a heavily greased rifle…a "Garand" or the "M-1" of World War II fame. There were hundreds of these weapons within the truck, destined for the Barrio Self Defense Units (B.S.D.U.) located throughout the province. The B.S.D.U.'s were paramilitary groups that the government forces used to supplement their troops in the field. With the Muslim insurgency breaking out through the whole of Mindanao, it was important to maintain control of key towns in each of the affected provinces.

I entered the main office of the Constabulary Commandant, Major Ramon Bautista. It was now about 2:15 P.M. in the afternoon and everyone was awake and busy. The Sergeant approached me and inquired what business I had with the Major. Briefly, I related the incidents of the last two weeks in Milbuk, emphasizing my need for armed escort. The sergeant entered the office of the commandant and quickly returned. He stood at the door of the Commandant's office and waved me inside.

"Good afternoon, Major Bautista. My name is Father Art Amaral. I am the parish priest of Milbuk in the Province of Sultan Kudarat."

"Ah, I see that you know my name."

"Yes sir. Father Albinus told me to relate to you all that has happened in Milbuk during the past two weeks. He said that you were a good man and soldier…and that I could count on you for help. I used to be stationed here in General Santos with Father Albinus some five years ago."

"Well, welcome back. Have you noticed any changes in the City?"

"Yes. It's become so much larger. There are new buildings everywhere. And the people…where are they coming from?" "The town seems peaceful enough…not like the "wild, wild west" of a few years ago."

"Indeed, there are so many new people here in the city and not all of them are good people. That's why we have such a large contingent of P.C. troopers stationed here in General Santos. How may I help you?"

"Your Sergeant probably related briefly some of the trouble I've been having in my parish. Milbuk is a logging camp with a population of about 5,000 people. The Weyerhaeuser Logging Company runs the logging concession in the Township of Palimbang. The township is predominantly Muslim with the exception of Milbuk which is practically 95% Christian. There are other small, scattered communities of Christians throughout the township".

Then, I continued, "On August the 8th, "a logging bus was ambushed in the mountains resulting in the death of 38 people. The Christians living in the nearby villages have flocked to Milbuk. Now both the High School and Elementary School is home to about 600 evacuees. I have traveled to General Santos to buy rice for the evacuees. Dominic Congson from Bula has provided an iron-hulled fishing boat to transport the rice to Milbuk. The trip is over a hundred and thirty kilometers by sea. Most of the way is safe. I'm concerned with the last 20 kilometers or so. The last part of the journey passes by five or more large Muslim barrios, anyone of which could be harboring the rebels. I am requesting an armed escort to Milbuk. We will be leaving from the barrio of Bula at 5:30 A.M. in the morning on Thursday, August the 15th. Can you help me?"

"I can help you," the Commandant replied confidently. "I will send five of my best men with you, a Sergeant and four troopers. Are there any P.C. troopers at Milbuk?"

"No! There aren't any P.C. in Milbuk at the present time."

"Then, I'll make sure that my men are at Bula by 6:00 A.M. on Thursday morning to accompany you to Milbuk", the Major replied.

"And I'll take good care of your men, Major. We will show them the hospitality of Milbuk. They will return to General Santos by Friday on the same fishing boat that they came on. I can't express adequately my gratitude for your generous assistance. God bless you. And thank you again."

"Think nothing of it. I am just happy to be able to provide assistance and security in your efforts for the people of Milbuk." And with that, I again expressed my gratitude and departed the P.C. compound.

That night, I slept soundly at the convento of Father Albinus, despite the loud, raucous noises of the city, in particular the tricycles. The "tricycles" are light weight motorcycles (90 cc.) that have an attached covered sidecar which can accommodate two passengers. Most of the vehicles had no mufflers. And there are hundreds of them plying their trade throughout the city. This low price transportation is very popular. There are no assigned routes or "tricycle stops", so that the tricycles can be found on every street and side alley of the city. The racket of their movements throughout the city continue well into the night, ceasing for brief moments of silence from midnight to 6:00 A.M. in the morning.

I had set the alarm clock for 5:00 A.M. and arose promptly at the first ring. Sleepily I groped my way to the bath room down the darkened hallway. I could hear Fr. Albinus shuffling around in his room. He was up and awake also.

"Hey, Art. I'll be down stairs in the kitchen heating up some water for coffee."

"Thanks a lot, Albi," I answered, splashing soapy cold water on my face, rinsing away the sand of sleep. After brushing my teeth, I finished my ablutions with a sprinkle of water on my hair, then ran the comb through it and arranged it exactly as my mother had taught me thirty years ago as a young boy. Nothing had changed in the appearance of my hair since then.

Down in the kitchen, both of us sat in silence at the table, slowly drinking coffee and eating a half stale "pan de sal" purchased the day before. The "pan de sal" was a form of bread fashioned like a small torpedo roll. Its name meant salt bread, a Spanish term for this bakery creation. After this monastic-like breakfast, I took my gym bag in hand and followed Albinus out the back door of the convento to the garage. We boarded the jeep and made our way through the center of town. Father Albinus was driving me to Bula, a short ride of only ten minutes. No traffic hindered our progress. There were only a dozen or so people awake, wandering here and there along the shore drive.

When we arrived at the home of Dominic Congson. His men were already up and working. "Thanks, Albi", I said. "Hope to see you next month in Calumpang, if all goes well in Milbuk. Otherwise, I probably won't be seeing you for a while."

"Have a safe journey, Art. God bless you and your companions." And waving one last time, Albinus drove away from Bula, his heart saddened by the uncertain events that faced his young friend.

Dominic Congson greeted me as he walked out the front door of his house. "Have you eaten your breakfast, Father?"

"Yes, I had some coffee with Father Albinus."

"Come then, let us see what condition the fishing boat is in." "Hoy, Ben," shouted Dominic as he approached the docked fishing boat.

"Good morning, sir."

"How's the engine acting?"

"It's a little rough, but it's running. It shouldn't give us too much trouble."

"When will you be able to leave", Dominic replied.

"We can leave in about an hour," Ben answered.

"Good. We still need to wait for the P.C. troopers." Turning to me, Dominic continued, "Come on, Father, Let's go back to the house and eat some real breakfast."

"All right, if you insist. Thank you."

As we entered the neat and tidy home, I was led to the dining room where places were already set up for breakfast. The women had been in the kitchen for at least an hour now and were bringing hot steaming rice, fried pork strips, fried eggs, bread and fresh papaya with small kalamansi on the side of the plate.

"This breakfast will keep me filled till Milbuk", I said, reaching for the bowl of rice. I ladled several mounds onto my plate. Fresh coffee filled out the menu...not the American kind but "made in the Philippines". This coffee was dark and somewhat bitter but delicious nevertheless. The caffeine content didn't seem as potent as Colombian brands.

Within twenty minutes, breakfast was over and I thanked my host profusely, making special mention of the fine breakfast that the women in the kitchen had prepared for me. The women all laughed and giggled as I attempted to relay my thanks in Cebuano.

Dominic and I walked outside the house as the weapons carrier of the Philippine Constabulary pulled up to the dock area. Four troopers exited from the truck with rifles slung over their shoulders and knapsacks in hand. The Sergeant in charge of the detail got out of the passenger's side of the truck.

I approached the Sergeant, a certain Elisio Gomez, and extended my hand in greeting, "Thanks for coming along with us. I really appreciate what you are doing. I presume your Major told you what troubles we are having in Milbuk."

"Yes, Father. He told us everything."

That's good. Now that you're here we can board the boat and leave for Milbuk."

The time was 6:00 A.M. and the sun was just rising over the distant hills. The five troopers, the captain of the boat and his mate were now all on board but the engine wouldn't start. "Now what's wrong?'" the captain muttered to himself. He left the wheel house and went to the large open hold aft of the boat where the engine was mounted. He climbed down the hold with pliers and wrench in hand to tighten and check each vital part. He returned to the wheel house to start up the engine. It roared to life but the sound didn't satisfy the captain. He turned off the engine and climbed back down the hold to undo some bolts to reveal that part of the engine that appeared to malfunction. Fifteen minutes passed…thirty minutes…then when it was almost 7:00 A.M. the engine started up to the delight of all on board. The captain announced that we could leave for Milbuk.

I yelled to Dominic as the boat was about to depart. "Dominic, thanks again for all your help. I'll take good care of your captain and mate and the boat as well, with the help of God."

"Safe journey, Father", Dominic yelled back as he raised his hand in farewell.

The captain carefully pulled away from the dock and headed out to the middle of Sarangani Bay. The fishing boat wasn't nearly as fast as my banca. Besides, the captain had no intention of over exerting the engine. As long as we arrived safely he would be satisfied.

The boat entered the mouth of Sarangani Bay by 10:00 A.M. and headed north along the shore of Maasim. The boat kept a steady course up the coast about two kilometers off-shore, far enough away to avoid hidden rocks and shoals, close enough to swim if the boat sank. The sun was now high in the sky. It was noontime and the captain kept a steady hand on the wheel... then it happened. There was a sudden change in sound coming from the engine room. The engine's exhaust began to emit strange belches of smoke that caused anxiety among the passengers and especially to the captain. The captain promptly turned off the engine. There wasn't much of a breeze on the sea but the current was running against us, pushing the boat slowly but definitely back to where we had just come. The captain assured his passengers, "This won't take too long to fix. We'd better drop anchor so we won't drift too far off course." So back down the black hold the captain went with a handful of tools. There was silence on the boat, except for the occasional clink of metal upon metal and the sound of the captain, speaking commands to his mate.

Twenty minutes passed and the captain scrambled up out of the engine hold to the wheel house. He turned on the ignition and the engine purred to life once again. A smile flashed across the captain's face as he ordered the mate to raise the anchor. And the boat was off again...slowly but deliberately.

By the time the fishing boat made Kiamba, it was already 5:00 P.M. Even in a fast moving banca, I could never reach Milbuk before dark. In this part of the world, sitting 6 degrees north of the Equator, darkness comes quickly. Twilight begins at 5:30 P.M. and in less than a half hour, total darkness, except for the moon and stars.

Arriving at Milbuk in the dark was one scenario that I dreaded. I never thought that the trip from Bula would take so long. My motorized banca could have covered the 130 kilometers in less than six hours. At the speed we were traveling, the fishing boat wouldn't arrive at Milbuk until 7:00 P.M. or later, a trip of 12 hours.

I approached the captain. "Captain, we will be approaching a group of about five Muslim barrios strung out along the coast to Milbuk. I suggest that you take your boat three or four kilometers off shore as you travel along the coast. You will reach the first barrio in about 45 minutes. From there, we will be about an hour away from Milbuk.

Sure enough, as the sun set in the West, the curtain of darkness fell dramatically upon us. From the boat, only pin points of light could be seen along the darkened coastline. A silence came over the passengers as each person strained to penetrate the black space, watching for any telltale movements of strange shapes that might cause harm. All lights were out on board the fishing vessel. Only the low roar of the diesel engines would possibly give us away. Everyone was now praying that the engines would not fail, no matter how loud they sounded.

As we neared the harbor of Milbuk, the captain brought the fishing boat closer to shore. It was then that tracer bullets could be seen arching across the sky in our direction. The boat was too far off-shore to be in any danger. What was of more concern was the passage into the harbor and the approach to the docking area. I was seriously afraid that some of the men on the evening "ronda" would become nervous over a mysterious fishing boat arriving at such an hour. I feared that some of the men would mistake the boat for Muslim rebels come to cause havoc in the camp. I hadn't told anyone that I would be arriving by boat on this day and at this time of night. I had planned to enter Milbuk in the clear light of day.

Turning to the captain, I made known my fears about approaching the dock area without some warning. "I have a plan", I said. "This is what I want you to do. Turn on all the lights on the boat, including the search light. I will walk to the front of the boat and you will shine the search light on me. Hopefully, they will recognize me. I will call out to the guards at the dock and tell them who I am. It should work. What do you think?" I was hoping that someone would try to discourage me from doing such a foolhardy thing. But this wasn't the case.

Everyone was in agreement. "Yes, that's a good plan", they said. I would be the one to stand on the open deck with the search light full upon me. All the passengers, however, huddled themselves within the tight confines of the wheelhouse for protection, including the P.C. troopers.

Slowly, the captain steered the fishing boat into the harbor of Milbuk in the direction of the docking area. I nervously walked from the wheelhouse toward the bow of the boat. Everyone else was squeezed into the protective womb of the wheel house and waited in expectation. Nobody wanted to offer themselves as a target to some nervous, tired logger with a rifle. I walked forward until I could go no farther. The search light not only illumined the deck but highlighted my whole figure. I held up both arms and yelled to anyone who might hear him... "It's me, Father Art. I'm Father Art. Is anyone there? Can you hear me?" I said all this in English, hoping that the guards would recognize me by my speech. By now the fishing boat had come within thirty yards of the dock when a man appeared out of the darkness, rifle in hand, "Good evening, Father", he said respectfully. "Oh, thank God", I gasped in surprise. "Yes, good evening. How are you doing?"

I turned around and faced the wheelhouse, directing the captain to bring the boat along the side of the dock. All the passengers slowly exited from the wheelhouse like dozens of clowns in a circus, tumbling out from a small car. Now their courage had returned and they headed to the front of the boat with me. "We'll tie up the boat for tonight. I'll arrange for a truck and some men to unload the rice tomorrow. In the meantime, all of you will spend the night at my house. We'll have a little party." "Sounds good, Father", the Sergeant replied with a smile. They all walked the half kilometer to the convento where I took them upstairs to the living room. "Make yourself at home. I'll be back in thirty minutes with some food."

I got into the jeep and went to my good friends, Norma Tibungcog and her husband, who ran a small restaurant. I purchased a case of San Miguel beer, a case of Coca Cola and whatever food I could lay my hands on. Upon returning home, I had the convento boys bring the food and drink to the visitors. They were quite pleased to be able to relax with a San Miguel in hand.

As the fishermen and troopers ate, drank and relaxed upstairs, I went to the boys' room and called out Mapandi Pantao, my Muslim "convento boy". He followed me to the office. We both sat on chairs facing each other.

I began to speak apologetically, "Mapandi, you are one of the best students who has ever lived and worked in this house. You work hard, study diligently and are always respectful. Your father can be rightly proud of you. However, you know all that has happened here in Milbuk. People talk silly sometimes and their thoughts and words become hateful. I am not sure that this trouble will be going away very soon. I am afraid for the people of Milbuk and I am afraid for you. You know how much I like you…how much I appreciate everything you do. Mapandi, it is not safe for you to remain here in Milbuk. I am not always around to protect you. I am writing a letter to Father Raymond in Surallah to accept you into their Notre Dame High School and to live in the convento. It causes me great pain to do this."

Mapandi lowered his head and uttered not a word.

I broke the silence. "Mapandi, I want you to get all your belongings together tonight. You will be leaving Milbuk tomorrow morning with the fishermen from Bula. They will make sure that you get on a bus in General Santos City for Surallah. I will give you money for the journey and some extra for your family. Your folks will be happy to see you again and know that you are safe. You are like my son, Mapandi. I will miss you very much."

Mapandi looked sadly at me. "Father, I thank you very much for everything. I know that you have no choice. I will be ready to leave tomorrow morning."

I rose from the chair and held out my hand to Mapandi. We shook hands, looking sadly at each other.

Early the next morning, the cargo was unloaded into one of the Company's trucks with the help of a dozen men taken from among the families of the evacuees living in the school. I thanked the troopers for accompanying me on the journey. I gave special thanks to the captain and his mate for sacrificing so much.

"Captain, I have a special favor to ask of you. This young man here is named Mapandi. He is like a son to me. Mapandi needs to leave Milbuk because of the dangers that being a Muslim place upon him."

I spoke loud enough so that everyone on board heard me. "I have given him money to purchase a ticket to Surallah. Could you please take good care of him until he is safely on the bus? I will be eternally grateful."

The captain replied without hesitation, "It will be my pleasure to help you, Father. I will take good care of him."

I then turned to Mapandi and shook his hand in farewell, placing my left hand upon his shoulder. "You'll be safe, Mapandi. God be with you."

Turning again to the captain, I continued, "Please tell Mr. Congson, that I am in his debt. Thank him very much for me."

The fishing boat left a little later than planned, at about 8:30 A.M. The return trip was as troublesome as the previous day's journey. However, they didn't have to contend with the prospect of a Muslim rebel attack on their boat. They all arrived safely in Bula about 8:00 P.M.

# CHAPTER 16

## *Cast Your Vote*

For the next two weeks, the people in the camp tried to occupy themselves. The women took the opportunity to visit and gossip. The men organized softball games and challenged the team from the High School. I loved to play softball and considered myself a good pitcher. "We can beat the loggers", I told the Notre Dame boys. "I'll pitch for you." Well, it didn't take long for the truth to be known. Every pitch that I threw, the loggers smashed almost as easy as felling a small tree with an axe. Their hand/eye coordination was remarkable. There were seven hits and five runs in the very first inning. Could these loggers hit! After the second inning and another four runs, I turned over the pitching to one of my students… and the slaughter continued. The whole game of five innings was batting practice for the loggers. These men, toughened by years on the job, cutting down trees, were vicious when swinging a bat. They were accurate too. Needless to say, the loggers won the game. The exact score has been lost to the ages, but the margin of victory was considerable.

A few days after my return to Milbuk with the boatload of rice, a small squad of Philippine Constabulary Troops, numbering about four, arrived at Milbuk by launch from Cotabato City. Ostensibly, their mission was to assist the local barrio self-defense force with their military knowledge and prowess. However, the sergeant in charge of the small squad of P.C. troopers was only intent on what he could receive from the logging company by way of food and drink... we are not talking about water here. The man was small and rotund in figure with a bad-tempered look about him. He was a nasty man but probably good at what he did in chasing down killers and robbers in the wild. When the manager closed off the donations of beer and liquor to this sergeant and his crew, the sergeant set up his thirty caliber machine gun and shot tracer bullets across the camp at 1:00 A.M. in the morning. Needless to say, this put the camp on edge.

A week later, another squad of seven P.C. Troopers arrived by helicopter led by a young lieutenant. These men were professional military types, namely, organized, respectful and trained to accomplish their goals efficiently. One of the soldiers was a sergeant, Tomas Ortiz, whose marriage I had celebrated to one of my Notre Dame High School graduate students only a year ago. The young woman was already with child and within months of giving birth. When the PC Sergeant heard that trouble had visited his town, he volunteered to serve in the area and to be close to his new family.

Boredom quickly set in among the camp dwellers. Anxiety of another kind fell upon the loggers and their families. Life and death issues were set aside by the more mundane considerations concerning work, money and food. The Company had allowed the employees to charge credit for their purchases at the Company Store. The money they owed was to be withheld automatically from their paychecks. But this generosity was not going to last forever. The Company needed the men to work, otherwise the whole logging operation would not be profitable anymore and the Company would have to abandon Milbuk.

## Saturday, August the 31st ⋯

The loggers had been out of work for 24 days. The Company's manager had arranged for a town meeting to take place at 10:00 A.M. A simple stage and sound system had been set up on a hilly slope of land just below the Company Store where most of the loggers purchased their food. The place was only a stone's throw distance from the main gate and a natural gathering place for the people who lived within and outside the camp. A series of speakers, representing the Company, the Philippine Constabulary, the Mayor's Office and the Church, would be addressing the loggers and their families concerning the all-important issue of returning to work. The loggers would then vote publicly whether to return to work or not.

The majority of the speakers emphasized the need to return to work. The ambush that took place over three weeks ago was an isolated incident, they argued. The Company will not need to log in that area. There are other more productive places to harvest the lauan… places that are safer. The logging franchise covered a vast area of land. The Muslim rebels cannot be in every place at the same time. Besides, there were assurances from the Muslim Mayor Druz Ali that the northern part of the Township did not harbor any dissidents or rebels. No one will harm any logger working in his part of the Township. These assurances came through the mouth of the Vice Mayor, Rolando Abary, the grandson of the owner of the large tract of land upon which the logging camp and all its facilities now stood. He resided in Milbuk on his own parcel of land.

Rolando Abary was a popular and generous person whose ability to speak several key dialects of the region fluently made him a favorite choice as a political candidate for Vice Mayor when the Mayoral candidate from Palimbang, Druz Ali invited him to run on his ticket three years ago. Druz Ali was shrewd. He knew that he could depend on Rolando delivering the Christian vote in the Milbuk/San Roque area if his running mate was a Christian. The incumbent Mayor at the time, Imam Ibrahim Malik, had his main constituency in the area between Kalaong and Malisbong. This was his first term as Mayor. Even though Mayor Malik was an educated and enlightened man, having attended college in Marawi City, Lanao Del Norte, he was beset by many problems stirred up by his arch political enemy Druz Ali. In the election results the margin of victory was narrow. Druz Ali was successful in discrediting this righteous man and installing himself as the Mayor, thus becoming the chief political power in the Township. Rolando Abary was all about doing the Mayor's bidding even though most of the time he was in the dark about Druz Ali's plans and intentions.

The Mayor would always tell you what you wanted to hear. He had such a knack for this. If you asked the Mayor in person, "Can we return to logging without being attacked by the rebels"? "Why of course you can", the Mayor would reply. "Isn't that what you'd want me to tell you"? The Mayor's perfidiousness and cunning would be more evident as this whole drama unfolded. Druz Ali was obviously in league with his Muslim brothers of the MNLF. He was no fool. He would play this game with the logging company, the military and the government itself rather than to risk any disfavor with his Muslim brothers. He would reassure safety and protection to the logging company all day long if they wanted. But the Mayor had no control over the rebels' decisions to attack again or not.

As intelligent as Rolando was, there were also weaknesses in him that placed this otherwise good person over on the "dark side". How many times had Mayor Druz Ali used his power of persuasion to manipulate Rolando in schemes that would further the personal interests of this "master puppeteer"? However, there was the real possibility that Rolando was fearful of losing his life to this unscrupulous Mayor, if he did not go along with his plans, whatever they were. Rolando was caught in the middle. Whatever he did, the result would turn out badly anyway. Here he was standing in front of all these hard working loggers. All eyes were upon him for words of consolation and assurance. How could he disappoint so many of his people? They were relying on him to give them the truth and as far as he knew, whatever the Mayor told him must be true.

Rolando stood tall before them and with a strong voice urged them to return to work. "I have come from the Mayor", he said. "Yes, I have traveled up the road to Palimbang myself. There were no rebels on the road to stop me. All was peaceful. The Mayor wants me to assure you that there are no rebels in his part of the township. The vast area of forests awaits your chain saws and axes. We want the Company to be successful and to remain in the township for many years to come. I am just as concerned with your safety as you are.

The buses that will take you to the area north of Palimbang will be escorted by armed Philippine Constabulary. You know me. I have lived with you here in Milbuk for many years. You can trust me when I tell you that it is safe."

Rolando turned away from the mike of the sound system and within his mind there was deep doubt that all would be well. He certainly hoped that what he said to his fellow Milbukians was true, that no harm would come to them.

There was no applause after these speeches, only silence. The loggers were deep in thought. After each speaker they would turn to each other and comment on something that struck them. Still, they wanted to hear more.

Finally, it was my turn to speak. I approached the stage and was well aware that my words would be the only ones in opposition for a return to work.

"People of Milbuk...I am a man without a family. I do not have a wife or children to clothe and feed. I know how urgent it is for all of you to return to work but I cannot agree with what has been said here today. There is no certainty that any of you will not be killed by the rebels if you return to the mountains. The words of the Mayor cannot guarantee that the rebels will not attack again. I know that there will be armed escorts with you as you travel to the logging site. But will this protect you from being killed? Your life is more important than logging. If you lose your jobs, you will have saved your lives. You can always move on...and start anew in some other more peaceful place. But this is your decision. You must vote to work or not to work. I give you God's blessing in the choice you are about to make."

With those words, I made my way down the hill and stood among the loggers. The Company's business manager called the assembly to order. He would call for a hand count. Each logger would vote only once...either to work or not to work.

"All those in favor of returning to work, please raise your hands."

Several supervisors began counting the raised hands of the loggers present at the meeting. "291...voting in favor of returning to work."... "I count 287"... "I have 282 YES votes". The business manager wrote down the numbers, added them up and divided by three. "The YES vote is "287."

"Now those who are voting NOT to return to work, please raise your hands."

This vote counting was much faster. The combined "NO" vote came to 87. The majority definitely voted to return to work by a 3 to 1 margin. The Company manager thanked the men. "You will be notified tomorrow who will be going on the first work detail. Thank you all for your cooperation."

I walked slowly toward the main gate somewhat embarrassed and saddened that I hadn't spoken more effectively to convince the men to remain off the job until conditions improved.

"It was too early to return to work", I muttered. "There are hardly enough troopers to protect ourselves here in the camp if the rebels choose to attack. It was a mistake to even take a vote. I should have prepared my talk a little better and spoken to the people entirely in Tagalog. It would have been much more forceful. Now the only thing to do is to pray that no harm comes to any of these men."

## Monday, September 2nd...

The High School had been closed now for almost a month, ever since the ambush in the mountains. The evacuees from the surrounding barrios had come into the camp for protection and were still occupying the classrooms. I still felt badly in sending Mapandi away from Milbuk. I was only thinking of his welfare. I also wondered about the young Muslim girl, Fatima Balitao, the working student who assisted the Sisters with some of their chores. She was a good student and most anxious to complete her studies in High School. Now she was living in the barrio of Wal, with her mother and other relatives. I thought it would be a good gesture to bring her some reading material and books to study. I contacted her teacher and asked her to put together some assignments for Fatima to work on while she was away from classes. My plan was to travel to Wal and deliver the books myself. I wanted to do something other than to wait till the next thing happened. Waiting around and doing nothing was not my virtue. Since the town meeting, the situation seemed a bit improved. One passenger jeepney even made a trip up the main road to Palimbang and back. Everything seemed somewhat normal again. The chances were slim that the rebels would venture this far off course. And so I placed Fatima's homework in my back pack and prepared to leave for Wal.

The Muslim village of Wal was about 4 or 5 kilometers from Milbuk, situated on the main road bordering the sea. I mounted the trail bike. I wore an old jet plane helmet on my head for protection, especially when taking trips outside the camp. The helmet had been left by the last priest, who was the pastor here. The trip would take about 20 minutes over a rough, wash-board like road.

As I left the camp, the sentry at the camp gate, looked at me with surprise as I headed north up the road to Palimbang. I hadn't told anyone where I was going. Only the teacher of Fatima knew something of my plans. It was 10:00 A.M., a bright, clear and sunny day. There was no other traffic on the road. I didn't even see another human being until I approached the village of Wal. The people heard the sound of my motorcycle even before they saw me. Everyone stopped what they were doing and gaped at me in amazement. What was this American priest doing here at Wal?

I drove into the middle of the barrio, stopped and turned off the engine to the motorcycle. I looked around at all the people coming out from their homes. They just stood there silently, staring…just staring at me. I swung my leg over the seat of the bike and set the kick stand. With a smile on my face, I approached one group of men and women and respectfully inquired if they knew of a young student who attended Notre Dame High School by the name of Fatima Balitao. Nobody gave the slightest indication that they even knew her name. However, one of the women in the group turned around and entered a house. In less than five seconds, Fatima appeared somewhat surprised and a little embarrassed. I took the knapsack off my back and went about a lengthy explanation to Fatima and to all within hearing, why I was at Wal. I next reached into the knapsack and brought the books out one at a time and gave them to Fatima, explaining to her and the whole village that I wasn't sure when the High School would be re-opened…but I wanted her to continue studying for the day when she would return. Everyone seemed satisfied with my explanation. I then said goodbye to Fatima and her family, waving to the whole village as I turned the bike around and headed back to Milbuk.

Well, that was rather strange, I thought. Filipinos, whether Christian or Muslim, are extremely hospitable, but nobody invited me into their home or even offered me a cup of tea or coffee. I felt a nagging certainty that all was not well at the village of Wal. I was now seven kilometers away from Milbuk on a very lonely stretch of road. My thoughts became troubled…almost paranoid. "What if… the rebels are camping out in this area? How easy it would be to kill or kidnap me here. Why didn't I think about this before I left Milbuk", I admonished myself.

I had only traveled half a kilometer when a feeling came over me as if eyes were watching me from everywhere. On my right side were coconut trees and a green mantle of grass leading to the sandy beaches bordering the Celebes Sea. But on my left was the heavy undergrowth of the jungle that swept down from the mountains. Groves of bamboo and palm grew here and there along the side of the road, good hiding places for an ambush. I kept reminding myself, "Look straight ahead at the road…Keep facing forward! Do not look to your left!" My bike maintained its speed. I was not driving fast…about 40 kilometers an hour. The temptation to open it up and speed out of this "danger" was compelling. Nevertheless, I kept looking straight ahead and maintained a steady pace. After about three kilometers, I no longer felt the eyes. A peaceful feeling of relief came over me as I increased my speed and proceeded more quickly to Milbuk.

# CHAPTER 17

# *The Betrayal*

**Tuesday, September 3rd...**

The rhythmic cadence of the loggers walking past my house broke the stillness of the early morning as the metal clanking of their lunch pails banged noisily against the sides of their legs. As with other mornings, they gathered in small groups awaiting the call to board the buses. The difference this morning was the seriousness of the men. There was no telling of jokes, laughing or loud talking. What little talk there was came in quiet, whispered remarks and solemn shaking of heads. The field manager went around from group to group, marking off the names of those assigned to work that day. All were present and accounted for...nobody called off sick or just didn't show up. The loggers had been out of work for one month now and their forced lay-off was not a paid vacation. They had to work if their families were to eat.

The sixty loggers would be riding in a convoy of two buses and three Toyota pickups. Their destination would be the main logging site in the mountains above Palimbang, about eight to ten kilometers within the interior. A combination of armed loggers, camp security personnel and P.C. troopers rode shotgun in the cargo bed of each Toyota, a total of 4-5 men in each pickup truck.

Chief Dorotheo would ride in the lead Toyota, spearheading the convoy. The field supervisor, Wil Ramchand would bring up the rear of the convoy in the third Toyota with Sgt. Tomas Ortiz, commander of the small P.C. force that had been sent to Milbuk several weeks before. Some of the loggers on the bus were also armed. This was not a formidable force by any means but it did give some confidence to the loggers on the bus.

Mr. Roberts the Company's manager was up early with his men. Contrary to all the assurances of Mayor Druz Ali, Mr. Roberts also felt uneasy in sending these men back into the mountains. His men would be working 30 kilometers away and it appeared unlikely that the rebels would bother them at that site. However, he just wanted to play it safe. And so, Mr. Roberts approached Chief Dorotheo and his field supervisor, Wil Ramchand and took them aside,

"Look, men, I feel a bit uneasy about the security arrangements for the men. I want you to bring the loggers back to Milbuk right after lunch. I don't want them returning late in the afternoon. Don't say anything until after lunch."

"OK, Mr. Roberts you're right. It is a good idea", both men chimed in.

The call went out... "Board the buses!"

Wil Ramchand opened the door of his Toyota pick-up, swung up onto the seat and greeted his companion, Sgt. Ortiz who was riding "shot-gun" with him.

Chief Dorotheo yelled from his pick-up to Sgt. Ortiz, "Are all your men on board, Sergeant?" "Yes sir, we are all set to go."

With that, Chief Dorotheo took the lead as the first bus pulled out behind him, followed by another Toyota pick-up and then by the second bus with the third Toyota bringing up the rear. The trip would take almost an hour and a half. It was 5:00 A.M. The weather was clear and the roads dry. The main highway was deserted at this time in the morning. It was still dark. No living person could be seen as the loggers drove quickly by the four or five Muslim villages strung out along this stretch of road.

The trip was uneventful. Upon arriving at the logging site in the mountains above Palimbang, the P.C. troopers dismounted from the vehicles and spread out through the area to make sure that there were no lurking rebels ready to spring an ambush. All the equipment had been left there for almost a month and was untouched. The bulldozers and log grapplers started up right away. The chain saws placed within the tool shed were all neatly hanging in rows waiting to be shocked into life. It was just another day on the job. Trees had to be felled and trimmed and the logs pulled and piled in the staging area to be later loaded onto trucks for the log pond. The men were working well. A month off the job had re-invigorated them. You could sense that they enjoyed being back in the forest.

A jeep pulled up to the logging site. Two men alighted from the jeep and approached two of the loggers and asked to speak with the supervisor in charge. Mr. Ramchand was called and he arrived shortly in his Toyota.

"What can I do for you?" he inquired.

"Sir, we were sent by Mayor Druz Ali to invite you and your men for lunch at Barrio Midol. It's a village, eight kilometers from here, along the main road at the foot of these mountains. The people of the barrio are preparing a lunch for you and your men, a feast to celebrate your return to work."

"Well, this is a surprise! Thank you very much," Mr. Ramchand replied. "Please thank the Mayor and give my regards."

"You can thank him yourself. He will be there to greet you and your men."

"Tell the Mayor that we will be there at about 11:30 A.M."

It was already 9:15 A.M. in the morning. The Mayor's two men returned to their jeep. Inside there were two other men, armed and silent. Most likely, these men were members of the Mayor's "blackshirts" squad or plainclothes policemen (it was all the same).

Wil Ramchand spoke with Chief Dorotheo and the other supervisors together and told them, "Round up the men in an hour. We will be having our lunch at the last barrio we passed along the way, a fiesta hosted by the Mayor. I guess it's the Mayor's way of saying thanks for returning to work. I don't know what the old fox is up to! But I was told by Mr. Roberts to bring all of you back to Milbuk right after lunch. Therefore, when the men finish eating at this village, I want them to board the buses quickly so that we can head back to Milbuk early. Any questions…?"

One of the men spoke up. "I'm a little bit suspicious that something may happen. What do you think?"

"I don't know. This is our first day back. So far it's gone quite well. You can tell the men now to finish what they're doing and put away the equipment. We've done enough for today."

The convoy made its way down the mountain deliberately, arriving at the Muslim village by 11:30 A.M. The convoy parked along the side of the road just across from the village nestled among the coconut trees. The barrio captain together with the Mayor came up to greet Mr. Ramchand and Chief Dorotheo, inviting all the loggers and security personnel into the village. Long rows of tables had been set up on one side of the village to the left. The Muslim men, arms folded, stood in small groups to the right at the doorway to their homes, looking on but showing no signs of welcome. The women folk were busy placing rice, vegetables and specially prepared goat meat on the tables, covering them with metal mesh-like covers shaped in the form of a hemi-sphere. Flies were endemic to this region and could be found anywhere there was food. Any food left unprotected would soon be covered with swarms of flies.

The barrio captain waved the loggers to the food laden tables. All of this preparation was done at the insistence of the Mayor. His request to the people of this barrio was an order, whether the villagers wanted to prepare the food or not. It didn't matter. The Mayor's word was law…and it became the villagers' duty to obey. Why was he doing this? It was anyone's guess. The Mayor never did a kind act for anyone but that he would receive as much if not more in return. You could be certain that the Mayor's action this day was part of some grand plan of his.

Slowly a line was formed. The loggers went first to the pump at the side of the road where the women would fetch water and wash their clothes. The men primed the pump and as the water flowed out, they washed their hands and headed for the buffet tables. They approached shyly and smiled gratefully toward the women who were looking on. There was no response to their friendliness, only a dull, serious stare. Uniform pieces of banana leaf were piled one on another like Styrofoam plates at a picnic. They placed their food on the plates of Mother Nature and used their fingers as utensils. Filipinos of all classes were most adept at using their fingers for eating, though in polite company, utensils would be available but not here.

Some of the loggers attempted to strike up a conversation with the Muslim men of the village. They would answer questions directed to them but were somewhat aloof from all these goings-on. It seemed that they couldn't wait until these loggers left their village. No one even attempted to speak to any of the women. The loggers knew the rules of such encounters…it was forbidden. As the last of the men filled up their "plates" with food, Wil Ramchand approached the Mayor and the barrio captain, thanking them for providing such fine food for his men. He bid them farewell, telling them that he and his men had to leave early for an important meeting with the manager back at Milbuk. He again thanked the Mayor and the people of Midol for their hospitality. Wil then turned to the other supervisors and gave the order to board the buses. Half of the men were still busy eating their food and hurriedly swallowing their bottle of warm coke. They brought their food aboard the bus with them and waved back at the villagers in thanks for providing such fine fare. The buses roared to life and the caravan, led by Chief Dorotheo in the lead Toyota, headed up the highway toward Milbuk.

The logging convoy covered the next twenty kilometers in record time. Surprisingly, there were no people out on the road. No one could be seen even walking around or working near the Muslim barrios they passed. Could they all still be having their siesta? This did not look good.

The convoy rumbled into the Muslim barrio of Wal. Now the loggers were only seven kilometers away from Milbuk. The time was about 1:15 P.M. in the afternoon. Again, no people could be seen even at this fair sized village.

In the meantime, Mr. Roberts had been informed forty-five minutes earlier by the radio operator, Virgilio Jayme, that the logging buses were about to be ambushed by the rebels along the road, upon their return to Milbuk near the barrio of Wal. Virgilio had obtained this information secretly from Mayor Druz Ali, his friend. Mayor Ali probably had a tinge of conscience and felt guilty keeping such harmful information to himself. Mr. Roberts quickly phoned Capt. Leonard 'Nards' Flores, the pilot, to meet him immediately at the office.

Upon his arrival, Mr. Roberts informed him, "There will be an ambush of the logging buses near the barrio of Wal. I want you to warn the buses of the impending danger."

"Where did you receive the information, Mr. Roberts"?

"Virgilio here, came to me a few minutes ago with the news. He got the information from the Mayor. We will talk about this later. I have typed out a message for the Field Supervisor Ramchand in this large brown envelope telling him to turn around and bring all the men to Wasag. We can safely transport them to Milbuk by barge. Get in the plane now and go warn the men of the ambush."

(Now Wasag was the port area developed by Weyerhaeuser for shipping out the large mahogany logs to ships anchored off shore. The place was fifteen kilometers or so beyond the town of Palimbang and very accessible to the main logging area of the concession. Wasag consisted of several large maintenance shacks. It was a large flat area along the coast that was built next to shore to facilitate the loading of mahogany timbers taken from the mountains nearby. The trucks would not need to travel the long distance south to Milbuk to deposit their load of logs. The logs would be stored on land until such time as a ship arrived to pick them up for shipment overseas. The timbers were placed one on the other, pyramid style, in such a way that they wouldn't roll off. Huge machines with tires 5-6 feet high and iron claw-like pincers would enwrap their mighty arms and lift 2 or 3 great logs at a time and carry them from their place on the ground at the storage area down to the edge of the sea where they would roll into the water with a mighty splash. There the logs would be herded together by the barge and fastened one to the other and taken out to sea, ½ a kilometer away, to be loaded onto a ship. The barge that

Mr. Roberts referred to was used in dragging the giant logs out to the waiting cargo ships.)

Hurriedly, the two men drove quickly to the airport and checked out the Cessna for fuel and oil. Everything was in order as Capt. Flores taxied the plane to the far end of the runway looking cautiously to his left and right for any suspicious movement in the jungle. Virgilio Jayme sat in the co-pilots seat. The plane ran quickly down the runway and within seconds was banking over the Celebes Sea and heading North up the road to Palimbang.

The road was relatively straight. Capt. Flores brought the plane down to about 100 feet off the ground, high enough not to clip any of the taller coconut trees. Virgilio strained his eyes as he tried to penetrate the foliage of trees below for any signs of life or movement. Nards stared straight ahead looking for the dust of the convoy as it made its way home to Milbuk. As the plane neared Wal, Nards could see the convoy in the distance. Just then, Virgilio let out a yell…

"Nards…they're down below us. There's a large group of men carrying rifles." Nards brought the plane down to tree-top level to warn the convoy of the impending ambush. The convoy was only two kilometers from the ambush site. Nards buzzed the buses, hoping someone would look up. How can he warn them? The brown packet of information that Mr. Roberts had given the men to throw from the plane to get their attention was useless now in this situation. They felt so helpless.

"Maybe I could distract the rebels below and draw their attention to the plane", Nards hollered to Virgilio.

He pulled the plane up sharply and banked left to make another run at the rebels. As he passed the rebels gathered below on the road, shots were being fired up at the plane. The plane took several hits. Nards cried out in pain as one of the bullets penetrated the under skin of the plane and exited through his foot. He pulled the plane sharply up and to the right, heading out to sea. "I've got to get this plane down before I pass out," he moaned.

Despite the pain, Capt. Flores was able to contact the radio shack at the main office in Milbuk and told the operator to get Mr. Roberts immediately. "He's here, Nards," the operator replied.

"Mr. Roberts, the convoy is now under attack as I speak. I tried to warn the buses but I couldn't get their attention. I came too close to the rebels in my attempt to distract them and they shot up the plane. I'm wounded in the foot. I'm bleeding quite a bit. Please have someone pick us up at the airstrip."

"It's O.K., Nards. Just land the plane safely", Mr. Roberts cautioned.

Mr. Roberts quickly called the assistant security supervisor to send out the alarm to the men in the camp to report to their posts. He also notified the hospital that there may be many casualties arriving within minutes.

At about the same time as the Weyerhaeuser plane came under fire, the convoy entered into the ambush area a kilometer past the village of Wal. Gunfire erupted from the jungle of trees and bushes on the left side of the convoy. The lead Toyota, driven by Security Chief Dorotheo, was the first vehicle to take fire.

The initial upward firing to down the plane gave warning to the convoy of the impending ambush, thereby giving the escorting security forces spearheaded by Chief Dorotheo a chance to take cover on the side of the road and return fire.

In the course of the firefight, a bullet, fired by a sniper hiding in one of the mango trees behind the stopped Toyota of the Chef grazed him slightly. Knowing the general direction of the shot, he sprayed that tree with a modified M16 Armalite rifle (on full auto). The Chief didn't know if he hit anyone, but there was no more sniper fire after that.

The driver of the first bus pushed down hard on the gas pedal, following the Toyota pickup of Chief Dorotheo. It roared through the ambush site with bullets whining over the heads of both driver and passengers. One, two, three of the loggers let out a scream as the bullets tore through their bodies. Everyone was now lying flat on the floor, cowering under the benches with fear. One logger lay draped over the back of the bench. His death came quickly.

By now everyone in the remaining convoy was firing their weapons wildly in the hope of hitting some of the ambushers. The second bus was hot on the heels of the second Toyota. Both raced forward with break neck speed through this gauntlet. The road had shallow irrigation ditches running along both sides and boarded by coconut trees every ten or fifteen yards. To drive off the road to the right would put you directly on the soft sandy soil that led to the beach. Taking a left off the road would plunge you into a jungle swamp.

The armed men in the back of the second Toyota pickup lay flat on the bed of the truck and fired their weapons blindly over the side without looking. Suddenly, the driver of the pickup was wounded by a bullet and lost control of his vehicle veering wildly to the right and catapulting through the air as the vehicle shot out of the ditch and onto the sandy soil near the beach. The driver was killed as he attempted to exit the vehicle. His companion in the front seat and the two armed men in the bed of the truck were able to leave the truck but were unlucky in finding shelter enough to fight off the attackers. Eventually, all the men were shot dead by the rebels who descended upon them in large numbers.

The fate of passengers in the third Toyota was similar. The logging supervisor driving this Toyota and his PC companion were hit by a barrage of bullets. The bullets from a high powered AK-47 of an MNLF terrorist entered through the open window of the driver's side of the last Toyota bringing up the convoy, and tore through the heads of the two men in the front seat. The skulls of both Wil Ramchand and Sgt. Tomas Ortiz exploded on impact, leaving only the fleshly mask of their faces hanging limply upon their chests. The Toyota careened wildly to the right and bounced in and out of the ditch several times, finally crashing into a coconut tree. The two P.C. troopers and a camp security guard in the rear of the pick-up were catapulted onto the sand. As they pawed their way onto the beach, three of the rebels came running up to them, firing their weapons into their battered bodies.

The Muslim guerillas seemed upset that so many of the loggers had escaped their clutches. They had anticipated a massacre of over sixty people. The rebels had been caught unawares. The armed killers looked down the road and saw the last speeding bus belch black clouds of diesel into the air as it escaped to safety. The ambush would have been a much greater catastrophe if not for the foresight of the logging manager.

Mr. Roberts had told the logging field supervisor, Mr. Ramchand and Chief Dorotheo, to bring the logging crew back home early, "Stop the work at noon, and as soon as the men finish lunch, head on back to the camp".

So when the convoy of two buses and three Toyota pick-ups approached the barrio of Wal, the Muslim rebels were unprepared for such an early return. The rebels expected the loggers to arrive about 4:00 P.M. It was only 1:30 in the afternoon and some of the rebels were just awakening from their siesta. Witnesses say that when the convoy approached the ambush site, many of the rebels were still running into position. They were firing their weapons as they ran.

While the lead Toyota and the two buses were running at break neck speed to reach Milbuk, the Cessna had headed south to Milbuk for the airstrip. The distance was only six kilometers, so it didn't take long for Nards to bring the plane around and set up for a landing. Slowly, he centered the plane over the water heading straight down the middle of the runway. The pain was pulsating. He could feel the wetness of the blood as it filled his shoe and left a small puddle on the floor of the plane. He turned to Virgilio and instructed him to put his feet on the rudder pedals so that he could land the plane. His left foot was useless now for flying. Virgilio had been with Nards on several trips so that he knew what he had to do if both of them were to leave the plane alive. Nards brought the plane down gently, while Virgilio kept the wings of the plane level with the ground, then, touchdown. The plane rolled down the middle of the runway and Nards turned sharply to his left and brought the plane right up to the maintenance shack where a pick-up was waiting to take him to the medical clinic for treatment.

While all this was happening, I was up in the convento, having freshened up after an hour's siesta. I was startled when I heard the blaring sound of the buses honking their horns frantically, speeding toward the main gate with the dead and wounded. I ran downstairs and across the street to the hospital just as the first bus was arriving. Not one to say, "I told you so!"...I couldn't help repeating to myself, "Why didn't they listen to me?" I told the people during the town meeting, "If you choose to return back to the mountains to log, you are placing yourselves in great danger."

Crowds of people appeared out of nowhere. The loggers on the bus took their wounded comrades into the clinic. I wanted to help bring some of the wounded into the clinic and so I swung myself up on the bus to see if anyone had been left. There, toward the back of the bus, slumped over on the bench seat, was another logger. "How could they have forgotten him?" I thought. Then I saw that the man was already dead. I called out to several loggers nearby to help me bring the body down and into the hospital. A morgue had been set up earlier during the first ambush and so all the dead were placed there for their families to identify.

The second bus arrived with its dead and wounded as well as the remaining Toyota that suffered one wounded. The entrance to the hospital was crowded with people. Dr. Domingo was besieged on all sides for his help. He ordered the nurses to triage the most serious cases and to provide first aid assistance until he could get to them. Dr. Domingo looked at me with some panic in his eyes and pleaded, "Father, could you help bring some order to this crowd. They will only interfere in the work that has to be done." Without hesitation, I spoke to the people and ordered those who were not wounded or directly assisting the wounded to leave the hospital and stay outside so that the wounded could be treated.

Twelve people were killed in the ambush and nine wounded. Nine bodies of the dead had not been recovered from the ambush site. The rebels continued to move by foot toward a small Muslim village, one kilometer from Milbuk, the very village where Mayor Druz Ali and I had held the "Peace and Reconciliation Prayer Meeting" one year ago. This was the same village that I had foolishly visited alone on my motorcycle two weeks ago when there was a report of gunfire coming from this village.

This area had two villages parallel to each other. One village was Christian and located by the shore; the other was Muslim and situated just a few hundred yards away, separated only by the main road. When word of the ambush spread to these communities, all of the Christians headed again to Milbuk and to their relatives and friends in and around the logging camp. The Muslims quickly left and headed toward the town of Palimbang. The Christian evacuees came inside the camp and showed up at the convento. The school had been closed for several weeks already and there were still quite a few families living in some of the classrooms. Now I had to utilize all the classrooms in the school and even open the church to accommodate the hundreds of people flowing into the camp.

On the same day, another unfortunate incident occurred by the shore near the Christian village, when some of the men, about to leave with their families for Milbuk, noticed a fishing boat with three Muslim fishermen landing just a few hundred yards down the beach from their village. They went over to the fishermen and questioned them. Soon the questions turned to accusations and tempers flared. The villagers accused the three Muslims of being involved somehow in the ambushes. The men pleaded with the angry villagers, arguing that they had spent the last several hours fishing. They knew nothing of what happened to the logging buses at Wal. The group of villagers, six in number, just grew more angry and distrustful of the Muslim fishermen, whom they knew. These Muslim men lived only a stone's throw from their village. One of the men pointed his gun at the more vocal of the fishermen, a young man, intelligent and tall. Suddenly, a shot was fired. The young man took a bullet to his chest and fell backward into the sea. The other two men panicked and began to run away, but were quickly shot on the spot. The six villagers came together and quickly walked away from the scene of their senseless slaughter. The people hesitated to tell me the story, but I insisted. They were embarrassed in the telling, since the people knew these Muslims even by name. The people knew that what the six men did was shameful.

A kilometer away, in a small settlement of several homesteads that butted up against the treed jungle hills, Romeo Mangahas, age twenty, was tending his father's small farm. The farm was situated about 900 meters from the shore and ran parallel to the main road, shielded by small groves of coconut trees, palms and bamboos. Romy heard the roar of the buses and the blaring horns filter through the trees and across the field of corn and soybean. He lifted his head and searched for an opening in the trees for a glimpse at the passing vehicles and some answer to the noise and speed of their passing. He could see nothing but flashes of yellow. Romy shrugged his shoulders and continued to work removing the weeds from the rows of corn and soy, loosening the soil and breaking up the clods to better aerate the plants and enable the rain to penetrate the roots.

A half hour had passed and Romy was still hard at work in the fields, intently focused on his hoeing, unaware that he was being observed. It must have been the strange silence that suddenly caught his attention. The farm was surrounded by trees and yet the chirping and singing of the birds was absent. Only the hushed blowing of the wind and the gentle rustle of the corn could be heard above the silence. Romy looked up from his hoeing and scanned the small four hectare of grain. Was he alone? His eyes focused on a grove of bamboo just north of the field. Were his eyes playing tricks upon him or did he see some movement there? Anxiety began to grip his mind. Mindful of the massacre in the mountains, Romy began to turn toward the small farmhouse just south of the field, situated beneath the shade of several large trees. He was alone on the farm, since his folks had moved out a month ago and were staying with relatives in Milbuk together with his two younger sisters who were still attending school.

Romy hadn't walked but ten meters when a shot from a rifle rang out from the grove of bamboo. He could taste the fear in his mouth as the adrenalin poured into his blood stream. Without turning to see who fired the shot, he broke into a run but seemed to be running on legs weighted with lead. The whole scene was becoming a nightmare in slow motion. Now the cracks of several rifles opened up and the sound of the bullets passed ever closer to Romy. Curiously, he turned his head in the direction of the shots as he ran toward the farmhouse for his rifle. A bullet from one of the AK-47s struck him on the lower side of his face, ripping away his lower jaw and teeth. The impact of the bullet sent Romy cart-wheeling onto the ground, finally coming to rest among the young husks of corn. He lay unconscious on his back, his body strangely contorted. Blood had flowed copiously from the gaping opening in his face, bathing his whole head with a veil of crimson liquid.

The group of three rebels came running up to their victim to observe the result of their marksmanship. An argument broke out among them. Who was the one who had shot this man from over fifty meters? They ignored Romy as they would ignore a head of cabbage. This was like a game to them. They didn't bother to check Romy for any vital signs of life. They just presumed he was dead from the severity of the wound. The rebels proceeded toward the farmhouse and found it empty, except for the old Springfield rifle that hung above the main doorway. Grabbing a kerosene lamp, they sprinkled the liquid over the floor of the nipa hut and onto the bamboo walls and set the whole house ablaze. The three young men joined up with the main rebel column as they continued up the road toward Milbuk.

# CHAPTER 18

## *Staying Alive*

The people of Milbuk were in a state of panic. There was no place for them to flee. During the past three weeks, the families of the logging supervisors had been secretly flown to Davao during this critical period. The ordinary employees and their families were aware of the special treatment afforded the supervisors' families. Some of the other leaders among the people pleaded with the manager to help evacuate the whole camp to Lebak or Kiamba where they could find transportation to Cotabato City or General Santos.

After the ambush, the logging manager again radioed the supervisor at Wasag, the log storage area 20 kilometers up the coast from Milbuk, to ready the log barge immediately and return to Milbuk. About four or five of the loggers that day had been dropped off at Wasag by one of the two buses that were headed into the mountains. Mr. Roberts had instructed Wil Ramchand in his brief letter to the returning buses warning of the ambush, to go to Wasag with all the men and use the barge to return to Milbuk as soon as possible. If they remained there, they would most likely be attacked by the rebels.

There was a Japanese transport ship, waiting to take on logs. "Tell the Captain of the Japanese logging ship to proceed immediately to Milbuk", Mr. Roberts radioed. "I will meet with him on board and explain our situation in person".

When the logging ship, which was quite large, arrived at Milbuk, the manager went by launch with his supervisors to speak with the Japanese captain. Mr. Roberts convinced the ship's captain to help in the evacuation of the people. The women and children would be brought to General Santos City. Then the ship would return and pick up the remaining people. In the meantime, preparations had to be made to select the first group of evacuees and to determine what they could bring with them on board. This whole process took the whole day of Wednesday.

## Thursday, September the 5th...

It was about 9:00 A.M. when the first batch of evacuees was loaded on the barge for the short trip out to the waiting logging ship. Just then, reports of snipers, firing from across the harbor, alarmed the people and they fled off the barge in panic. The sounds of gunfire were suspicious. Were there really rebels on the other side of the harbor or did elements of the P.C. troopers or even members of the militia, fire the shots to keep the people of Milbuk from fleeing? There were some who did not want to fight off the rebels by themselves. Now the people would just have to wait until more soldiers arrived before they could even think of leaving. The Captain of the logging ship became afraid that some harm may come to his ship and crew. He was not willing to wait any longer and so he sailed away later that afternoon.

When Mr. Roberts radioed his main office in Davao on Tuesday afternoon concerning the latest attacks on his loggers, he pleaded with them to contact the Manila office for Government assistance in this critical situation. The security of Milbuk was weak and indefensible. Where was the battalion of soldiers promised by the Government? For two days, all of Milbuk was filled with rumor and fear. When the attempt at evacuation had failed and the logging ship sailed away, the people were deeply agitated. Then, no sooner had the logging ship sailed out of view, when wonders of wonders, a Filipino Naval vessel entered the harbor of Milbuk. The inhabitants of Milbuk were overjoyed. About eighteen regular Army troopers, fully armed, disembarked from the ship. They brought with them boxes of ammunition and crates of Garands (M-1s) to arm members of the B.S.D.U. and increase the fire power of the defense force. The mood of Milbuk changed from that of a funeral procession to a spirit of fiesta. The people knew that the situation was still somewhat grim but nonetheless hopeful. Maybe conditions will improve, they thought, since even the sailors from the naval vessel were given a brief R & R to play basketball at the High School Court across from the convento. The townspeople surrounded the soldiers and sailors, welcoming them with open arms. They were truly relieved to see the additional armed forces personnel being sent to Milbuk to protect them.

The rebels had taken up positions about a kilometer north of the main camp along the main highway near the Muslim barrio. The naval vessel upon its departure from Milbuk had been informed of these rebel emplacements and shelled their positions, routing the force of rebels and driving them back down the road toward Wal. The naval vessel continued to shell the rebel positions along the road as the combined units of P.C., regular Army and B.S.D.U. pursued them for the purpose of retrieving the bodies of their slain comrades. The Milbuk force was unable to retrieve the nine bodies since the resistance of the rebels grew more intense, the closer they approached Wal. The Milbuk force withdrew within one kilometer from Milbuk and set up defensive positions at the two twin barrios of Kanipaan and Sinangkangan, straddling the main road.

As the Milbuk force was heading back from their attempt to retrieve the ambushed victims at Wal, they scoured both sides of the road for the presence of rebels who may have been hiding during the retreat. Several members of the Barrio Self Defense Unit went purposely to the farm of Romy Mangahas, since he was a companion of theirs in the Unit. They saw from a distance that the rebels had burned down Romy's farmhouse. Cautiously, they moved across the field and there to their surprise lay the body of their companion. Romy was barely alive having lost a great deal of blood. His eyes opened slowly and he groaned when he heard his name. He couldn't speak, of course, but his fellow guardsmen knew he was terribly thirsty. Slowly, they let small drops of water fall upon Romy's blood caked tongue, and roll gently down his parched throat. Miraculously, his tongue was intact, being slightly cut and bruised by the violence of the gunshot. Carefully, they lifted him from the ground and carried him between them, making their conjoined arms as a stretcher for his body. Once they reached the road, they hailed their commander who, in turn, was able to get one of the company's Toyota pick-ups to transport Romy to the hospital. Doctor Domingo could hardly believe his eyes. Romy had lost several pints of blood and had lain in the corn field for almost two days without food or water. The doctor quickly set up a saline solution in his arm and began to type Romy's blood.

"We are looking for blood donors with A-positive blood", the doctor yelled at the crowd of men gathering in the front of the clinic.

The men did not hesitate. One by one they lined up to be tested. Before long, several men had been chosen. They all quickly cleaned up their hands and arms and waited their turn to lie on the hospital gurney next to Romy and transfer their precious liquid into his body. Romy remained in the hospital for over a week. There was little the doctor could do for this young man. Romy would need extensive operations by a plastic surgeon to return his face to one recognizable as human. His countenance was grotesque. A large gaping hole where his whole lower jaw had once been gave clear view of his limp and languid tongue that had no place to rest itself. He was sent home in this condition, holding a white hand cloth up in front of his face to shield his misshapen mouth from the curious. His parents would later take him to live with some relatives just outside the main camp.

In the meantime, the rebel force, which had withdrawn under fire from the naval bombardment, entered the thickly wooded mountain hills above Wal and headed south to trails that led around Milbuk to the east. Their destination was the Company airstrip. The airstrip ran from East to West. The east end of the airstrip began on a level stretch of land just below a low lying hill that resembled a loaf of bread. The strip extended for a distance of 600 meters almost to the shoreline bordering the Celebes Sea. A roadway ran midway between the end of the airstrip and the beach. The Company's land movers, graders and bulldozers had fashioned a firm, solid surface to the airstrip. Fine gravel mixed with clay soil enabled the strip to quickly absorb the daily monsoon rains keeping the ground firm, dry and safe for landing. A thin layer of grass covered the strip, a type of grass similar to the hair on a balding man, not growing in clumps but standing apart from each other revealing the gravel soil below. The airstrip was a bit wider than the width of a football field.

The north side of the airport held the maintenance shacks for the airplanes. There were no hangars to house the two planes. Besides, one of the planes was usually housed overnight in Davao where hangar facilities were available. A large barrio of non-descript homes backed up against the airstrip, leaving only a distance of a few hundred meters. On the south side, there was a small community of about eight well built homes scattered about and distanced well away from the airstrip itself so as not to be a hindrance to landings. These homes belonged to the owners of the farms and coconut plantations. However, there was a slight problem at times with certain of the animals that belonged to the people of this community. On occasion, some of the carabao and goats would wander off and find themselves grazing on the thin grass surface of the airstrip. Company employees would have to run the jeep after the animals and chase them off the airstrip so the plane could land safely.

The movements of the rebel force over the mountain trails went unobserved. So it was a great surprise to the Milbuk force at the airstrip when columns of smoke began to rise from the eight homes in the small settlement, nestled at the bottom of two intersecting hills. This community was located at the far end of the airstrip, about seven hundred meters away. There were no people living there since they evacuated their homes almost a month ago after the first ambush. No gun fire was exchanged. The rebels were simply announcing their presence. No, they were not being chased away by a few naval shells.

The rebels would continue to harass the community at Milbuk and the American logging Company in particular.

The Milbuk force of defenders had set up a defensive perimeter along the south rim of the airstrip. Foxholes were dug and protective barriers set up at the emplacements to repel any attempt by the rebel force to destroy the airfield and to prevent them from entering the neighboring barrio. The barrio of San Roque was a buffer that lay between the airstrip and the Camp complex. Most of those who were stationed at these posts were members of the B.S.D.U., the local militia. They were armed with old Springfield rifles. The rifles themselves were in good shape and reliable but they had seen their day. These rifles were not automatic. The Springfield rifles had to be loaded by hand, placing the bullets, one by one into the loading chamber. No more than six bullets could be loaded at any one time.

However, there was good news. On Thursday, when the Navy had dropped off the 18 or so regular Army troopers, the soldiers had brought with them six crates of Garand rifles of World War II fame (about fifty in all). The Garand or M-1 was a sturdy, reliable weapon. Though not automatic, the M-1 could fire bullets in a matter of seconds. The M-1s were cartridge loaded, which made it fast and convenient when re-loading. This would definitely increase the fire power of the Unit. The Army would first need to uncrate the fifty rifles, remove the grease and oil placed on the rifles for storage and clean and test each rifle to insure that the rifles were functional. This would take a whole day to complete. Thus, at the end of Friday, all the M-1s were ready for distribution to the B.S.D.U. members.

## Saturday, September the 7th ...

Early the next day at 6:00 A.M., the volunteers of the B.S.D.U. were stationed in the foxholes and barricades set up along the southern perimeter of the airport. They were called away from their posts by the commander, in order to be given new weapons. The B.S.D.U. members gathered together near the airport's maintenance shacks to receive their new Garand rifles (semi-automatic) in exchange for the older Springfield rifles (bolt action) that they had been using. They were all neatly lined up, as they received their new weapons, listening to directions and receiving instructions for the day's guard duty. As they stood at attention, they were suddenly surprised to see rebel troops running toward their emplacements on the far side of the airstrip and occupying their positions. In their brief absence, the rebels had taken the opportunity to capture the emplacements and were soon opening fire on the startled troops.

All hell broke loose at the airport. The Army soldiers, the PC troopers and members of the B.S.D.U. were all caught unaware. Everyone was now involved in the fight. Fierce fighting enveloped. There were casualties among the defending force. Two B.S.D. men were killed and 3 soldiers wounded. Bullets were flying everywhere.

I could hear the sounds of the rebels AK-47s and the answering salvos of the M-1s. I left my house and went outside to get information of what was happening. Several loggers came running up to me and told me that we were under attack at the air strip. I, then, ran to the Sister's Convento. Banging on the door, I entered unceremoniously and shouted at them, "Get out of the house and stay in the school with the evacuees". I instructed them to tell the people to remain seated on the floor of the classrooms and not to venture outside at all since there were many stray bullets entering the camp area.

Shortly after the attack began, a mother brought her four year old daughter to the Medical Clinic. The little four year old girl had been shot in the upper part of her chest. The spent bullet had force enough to penetrate the skin and muscle in the child's chest and then simply dropped within the chest cavity. The bullet was still lodged within her and she would need a specialized surgeon at one of the major hospitals in Davao to remove the bullet. There was nothing that Dr. Domingo could do but to sew up the entrance wound and give the child antibiotics to ward off infection. The girl was not presently in danger of death. It would take almost a week before the young girl could be airlifted to Davao.

People lay flat on the floors of their homes, not daring to venture outside. I, however, sat impatiently on the sand between the garage and the convento with my back against the wall of the garage. As I was sitting on the ground with Julio, we could see spent rounds kicking up the water along the beach thirty feet from the convento. Bullets whined over our heads striking the walls and ricocheted off the corrugated iron of the convento's roof. I couldn't sit here and wait patiently anymore. So, I brought out my trail bike from the garage and ventured through the camp in the direction of the front lines. I tried to stay close to the buildings along the road as I passed through the barrio of San Roque. All I could imagine was being hit in the face with some stray bullet. "Why am I doing this?" I mumbled to myself. I stopped at one building where a group of people were huddled inside the structure close to the ground. I encouraged them to make their way into the camp area and seek shelter in the church. "When the shooting stops, try to travel to the camp and find shelter at the school or church. It will be safer there", I counseled them.

Most of the people chose to remain in their homes, hiding behind some barricade or other that they had made. I joined one group of about five men hiding behind a concrete stage used by the barrio for their assemblies and for drying rice. The stage was about 20' x 20' and 3 feet high. I carried on a conversation with them for about ten minutes and then prayed with them briefly that they would be safe. Quickly mounting the trail bike, I sped back into the camp to check out the medical clinic for casualties, remaining in and near the clinic for the remainder of the day.

By now there were about 800 evacuees in the school & church. I only had limited supplies to feed these people. The people would need to share some of the bulgur that I had set aside to feed the Manobo children. I continued to caution the evacuees to lay low in the classrooms and church and not to go out into the open lest they be hit by stray bullets. Several bullets had already struck some of the buildings. One bullet went into one of the blackboards in the building that housed the Manobo students. Rounds from the AK-47s and 30 ca. machine guns were hitting the convento in the upper floor since it stood tall over most of the other homes.

All day long there was sporadic gunfire along the airstrip. Later in the afternoon, as the sun was about to set, the rebels withdrew from the emplacements captured during the morning "line-up". But they still continued to snipe and harass the Milbuk force until nightfall.

During the dark of night, the men of the B.S.D.U. returned to their emplacements along the southern rim of the airstrip. In several of the fox holes, the rebels had left parting gifts of excrement mixed with their urine. This only inflamed the men's passion for revenge. The commander of the combined forces, a certain Capt. Alonzo Tejano, cautioned the troops to be patient. It would be foolhardy to chase after these rebels with such limited personnel. This is exactly what the insurgents expected them to do. The rebels were waiting in ambush for any attempt by their enemies to chase them down. The Captain of the Milbuk force assured his troops that in a few days, there would be many more soldiers arriving. The battalion commander himself, Colonel Laraya would be here to set up his command post. But for now, the Captain was very concerned with the lack of ammunition among his soldiers. It was paramount to conserve ammunition in the event that the rebels would counter-attack.

The soldiers and the men of the Barrio Self Defense Unit had been fighting since early morning and everyone was low on ammunition. As in any war, there is an extravagant use of bullets in relation to the number of men wounded or killed. In other words, hundreds or thousands of rounds of ammunition are expelled during any fire-fight or battle and is almost always disproportionate to the effect intended, namely the wounding and killing of the enemy. In fact, most of the men of the B.S.D.U., inexperienced as they were in war, had almost used up all their supply.

I was told that the B.S.D.U. was down to only 300 rounds of ammunition for their Garands. The ammunition supply or lack of was critical. Frantic calls were made to the military command in Cotabato City to send ammunition, supplies and additional troops immediately. Then, just before dusk, as the sun was rapidly descending into the West and the darkness of night was about to envelope the whole of Milbuk, a lone helicopter suddenly appeared flying out of the sea and noisily circling the camp. The helicopter swung low over the elementary school and came across the open field, landing directly in front of the Notre Dame High School no more than fifty yards away. It was midpoint between the High School and the Medical Clinic. Half a dozen soldiers, fully armed, piled out of the helicopter and began to unload crates of ammunition and other necessary supplies.

The helicopter only remained at Milbuk for about fifteen minutes, just time enough to load a wounded member of the B.S.D.U. He was one of several pilots employed by Weyerhaeuser. The senior pilot, Nards, had been shot in the foot earlier in the week when he tried to warn the loggers of the impending ambush. He had been airlifted to Davao for medical treatment. This other pilot, Ray Johnson, was a Filipino of African/American descent. He was born in the Philippines, an educated young man with great energy. When the fighting broke out, he wanted nothing else than to participate in the battle. Unfortunately, he was one of the three wounded during the attack at the airport. The medical personnel from the hospital helped to load Ray onto the helicopter by stretcher. Once on board and secured to the floor, the helicopter quickly lifted off, hovering momentarily in the air and then rocketing with a great surge of power over the High School building out toward the Celebes Sea and northward to Cotabato City. The wounded pilot never made it alive to the hospital. He died on board the helicopter in route.

## Sunday, September the 8th ...

The people of Milbuk had slept fitfully through the night, especially those living within the school classrooms and church pews. I went to the church early as I did every Sunday morning, to celebrate the Holy Mass. The refugees placed their few belongings along the side and back of the church to make room for the parishioners to attend Mass. I didn't preach long during the Homily of the Mass but limited my few words to an exhortation to courage through faith and prayer, urging the people to show love for one another by being considerate to others needs. "As we all share the one faith, let us in love share what we have with those in need." I left the church soon after Mass, only taking time to inquire among the refugees if there were any special assistance that I could give them. I would be holding another meeting with Mrs. Gaviola and the teachers to obtain an update on the conditions at the High School.

People took advantage of the lull in the fighting to buy whatever food was available and hurriedly returned home again. The silence and peace of this Sunday was somewhat disquieting. Ears were attentive to the smallest noise and neighbors gathered together to pass the time and to share the latest rumors. The night came and darkness fell. All the fears that the mind could conjure up filled the thoughts of the people as they lay awake, listening to the silence and awaiting the light of another day.

# CHAPTER 19

# *Hope Returns*

**Monday, September the 9ᵗʰ...**

Excitement filled the town. Two helicopters encircled the camp. One by one they landed in the large open field between the two schools. Half a dozen fully armed troopers leaped from each copter. Boxes of ammunition and medical supplies followed. The second helicopter had landed closer to the High School. The first to disembark was a tall, (5' 9") handsome and well-built man in his late thirties. He wore the insignia of a full colonel. His name was Colonel Carlos Laraya a graduate of the Philippine Military Academy. He was among the top five in his class. Following him out of the copter was another half dozen fully armed soldiers who quickly unloaded ammunition and supplies for the Milbuk force.

The Company's Toyota station wagon drove up about 10 meters from the helicopter. Mr. Roberts exited the vehicle and went directly toward the Colonel to graciously welcome him to Milbuk. I stood back out of the way with the teachers and two of the Sisters along the sidewalk fronting the Notre Dame looking upon this whole scene. I planned to visit with the Colonel later that afternoon. For now, I would let the Colonel enjoy the hospitality of the Company's guest house and have time enough to prepare for the task ahead. I looked at my watch. It was 8:45 A.M.

Within an hour of the Colonel's arrival, a Philippine Naval boat appeared on the horizon heading toward the Milbuk harbor. By 10:30 A.M. sixty regular Army soldiers of Colonel Laraya's battalion came ashore. This was part of a promised 250-300 troopers from the battalion. More crates of ammunition and other military equipment were unloaded from the ship…guaranteed to dislodge the rebels.

After the disembarking of the soldiers, some of the naval crew of about 30 sailors, once again, came ashore for exercise. They walked to the High School campus and played basketball. Others chose to intermingle with the local people and take refreshments as they were offered. The ship on which they sailed had been on operations for over a month. This was their first shore leave in all that time. The sailors stayed in Milbuk until early afternoon.

The captain of the naval ship was impressed with the hospitality of the Milbuk people and invited over a dozen of its citizens on board to tour the fighting ship. Among those invited were the three Oblate Sisters. Upon their return to Milbuk after their hour and a half cruise, Sister Ana reported to me what she had witnessed while on board. A small boat from the naval vessel had ferried them out to the ship and once on board, the ship weighed anchor and headed north up the shore toward the barrio of Wal. While on the way, spotters on board ship had sighted movement on shore, allegedly rebel troops on the move. The naval ship opened fire on the rebels and dislodged them from their positions near Milbuk sending some fleeing toward Wal and others into the jungles. The group was shadowed by the naval vessel whose six inch guns hastened the retreat. When I started to go into detail with Sister Ana about the bombardment, the only thing she clearly remembered was the noise of the guns.

Later in the afternoon, after the naval ship had shelled the barrio of Wal and adjoining areas, a large twin engine plane suddenly appeared, hovering in the sky and circling the jungle area north, two kilometers from Milbuk. Like a hawk searching for its prey, the plane hung silently above waiting for the moment to strike. Many of us rushed up the hill overlooking Milbuk, where the Manobos had built homes along the ridge, to get a better view of the action.

Some soldiers stationed on the hill remarked to me that the rebel force at Wal was making their escape into the mountain jungles as a result of the naval shelling. The plane I saw was a Douglas AC-47D, otherwise known as "Spooky" or "Puff the Magic Dragon".

This unusual gunship was equipped with three 7.62 mm "miniguns" with a 6,000 rounds per minute rate of fire. The miniguns were mounted in the aft left fuselage; one gun was installed in the aft passenger door area. The other two guns were mounted just forward of the passenger door with the gun barrels pointed out window ports. The initial attack procedures began with the aircraft in straight and level flight, and the target just outside and forward of the left prop dome. Usual altitude is between 2500-3000 feet above ground level with an air speed of 120 knots. As the target passed under the engine cowling, the aircraft was rolled into a level 30 degree bank turn. When the gun site came on target, firing was commenced in bursts of 3-7 seconds as required. As the gun site moved off the target to the rear, the firing was ceased and a slight turn was made away from the target for repositioning and subsequent firing passes. Each minigun fired at a rate of 6000 rounds per minute. This provided coverage over an elliptical area approximately 52 yards in diameter, placing a projectile within every 2-4 yards during a 3 second burst. Whenever a human target was caught within this killing zone, hardly anyone survived.

We, onlookers saw the gunship go through its maneuvers and could hear the rapid seven seconds of firing and the telltale smoke belching from the windows and door of the plane. It was all over. The plane performed only two passes in its mission and headed back to base. What the results were of its firing, if any, is not known to this day.

In the meantime, a command center had been set up on a hilly slope of land bordering the main road, parallel to the camp. Two well-built one story company buildings had been turned over to the Army. There the new Battalion Commander, Colonel Laraya set up his offices. The soldiers also built a stockade for any prisoners that they might capture. With the added strength of additional troops, the security chief of the camp came together with the Colonel to plan the recovery of the bodies from the second ambush near Wal.

## Tuesday, September the 10<sup>th</sup>...

Colonel Laraya wasted no time in employing the additional troops to expand the defensive perimeter of the camp two kilometers beyond the airstrip. This would insure that flights in an out of Milbuk would be protected. The increased military forces also enabled the Colonel to likewise expand the northern defense perimeter and even advance five kilometers all the way to Wal and to the second ambush site where the bodies of the nine men still lay where they had died. There was no opposition to the movements of the combined force as they proceeded up the road toward Wal. The rebels had simply disappeared into thin air. They had melted away into the green foliage of the mountain jungles.

The soldiers advanced with caution as they neared the ambush site. The first thing they saw was the olive green Toyota pickups that stood silently where they had crashed. Two vehicles had been brought along to haul the wrecks back to the Camp maintenance area. One of the soldiers approached the first Toyota, the one driven by the field supervisor, Wil Ramchand and his companion, P.C. Sergeant Tomas Ortiz. He slowly opened the driver's door and looked upon the gruesome site of the two men slumped over in death. There were no heads to be seen, but only the fleshly masks of their faces that hung limply onto their chests. The cab of the Toyota was sprayed with blood and the bone fragments of the two men's skulls. The bodies of the other two troopers lay face down on the sand where they had been gunned down in their attempt to escape along the beach. The scene was similar at the site of the second Toyota. The lone driver, also one of the field supervisors for the Company, had been riddled with bullets that penetrated the door of the pickup. He was recognizable but the stench of the putrefaction was almost unbearable. Two of the armed loggers who were riding in the back had also been cut down by the terrible fusillade of automatic weapons. Nevertheless, the loggers and members of the Philippine Constabulary lifted each of the nine bodies with care and reverence, placing them gently onto the beds of the pick-ups to return them to Milbuk and to their families.

When the men returned from the ambush site with the bodies of the dead Philippine Constabulary troopers and loggers, Rudy Alameida ran upstairs to the living room of the convento where I was busy looking over the school's finances. "Father, the men have returned from Wal with the bodies of those who died in the ambush." I went without hesitation to the hospital and found two bodies lying side by side along the wall of the lobby. The two men were Wil Ramchand and Sgt. Tomas Ortiz. They had ridden in the Toyota that was bringing up the rear of the bus convoy. I gazed upon the fleshly mask of the man dressed in khakis with a Sergeant's insignia patch on his shoulder. I recognized him as the husband of one of my former students. I had witnessed their marriage less than a year ago. She was now pregnant with his child. They were a happy couple, well suited to each other.

I kept on staring at the face mask of the second man, a civilian. I couldn't recognize him. Chief Dorotheo came up behind me and we both silently acknowledged each other as we gazed upon the dead men.

"Chief", I whispered, "Who is this man?"

"Why, can't you see, it's Wil Ramchand. See here at the right side of his mouth," he pointed, "that dark brown oblong birth mark." That's Wil alright!"

"Ah", said I, "I recognize him now. He was such a good man. What a shame."

Silently, I prayed for the two men. My attention was abruptly interrupted by the unearthly wail of a grieving woman. I turned around. There coming through the swinging doors of the hospital entrance was Evelyn Ortiz, the wife of the P.C. Sergeant. I turned to meet her. She was hysterical. "Evelyn, you shouldn't see him now... not like this", I cautioned her. My hands held the sides of her arms to gently restrain her from viewing the body of her husband lying so grotesquely upon the floor of the hospital. But she would not be stopped. Evelyn broke from my grip and ran screaming toward the dead body of her husband, falling to the ground on her knees, her tears raining down on his fleshly mask, her hands upon his chest. Her companions, women relatives and neighbors, knelt down in a semi-circle around her and placed their hands and arms upon her in comfort. Slowly, as several minutes passed, they gently raised her from the floor and embraced her heaving body as she cried inconsolably. Orderlies came soon after to remove the bodies and place them in the room where Dr. Domingo would embalm them for burial.

## Wednesday, September the 11th...

A large combined force of Army, P.C. and B.S.D.U. fighters pushed out from the airport emplacements and headed south along the coast to remove any remnants of the rebel force remaining from the previous days. The force met strong opposition at first but was able to push back the rebels about 2 kilometers along the coast and inland for about another kilometer. The battle produced six casualties; 5 Army troopers and one civilian from the B.S.D.U. One of the regular Army soldiers had a bullet ricochet off his helmet from a sniper's rifle. He laughed and joked around with his fellow soldiers over his good fortune. Two minutes later, as he peered over the barricade, he was shot dead by the same sniper with a bullet through his head. The lone B.S.D.U. fighter killed in this action was hiding behind a large trunk of a coconut tree when a bullet from a sniper's rifle penetrated the soft outer edge of the tree and struck the man in his chest, killing him instantly.

The Milbuk force set up a line of defense that was more advantageous to them than the former emplacements at the airport. The large loaf-like slab of a hill that ran east to west parallel to the airstrip was now behind them and offered a good vantage point to spy upon the activities of the people of Kulong-Kulong, three to four kilometers away.

Everyone presumed that the rebels retreated to Kulong-Kulong to hide in the forest of coconut trees. Or did they simply melt into the mountains to the east? The Army had no intention of pursuing them, at least not at this time. The military objective of Colonel Laraya's battalion was to insure the safety of the people of Milbuk and to protect the interests of the Weyerhaeuser Logging Company. There were millions of dollars' worth of equipment and vehicles which the logging company did not want to lose.

There was a plan in the works, which the occupying Army under Colonel Laraya was not telling the people of Milbuk. Mr. Roberts however was taken into the confidence of the Colonel since the manager would be performing an important job for the Army that would enhance their presence in the area.

Weyerhaeuser Logging Company was one of the top U.S. Companies doing business in the Philippines. It was important to the Marcos regime to insure that foreign investments in the resources of the Philippines not be affected by the violent insurgency of the Muslims in the Southern Philippines. To this purpose, Marcos was spending large sums of money on national defense, and also receiving arms and ammunition from the United States. Fighting during 1974 was no longer centered in the troublesome Sulu Islands but now was widespread throughout the Zamboanga region, Lanao and the whole western section of Mindanao, especially in the Cotabato Provinces. Attacks against government troops and installations as well as the take-over of provincial towns were now becoming common place. When news of the attack on the logging bus and the resultant massacre of 38 people reached the Offices of Weyerhaeuser International, the CEO of the Company immediately contacted the Office of President Marcos and strongly petitioned him to protect the interests of the Company if Weyerhaeuser was to continue to remain in the Philippines and conduct logging operations. But where was Marcos to get these troops from? Most of his Army, Navy and Air Force were tied down in the Jolo area attempting to maintain control of the towns which only a few months ago had been controlled by the rebels. It would take time to juggle military resources and provide the

Milbuk area with sufficient and effective military assistance. Thus, token military help was sent to Milbuk in the form of Philippine Constabulary troopers together with weapons for arming the loggers and forming a Barrio Self Defense Unit until such time as regular Army soldiers could be sent.

The movement of troops in any given situation is of its nature slow even for the United States. There was no rapid deployment of troops or Delta Force-like platoons in the Philippines that could be dispatched at a moment's notice and appear on the troubled scene in a matter of a day or two. The military was hoping against hope that the situation would not become worse and perhaps might even improve. This may be an isolated incident, some thought, just a warning by the militant rebels to stay away from a certain area of the mountains. But when the second ambush occurred, there was no doubt that the rebels meant to control the whole township of Palimbang, free from the exploitation of this American Company. Thus, within ten days of the second ambush, Colonel Laraya arrived with the promised battalion of soldiers.

# CHAPTER 20

# *The Invasion*

**Sunday - September 15th ...**

The last five days were somewhat normal after the arrival of Colonel Laraya and the contingent of regular Army troops. The battalion was not at full strength but had grown considerably. The prospects for safety looked good. The people of Milbuk began to be hopeful again. They may not need to evacuate after all. Yes, today was a good day and pleasant.

I was in a fine mood this morning as I stood at the bathroom sink about to finish my morning shave, in preparation for Holy Mass. A loud noise reverberated from the sea and filled the whole house. I ran out of the bathroom across the living room with razor in hand and placed my face just inches from the screened window. There, down the coast, opposite Kulong-Kulong was a Philippine Naval vessel anchored no more than two kilometers off shore. Ka-boom! The 5 inch shells rocketed point blank into the coconut plantation, snapping trees in half as they sped by. The invasion had begun. I watched transfixed as the bombardment by the Navy continued. The time was 6:15 A.M.

After about five minutes, I returned to the bathroom to quickly complete my grooming, all the while the crash and thunder of the naval guns continued to pierce the stillness of this Sunday morning. Heading off to the church, I tried to concentrate on the religious duties for the day. I knelt down in the front bench of the church and began my meditation before Mass, but my mind was so distracted by the activities of the Philippine Navy. The shelling continued sporadically for another half hour. What horror it must be for the people in these villages.

The Muslim villagers knew beforehand that something bad was going to happen when some of the fishermen from the area failed to return before dawn to their villages. Philippine naval PT boats had been picking up fishermen all along the coast. Several of the fishermen were able to put out the light in their lanterns so they wouldn't be detected by the Navy. They slipped off quietly avoiding the fast moving patrol boats that were scouring the area. Then when the light began to filter through the darkness of the failing night, the people stood curiously at the shore and could see the large unmistakable outline of the Philippine Naval ship taking up position directly off shore in front of their village.

Seeing this sight, fear gripped the people and they ran in panic throughout the village crying out the alarm to those still asleep...to their family and neighbors. "We must flee now. The Navy ships will destroy our village and kill all of us if we do not escape now."

Hundreds of villagers along the coast fled in-land from the impending disaster. There wasn't time to pack a bag or bring along provisions. The people simply ran from their homes with the clothes they were wearing and little else. Mothers were herding their children before them and others holding infants in their arms... all following the men who led the way through the darkness of the coconut plantation. Fear of a violent death for them and their children paralyzed their minds. Escaping...running...hiding from the guns of the Naval ship was all they could think of. The men guided their families through the pathless maze of trees to several of the small villages in the interior. Here they would stop and wait in dread for the next troubling event, whatever that might be.

The people had no weapons to defend themselves...no barricades behind which to hide...no secret bunkers bristling with machine gun emplacements and mortars....no weapons at all. Why should they defend themselves against the armed forces of their own country? They were not the enemy. Why would the Navy and Army battalions invade their peaceful shores? And yet here they were, fleeing from those sworn to protect them…fleeing from other Filipinos.

These Muslim villagers had always been the subject of the worse rumors concerning the smuggling of goods and weapons. But what was the truth? Were these people really guilty of participating in the terrible ambushes of the loggers from Milbuk? Were their alleged offenses some kind of vendetta…a revenge for the loss of jobs with the Weyerhaeuser Logging Company simply because they were Muslims? Or were these people the dupes in the political intrigues and conspiracies of the powerful?

The Navy had started the shelling of Kulong-Kulong at 6:15 A.M. Elements of the 15th Battalion Army strike team had been ferried ashore by Navy landing crafts. For the next hour, the Garcia Class Frigate would sporadically shell the area for effect. A few homes had been hit. The whole exercise was more to frighten the inhabitants and have them flee to the interior, rather than to destroy the villages. The Army had already landed close by Malisbong and easily corralled the panicked population. Not a shot was fired in return. There was no opposition at all as the landing crafts sped toward the beaches and unloaded the running, screaming soldiers. Like ants at a picnic, the young soldiers swarmed into the villages, searching home after home for any combatants at all. There were none. All the people had fled. Only one ancient weapon was found, hidden beneath the floor boards in one of the houses in Kulong-Kulong. It had laid there for many years undisturbed. Where were the rebels?

The order went out to all platoon leaders, "Head into the interior. Capture all whom you find. Bring all prisoners to Malisbong." It didn't take long for the horde of heavily armed troopers to catch up to the fleeing mass of villagers. Horror filled their eyes as the women clutched their children in desperation. The men yelled out their surrender with hands outstretched over their heads, quacking in fear as the soldiers separated them from their families. All the men were searched for weapons and made to kneel in rows with hands clasped behind their heads. The women and children let out a continuous howl and cry as the troopers roughly handled the men prisoners.

A command for silence rang out over this crowd of several hundred people. Slowly, the noise subsided. Only the whimpering cries of the children could be heard. An Army Captain stood upon a sturdy table taken from one of the houses. He addressed the people in Tagalog, telling them that they would be taken to the town of Malisbong. When they reached there, further information would be given to them. The military had identified one young man, a High School student, who translated the Captain's message into Maguindanao, the language these people spoke. "Just follow the orders of the soldiers and do everything they tell you." This scene repeated itself many times throughout the delta as the inhabitants of the area were all herded together at Malisbong. The five villages scattered throughout the delta were now vacant and empty of people. The civilian population had quickly surrendered and complied obediently with every command given by the military.

The Muslim men led the procession, filing in twos through columned corridors of coconut trees. There was no road to Malisbong, only the trail that these hundreds of people would make in their passing. The woman and children brought up the rear with soldiers walking in staggered positions along the side. The final group of captives reached Malisbong in under an hour. Other groups had preceded them from neighboring villages so that the whole town was congested with upwards of 2500 people or more. The men between the ages of 16 and 45, considered to be of fighting age, were all imprisoned within the town's Mosque, the largest building along the coast. The women, children and older men were left to mingle aimlessly under the shade trees that lined the shore of the town.

As the last of the Muslim men to be captured were led to the front entrance of the Mosque, they hesitated when they saw how packed the building was. There didn't seem to be any room for the final hundred men. The soldiers screamed at the prisoners to make room. Grumbling moans went up from the crowd as the new arrivals pushed into this mass of humanity to find some vacant spot on which to squat. From front to back within the Mosque, the men squatted in rows as at a prayer service, filling up every square inch of space. There were no fewer than 500 men imprisoned within the Mosque.

Silence was ordered. No one was to move from his spot on the hard packed earthen floor without permission. Those who had to relieve themselves were allowed to go one by one a few feet beyond the building, along the right side of the Mosque, where a deep hole had been dug. No modesty screens were erected. The men did their business in full view of their guards. Machine gun emplacements were set up at key points around the Mosque to prevent any mass escape. Soldiers stood at the two entrances to the Mosque and kept guard throughout the night. Moaning could be heard in the darkness. The only light was the one coming from several outside bulbs powered by one of two generators owned by some well-to-do business man in the town. In the morning, the men in the Mosque were fed by groups of women who had been picked by the Army to handle this operation. Water was brought to them in buckets to be ladled out to each man as needed.

It didn't take long for the Army to begin its interrogations. Two non-uniformed men, armed with a .45 Magnum on their hip, wearing khakis and loose fitting, light colored shirts began the selection process almost immediately upon the arrival of the first prisoners to Malisbong. Ten men had been chosen to undergo the hard questioning of the two Army intelligence men early the next morning at first light. It was necessary to list down the identity of all these male captives so that the names might be shown to key informants who allegedly had important information concerning membership in the Muslim rebel cause. These informants would be arriving early in the morning to assist the intelligence men in their investigation.

On the same day of the naval bombardment, farther down the coast, a company of soldiers had proceeded overland, arriving at their destination just before dawn. They silently encircled the Muslim barrio of Kalaong. The three platoons of soldiers had been trucked in from General Santos City the day before and had ridden along the coastal road to Kiamba and then to Maitum. From there, the road became nothing but a foot path. When the terrain became impassable to vehicles, the soldiers then bivouacked at the site, waiting for the cover of darkness to march the remaining eight kilometers to their destination. The plan was to form a pincer–like movement that would enable the military to cut off any rebels who hoped to escape along the coast or into the mountains. Their mission was to conduct a surprise attack on this Muslim village which 'sources' stated, was a beehive of rebel activity and a center for the smuggling of arms. It was situated about six kilometers from Malisbong,

The Captain glanced at his watch every few minutes, waiting for the moment of attack. His assault upon this barrio was to be synchronized with the main attack on the delta of villages from Kulong-Kulong to Malisbong. As soon as the minute hand indicated fifteen minutes past six, the distant roar of the five inch shells echoed across the bay signaling the beginning of hostilities. Many of the people ran in panic from their "bahay kubos". The soldiers fired upon the frightened, unarmed Muslims with impunity, continuing their attack until there was no one standing to run away from them.

People lay all over the grounds of the village, some dead, others wounded and writhing in agony. Children too had become victims to this slaughter. The remnant that remained unscathed by the attack remained within their homes and lay motionless on the ground, fearing that they too would be gunned down. The soldiers gathered up these people from their homes and herded them into a large open area at one side of the barrio. The whole nasty operation took but five minutes. The eighty or so troopers surveyed their work and seemed happy with the results.

The young officers, two Lieutenants and a Captain were busy speaking with their Colonel over the phone, telling him the outcome of the attack. "There are about one hundred and eighty people in the village. We have already killed or wounded about thirty of them. There are over a hundred others whom we have rounded up as prisoners. There are many women and children among them. What shall we do now?" The Captain listened carefully as the Colonel gave his instructions. The Captain replied over the phone, "Pardon me sir. Let me repeat your instructions. You want us to kill the rest of the people and burn down the village. Is that correct, sir? ...No sir, nobody escaped from the village. We had it completely surrounded. Let me repeat that sir...you say that the Navy will be sending a landing craft to this village within the hour. And you want us to put all the bodies on the landing craft. Yes, Sir, we can do that. I'll tell the men now."

The Captain sent his lieutenants to gather all the people who could walk and bring them to the shore. He instructed them, "Let them all sit close together by the edge of the sea." The men, women and children huddled together on the beach shivering and afraid. A dozen soldiers stood guard over them. The Captain then instructed his lieutenant to have the soldiers carry the dead up to the water's edge next to the squatting prisoners. The women and children cried, wept and moaned as the bodies of their families and neighbors were thrown in heaps upon the sand.

"Sir", one of the soldiers asked, "what are we to do with the wounded that can't walk to the beach?" "Kill them, he said, and then carry their bodies to the shore." For almost five minutes, sporadic gun fire erupted from within the village as the wounded were dispatched and their bodies carried to the beach.

In the distance, a landing craft could be seen making its fateful journey to this nightmare of a village. The Captain gathered his troopers together at the edge of the village away from the hearing of the Muslim captives and gave his orders, "Men, the Colonel gave me instructions to kill all these rebels, leaving no one Alive. As you know, we were ordered to enter this village and to destroy the enemy. This is our job for today. This is the mission we were given. We do not hesitate now and think in terms of men, women and children. They are all the same. In a few moments we will form a line behind this remaining group of rebels and we will shoot them at my command. Do you understand?" "Yes sir", they all chimed in. The Captain continued, "We must teach these people a lesson. You know how many of our men were killed in Jolo and Basilan. How many of your friends are dead today because these people rebelled against the government. We need to do this."

"Yes sir"', the young soldiers answered enthusiastically.

"Alright then, on my command, we will open fire upon them."

"Yes, sir!" the young soldiers replied in unison.

The soldiers walked slowly and deliberately to the shore. The landing craft was close now, no more than a kilometer away. Only one platoon of soldiers could be conveniently grouped together behind the Muslim prisoners. The other two platoons just simply looked on at the drama unfolding before them. The soldiers stood only five meters from the squatting, defenseless captives. Many of the victims looked apprehensively back over their shoulders at the assembled and somber soldiers and instinctively knew what was about to happen. This was a firing squad. Some of the people began to stand and others started moving out from the crowd. The voice of the Captain rang with a shrill and echoed down the beach with finality: "Ready, Fire!"

The continuous volley of automatic weapons erupted so loudly that flocks of birds nestled in the nearby forest burst forth from the trees, seeking shelter in the mountains. Most of the people died instantly, still sitting upon the sand, others fell headlong into the sea as they tried to escape the barrage of bullets. The innocent, tear streaked faces of the children were shattered and their doll-like figures danced upon the sand as the bullets ripped into their tiny bodies. It was a wonder that anyone could survive such an onslaught of killing metal but there were some who still lay writhing on the beach. Some of the soldiers, who were unable to join the others in this bloody slaughter, stepped up into the ranks and blasted away at this gruesome mound of humanity while their companions re-loaded their empty weapons with fresh cartridges of bullets.

They were all dead now. There was nothing else to do but to load all the bodies on board the landing craft and dump the remains far out to sea. The sharks will have a feast. Some of the deepest waters in the world lie off the Islands of the Philippines. Here in the Celebes Sea, the waters go to a depth of 6,216 meters below sea level or four miles to the bottom. Once the bodies were dumped into the sea, there would be no trace left of any remains.

The landing craft pulled up close to the mounds of corpses. The soldiers broke into pairs and formed a procession to the landing craft, carrying the lifeless bodies of the massacred between them. Like cords of wood, the corpses were laid one upon another, forming a solid five foot wall of human flesh. It's amazing how much space can be saved when human bodies can be stacked so conveniently. The Captain ordered his first Lieutenant to take part of his platoon of soldiers and help the Navy men unload all the bodies when they get out to sea. The rest of the soldiers would remain in the village. "We will meet you back here when you return", the Captain instructed.

No weapons were found in this village either. There was nothing to indicate that this village of farmers and fishermen were anything but peaceful, law abiding Filipinos. Their only crime, apparently, was being Muslim. The mission of the soldiers was almost complete. They were hungry. It was now time to serve up some breakfast. The soldiers found rice, vegetables, some fresh fish caught earlier that night and then there were the goats. Some of the goats had been killed during the attack but other goats were still tethered to stakes in the ground.

"Captain", one of the soldiers inquired, "Will we be here long enough to cook up some goat meat?"

"I don't see why not. The others won't be returning with the Navy for at least three or four more hours, maybe longer. However, once they arrive, we will demolish this village and burn everything to the ground. What you don't take with you, destroy. This village never existed. If there were people here, they all fled to the mountains. That's the story."

"Thank you; Captain... ...Understood, sir", was the obedient reply. And all was accomplished according to orders.

# CHAPTER 21

# *Beneath the Sun*

I had no idea that anything like a massacre was happening in Kalaong, only forty minutes away by banca. I had passed this village many times, never stopping of course, since I had no business there nor invitation. Now I was in the midst of celebrating the Holy Mass where the symbolism and prayers emphasized the unity and love of those assembled with the all-forgiving Jesus, who gave His life for all humanity on the cross. "This is the cup of my blood, shed for all men for the forgiveness of sins." The symbolism of Christ's death was actually being enacted by the innocent men, women and children whose blood flowed copiously upon the sands of Kalaong. "Whatever you do to the least of my brethren, you do unto me."

The Mass was completed in thirty-five minutes. I preached only four or five minutes, aware that the people's mind and attention were on the activities of the military. Having spent ten minutes in troubled meditation, I departed the empty church after Mass. My breakfast lay cold on the dining room table, having been prepared over an hour ago at the house of my cook. Nobody was in the convento. I sat down and poured hot water from the thermos into a cup of Ovaltine. Brushing away the few ants that had come for breakfast ahead of me, I chewed on the 'pan de sal' and mopped up the yellow yolk of an egg with the bread.

"Father... Father Art", Rudy shouted as he ran up the stairs to the living room out of breath. "Father, the Army has about thirty prisoners down at the landing dock near the veneer mill. Crowds of people are gathering and they're angry."

I quickly jumped up from the table and followed Rudy to the end of the camp road near the Company's guest house. There was an opening in the fence through which we entered. The large open area that lay between the sea and the veneer mill was about four acres in size with a width of about three football fields. The landing dock lay hidden along the bank of this great expanse of land. Concrete steps had been laid at the edge of the embankment, leading down twelve feet to a large wooden floating dock. The landing dock measured 16 x 30 feet long.

As I approached, there was a large crowd hovering at the edge of the embankment, shouting and gesturing wildly at some unseen phantoms. Other people were streaming toward this site as if to a ball game to cheer on their favorite team. They had their backs to me and did not know that I was now among them. "Excuse me, please. Let me pass", I hollered above the din. A few men looked back with anger in their eyes, but when they saw my white face, the face of the priest, they weakly apologized and made a way for me.

The first sight that caught my attention, as I descended the stairs, was the frightened faces of the Muslim "prisoners", squatting helplessly under the guard of two armed soldiers. I approached the soldiers saying, "I am Father Art, the Catholic priest of Milbuk. Will you let me stay here with your prisoners?" "Yes, Father", they answered, evidently relieved that the priest had arrived and would quiet down this rowdy crowd. Anything could happen. Some of the crowd may even be armed. They could begin killing these prisoners and the soldiers would be helpless to stop them.

There were twelve men among the captives, all lined up in two straight rows of six. Next to them were the women and some children, eighteen in all, dressed in their Muslim clothing. No cries came from their lips, but they were in great fear and avoided raising their eyes toward their tormentors. The roar of the crowd was incessant as they vented their anger and cried out their accusations and threats.

I turned sharply around and looked up at the crowd, perched high above on the bluff overlooking the landing. "Be silent", I demanded. "This is not the way we Christians act. Leave these people alone!" The crowd slowly stopped their noisy shouting, but some continued to babble on in their dialect, voicing their opinion that this American just didn't understand the way things are. I then turned my attention to the Muslims and spoke to them in Tagalog saying, "I hope you can understand me. I will remain here with you until the Army decides what to do with you."

It was 8:45 A.M. and the sky was cloudless. The heat of the sun was already bearing down upon the prisoners. I didn't dare move from my position on the landing. Every once in a while I would gaze up at the crowd above and look at each face. Slowly, gradually, people began to walk away. Others, however, took their place. Some would begin to blurt out some insult but would be quickly silenced by others who knew that I would not hesitate to scold them publicly. Embarrassment must be avoided at all costs.

After an hour, I too began to feel the heat of the sun. Then I realized that I left my hat in the convento in my rush to the landing. How must these people be feeling? They have been without water and food for hours now. It was then that I searched the crowd above for a familiar face, maybe one of my teachers. Sure enough, there was old Rudy. "Rudy...go to the convento. Bring water and crackers... bread...something for these people to eat. We need water!" "Alright, Father...I'm on my way."

Just then, one of the young men squatting by my left side spoke softly to me, "Father, my name is Ahmed Khalid. I graduated from Notre Dame several years ago. I knew Father Henry. I worked with him as a student. Can you help me?"

"I will stay here with you until I find out what the Army intends to do with you. Don't worry. It will all work out well."

The young man was very worried that something bad was going to happen to him and to his companions. He told me that he was not a rebel. He had nothing to do with the attacks on the loggers. I began to be worried too. What could I do under the circumstances? I was under the presumption that the rights of all prisoners were protected under the Geneva Convention Accords. How much more should the rights of civilians be protected and upheld. The Philippine Army soldiers were not the bad guys, or so I thought.

Another hour passed during which Rudy returned with the water and some crackers. I got permission from the soldiers to pass around the water so that all the prisoners could drink. At about 11:30 A.M., a detachment of soldiers accompanied by a Lieutenant came to escort the twelve Muslim men to the Army's command post for interrogation. The young man, Ahmed, looked sadly at me as he was being led off the landing, like a man being marched off to a firing squad. The women and children remained. There were no words exchanged among them as their men departed. The women remained squatting, stoically enduring the hidden sorrow and pain of this ordeal. The officer did say that the Mayor was sending a launch to take the women and children to Palimbang. In fact, the launch had already left some time ago, and would be arriving shortly. This was good news.

I really began to feel the heat of the sun. "We all need to get off this landing and under some shade", I said to the soldiers. And then the launch appeared in the distance. It slowly maneuvered across the shallows fronting the logging camp and entered the deeper water near the landing dock. The lieutenant returned to the landing and supervised the loading of passengers. I stood upon the dock and gently waved my hand in farewell. I thanked the soldiers for keeping the prisoners safe. Gratefully I retraced my steps to the convento. Peering into the bathroom mirror, I could see the red tinge of a sun burn on my already tanned face. Turning on the faucet of water, I splashed my face with the cool liquid till most of the heat evaporated from my skin.

Later that day, I inquired about the 12 Muslim men who had been taken off the dock earlier that morning. Some of the loggers who were "hanging out" with the soldiers at the command post told me that all the men were questioned about their involvement with the Muslim rebels. Needless to say, the questioning was hard and torturous. Whatever was the result of the questioning, I never found out. But I was told, as a matter of fact, that the 12 men were taken away by naval launch out to sea. They were never heard of again.

After lunch, I walked through the camp. It was about 2:00 P.M. Most people were still within their homes sheltering themselves from the day's heat and seeking rest from the morning's excitement. Few people passed me on the way. The security guard at the main gate looked casually at me and then turned away as if no one was there. Walking up the main road, there was a hubbub of activity near the command post with small bands of soldiers coming and going along the highway in groups of three and four.

The command post was likewise busy with a group of officers crowding around a map on a table in deep conversation over their next mission. Sergeant Romero was the first to notice me as I entered the large reception room.

"Father, I'm glad you're here. Colonel Laraya wants you and me to travel tomorrow morning to Malisbong to speak with Colonel Molina about the large number of Muslim women and children evacuees. He's appointing you as civilian liaison for the rehabilitation of the evacuees."

"I can do that", I volunteered, "but I'll let him tell me first. Is Colonel Laraya busy now?"

"He's just finished lunch. Let me find out what his schedule is like."

Within a few minutes, the Sergeant returned and escorted me inside the Colonel's office.

"Good afternoon, Father. I have an important request to make of you. Will you be willing to serve as civilian liaison for the Muslim evacuees over at Kulong-Kulong?"

"Yes, Colonel, of course I will."

"Good. I want you and Sgt. Romero to travel to Malisbong tomorrow and speak with Colonel Molina, the battalion commander. Find out what his plans are for the prisoners and their families."

"We can use my banca to get there", I added. "It won't take us but thirty-five minutes or so to reach the village. If Sergeant Romero could be at the convento by 8:00 A.M., tomorrow morning, we can leave there by boat. I'll be taking my two teachers and the two men I employ at the convento."

"That's a good plan", the Colonel replied. "I wish you success."

# CHAPTER 22

# *Kill or Feed?*

**Monday, September the 16th...**

Sergeant Romero arrived at the convento promptly at 8:00 A.M. by jeep. All my people were standing on the beach near the banca, ready to go. Cecilia Ramos and Lisa Alcera boarded first, then Sgt. Romero and I. My two boatmen pushed the banca out from the shore and fired up the engines. We sped along the shore fronting the camp. The day was pleasant and bright. The sea lay still as we skimmed the surface heading out to sea. Before we knew it, we were already approaching Kulong-Kulong. From the boat, we could see no movement in the village. There didn't seem to be any damage at all from the shelling on Sunday. The village seemed intact. We swung around the point of land leading to Malisbong. There, speeding across the bay was a PCF (Patrol Craft, Fast). This 17 ton naval patrol boat had a six man crew. The boat was armed with machine guns and a mortar. We were only 300 meters away.

As my companions and I approached Malisbong, there was a naval landing craft anchored 900 meters from shore far to the right of the village. Malisbong was perched several feet above the sandy shoreline on an embankment that rose slightly from the waters' edge to a grass covered mantle that held back the erosion. A large, concrete, hollow brick mosque dominated the town. Its minaret rose forty or fifty feet high, a little higher than the tallest coconut trees that sheltered the town. You could always see the peculiar and unique spire of the building while at sea, whenever you passed by the town. If not for the prominence of this edifice, you could easily sail by and miss the village completely, being unaware that a large thriving community of almost a thousand people lay beneath the thick groves of coconut. There is no main road leading to Malisbong. Access to the town was only by sea. Only the paths trodden down by the townsfolk as they passed from one settlement to the other was evidence of any traffic.

If there was a center to the town, the place definitely was the one occupied by the Mosque. The homes closest to the Mosque were 10 to 12 meters in distance, forming somewhat of a square around the perimeter. The culture and religion of these people spoke volumes to any visitor. Islam was not a religion practiced once a week, but a life lived each day.

Everyone disembarked from the banca. The two boatmen with arms under the main struts pulled the boat halfway out of the water. They remained with the boat so as not to be involved with any activities at the village. The sergeant and the two teachers accompanied me as we walked up the slightly sloping beach and approached the main body of refugees milling about on the grassy mantle of the town under the shade of various trees.

The soldiers were in and among the hundreds of refugees, women and children, who congregated under a great, old shady tree, much like our oak tree. Around the fat trunk of the tree were stacked sacks of grain, probably rice or wheat bulgur. None of the food had yet been distributed. The crowd of women and children were strangely silent. This was not market day! For such a large group of people there was hardly a sound of talking and certainly no laughter. The eyes of the women were questioning, sad and uncertain of what the next move or command would be. The children like children everywhere were curiously running here and there, not playing but just observing... not wanting to miss any of the action. I instructed the teachers to mingle with the Muslim women and find out what transpired during the last twenty four hours.

The Sergeant and I next approached a group of three soldiers who were nonchalantly leaning up against the wall of stacked sacks of grain smoking cigarettes and observing the milling crowd of women and children with bored looks. Our presence disturbed them a bit but they were polite enough to listen to our request for directions to Colonel Molina's command post. One of the soldiers slung his Armalite rifle over his shoulder and directed us to follow him. The sergeant and I followed the soldier to the interior of the village toward a group of well-built homes that lay about thirty meters from the Mosque over to the left of the village.

The soldier then directed us to a small square table encircled by three chairs. An umbrella- like covering hung above the table to provide shade from the day's sun. Within seconds, a middle aged man, about 40, dressed in the khaki of his profession and wearing the insignia of a colonel moved smartly toward us and greeted us.

"I'm Colonel Mateo Molina", he said business-like.

"I'm Father Art Amaral, parish priest of Milbuk and this is Sergeant Romero. We've been sent here, sir, by Colonel Laraya to confer with you about your plans for the refugees."

"Please be seated, Father, you too Sergeant." The Colonel then called to one of his aides and instructed him to bring us all some tea.

"Well, Father, how do you find this place?" he continued.

"It's quite crowded, Colonel. Where did all these people come from?" I inquired.

The Colonel replied to my question with a definite air of authority, "We gathered them all from the villages in the area. We wanted to make sure that no rebels escaped into the mountains. Now we are questioning the men about their involvement in this secessionist movement of theirs."

The Colonel was obviously intelligent. He appeared to be a learned man and one whose authority was not to be questioned. I informed him again that Colonel Laraya had commissioned me and Sergeant Romero to set up refugee services for the hundreds of displaced evacuees. And so I said to him...

"Colonel, where do you intend to set up the evacuee camp?" I inquired.

"The women and children will be sent to Kulong-Kulong" he replied. "You can take care of them over there. The men remain here with me."

Then the Colonel's face grew dark and his eyes stared at me as he said, "Let me ask you, Father…is it better to feed them or to kill them?" (The Colonel was speaking of the 500 Muslim men that he had imprisoned in the Mosque under heavy guard.)

I was visibly shocked at these words…words that seemed unbelievable from a responsible Officer of the Army of the Philippines.

I thought to myself, "Am I really hearing what he said? If he was trying to shock me, he succeeded. What kind of man am I dealing with?"

I began my defense of the detainees by stammering out… "Of course it's better to feed them than to kill them."

The Colonel replied…"If we feed them, then we will have to fight them another day."

"And if you kill them," I replied, "you will have their sons growing up to hate you. They will fight you and the violence will continue out of revenge. It is better to feed them and win them over to your side in the hope that one day they will see themselves as true Filipinos and not demand secession."

I could tell that Colonel Molina was not convinced by my words. He stared at me in silence and then the conversation came to a sudden halt. As we sat in silence, the tea arrived and the three of us sipped from our cups until the Colonel abruptly rose from the table, wished us a good day and directed one of his officers to accompany me and the Sergeant around the village to see whatever we wanted. I bid farewell to the Colonel and courteously thanked him for his time.

Numbly I walked off with the Sergeant and the Officer assigned to us by Colonel Molina to tour this place of sadness. It was only too evident to me that something horrible was about to happen.

"I want to see the Mosque", I said to the Lieutenant. Without a word, the Lieutenant led me sixty meters over to the right of the

Mosque to a side door that led to the darkness inside. By now, the sun was high and the brightness of the day made it difficult for me to see inside this almost windowless building. No noise or sound could be heard within, only the voices of the soldiers outside as they patrolled the village and kept order. Then slowly, as my eyes became accustomed to the darkness of the room, shadowed images began to appear from across the expanse of floor. From the front of the large prayer area and all the way to the back of the Mosque, the floor was covered with the squat figures of 500 men huddled together, and cramped into this tight space.

I gazed upon these frightened men, strangers to me, nameless, faceless people. All eyes turned toward the doorway which I now filled. There was expectation...but only silence came. What could I say to them that meant anything at all? What words of encouragement could I give them from a mind so confused by this whole situation? I never felt so helpless...and so embarrassed at my powerlessness. I was a missionary priest after all. I must be able to do something. No more than a minute or two was spent peering upon this scene of tragedy. I wanted to get away ...to leave this place.

Turning about, I walked slowly from the Mosque in the direction of the beach, eyes downcast. After walking about twenty paces, I quickly looked up to find myself staring into the barrel of a .30 caliber machine gun positioned on the back porch of one of the houses and directed at the Mosque. There were no soldiers attending this weapon. How strange, I thought, "Like sheep led to the slaughter..." These Muslims were silently submissive to this army. There was no revolt here. Where were these rebels that caused so much trouble for Milbuk?

News had come to me later on that there was no opposition to the troop landings at Malisbong or at any of the other villages along the coast. No weapons were found on any of the people or in their villages.

Nevertheless, "We will interrogate the men to find out who the rebels are", said the Colonel. Did the AFP really want to find out the truth?

As I approached the area near the old shady tree, several of the Muslim men were being taken to a house near the shore. The house was elevated some five to six feet from the ground with a two foot wide ladder leading up into the doorway. I saw one Muslim prisoner being guided up the ladder under the guard of a soldier beneath him. Another soldier grabbed him by the arm and pulled him into the doorway of the house. Loud voices could be heard emanating from the room above. "We need to leave", I told my companions. "We can do nothing here."

The attitude of the Colonel agitated me as his words played over in my mind like a broken record, "Is it better to feed them or to kill them?"

"Is this man playing with my head'" I wondered, "or is he really intent on killing these 'rebels'?"

Like a man hypnotized and in a trance, I walked almost aimlessly across the sandy beach to the waiting banca. Stopping before the water's edge I turned and gazed at the people huddled beneath the trees. My eyes then focused on the house of interrogation where I had seen some of the prisoners enter. I was not that naïve to think that the prisoners would not be tortured in some way to "tell the truth" of their involvement and to give the names of the resistance leaders in their community. Torture and martial law went hand in hand.

What an awkward situation to be in. The teachers looked at my troubled face and could see that I had experienced something that deeply disturbed me. "We will be looking after the women and children over at Kulong-Kulong", I informed them. "It probably won't happen for a day or two. This will be your work from now on until this emergency is over." The two teachers shook their heads in agreement.

We all boarded the banca. Once out of the shallows, the motors turned over noisily and the boat headed straight out to sea for about 200 meters before turning northwest, running parallel to the shore. What happened next was truly frightening.

*"I turned my eyes to the shore and looked back at Malisbong. I noticed a procession of eight Muslim 'prisoners' on the beach, guarded by a detachment*

*of about 6 soldiers. They were marching them along the sandy shore, in single file with about two or three meters separating each prisoner. The soldiers walked parallel to and above the prisoners along the grassy mantle of the beach. Gunshots rang out…the neat row of Muslim captives broke apart and they started running in all directions. Some ran down the beach away from their captors, others ran straight into the sea and started to swim. I snapped out of my dazed stupor and strained my eyes toward the sound of the gunfire. It was a turkey shoot. Soldiers came running from all over the village. Four of the original guard detachment gunned down two of the Muslims right where they stood. Then they pursued the other six with the help of their comrades. There was no place to flee. One by one, the captives were killed. Several prisoners reached the water but there they were, floating face down in the sea, waves washing over their lifeless bodies."*

*"When the firing began, everyone in the boat riveted their eyes in the direction of the shooting. Julio even slowed down the boat to turn his attention to what was happening. It took me several seconds to realize that the soldiers on shore were now shooting at the several Muslim prisoners who had chosen to flee into the sea in order to escape. We seemed to be in the line of fire. I shouted to the boatman, "Julio, get moving. This is not a movie!" I was concerned that with all the shooting that was taking place that some of the bullets could ricochet off the water and reach us in the boat. The boat lurched ahead but our eyes were still drawn to the bizarre scene on the beach."*

*"We did not return to Malisbong but continued our trip back to Milbuk. As we all sat silently in the boat remembering the incident of a moment ago, I turned to the Sergeant and yelled, 'This Colonel intends to kill all those men in the Mosque.' Sergeant Romero only shook his head in agreement."*

Kill or Feed: (Top) A Sergeant is explaining to the Muslim Evacuees at Malisbong that they will be sent to Kulong-Kulong where the Army will assist them with food and shelter. (Below) A thousand and more people were made evacuees on the day after the AFP invasion of Kulong-Kulong, Malisbong and neighboring barrios in September, 1974.

# CHAPTER 23

## *Upon Deaf Ears*

I didn't remember the journey back to Milbuk. I was deep in thought, troubled over the events of the last hour. The gentle jolt of the banca as it rode up onto the sand in front of the convento awoke me from my trance. I snapped immediately into action, swinging myself over the side of the boat and into the knee deep water. I was heedless of the other passengers on board and much too impatient to wait my turn to disembark. Not a word was spoken. I departed from my companions abruptly and headed directly to the convento.

"Good afternoon, Father Art," Rudy said, greeting me as I stormed through the kitchen doorway.

"Good afternoon, Rudy," I flatly answered, not looking at him but quickly brushing past him toward the flight of stairs to the second floor.

"Father, there's a message for you from Sister Helen," he shouted after me. "What is it?" I impatiently growled.

"Sister Helen says that you're invited to the manager's house at noon today. It's Mr. Roberts birthday. Everyone will be there."

"A birthday party... today... what are these people thinking about?"

I ran up the stairs and pulled off my shirt, pants, wet socks and sneakers. I quickly cleaned up and put on fresh clothes, I gazed in the mirror to assure myself that I was presentable. Now I was ready to attend the party where "everyone" was invited....that meant, of course, the important people in Milbuk…the supervisors and their families as well as the Vice Mayor, Colonel Laraya, the Sisters and of course Father Art. This was my opportunity to report to the Colonel all that had happened at Malisbong earlier that day.

I walked the fifty meters to the manager's house that lay along the row of cottages overlooking Milbuk Bay and the Celebes Sea. A tall, wooden stockade fence surrounded the house and afforded some privacy from curious eyes. I pushed open the wooden gate and entered the enclosure. At least forty people were crowded into the yard. Most were seated at long rectangular tables, each covered with a simple white table cloth and two vases of colorful flowers. Eight or ten people occupied each of the tables. Over to the right of the yard parallel to the stockade fence were two long tables also covered with a white cloth but loaded down with food. Three women, wives of company employees, stood by the food to ensure that the plates and bowls of various Filipino delicacies were amply full and that the guests were satisfied.

The party was scheduled to begin at 12:00 noon. I arrived at about 1:15 P.M. All the guests had already gotten their food from the buffet and were busy eating and talking. As soon as I arrived, Sister Helen approached me and led me to the buffet table, handed me a plate and pointed the way to the food. I thanked her for being so solicitous. But first I needed to greet Mr. Roberts and his wife, wishing him a happy birthday even on such a day as today. I then excused myself and headed to the food table.

Having filled up my plate, I scanned the tables of assembled guests. The only place I saw vacant was next to Jim Woods, the assistant manager of the camp. Mr. Woods was a tall, well-built man, tan and swarthy, still handsome at fifty years of age. Jim was appropriately named since his position as assistant manager was to oversee all logging operations on site in the woods or forest. He impressed me as a man's man, someone who knew how to deal with other men in a direct and frank way but still uphold their dignity and cultivate their loyalty. The men knew where he stood on all issues relating to the logging operations. His instructions were clear, concise and without any shade of uncertainty. When he saw the loggers successfully complete some project, he was quick to acknowledge their achievement, but just as quick to vent his displeasure when their efforts failed.

Mr. Woods had worked as a logger for many years in the States right out of high school. He knew the rough and tumble life of these men first hand. Aware of the dangers of this profession, he always preached safety to his men. The loggers liked Mr. Woods to a man... he was, after all, one of them. Mr. Roberts, on the other hand, was a college educated, pencil pusher, trained in business accounting. His world was the world of ledgers. His main concern was always the bottom line. Is there profit here or not? He relied heavily upon the experience and expertise of his field supervisors, especially Mr. Woods.

I approached the empty seat next to Jim Woods and greeted him with, "Hi Jim. Is this seat taken?"

"No, Father, come on have a seat. You're late," he said.

"Yes, I just arrived from Malisbong", I replied.

"You don't look too happy", he observed.

"You got that right", I answered.

"What happened over there?" he curiously asked.

"It's tragic! Colonel Molina has 500 Muslim men imprisoned in the Mosque. The soldiers packed them into the building like sardines. I think he plans to kill them all. Can you imagine that...? And guess who I saw in the village being real familiar with the Army? It was Rolando Abary the Vice Mayor. Whenever I see him, I think of Mayor Druz Ali. The Mayor is like a puppet-master. I'm getting the feeling that the Druz Ali is mixed up in all of this...but I have no proof. He is a Muslim after all, but I'm not sure where his loyalties lie."

"Well, I told some of the loggers", Jim interjected, "that they should have gotten rid of that Mayor a long time ago. Druz Ali is a snake. You can't trust him. They should have killed him when they had the chance."

I tried not to show any surprise at Mr. Woods' comments. I wondered when it was that the loggers had the chance to "get rid of" the Mayor. I listened with interest. There was more going on in this township than I ever imagined: intrigue and conspiracy. It will make a good novel someday.

I continued to eat in silence as Mr. Woods gave a running commentary on various subjects as they crossed his mind. One in particular was rather interesting. As he gazed over the noisy guests, his eyes fell upon Sister Ana, who was sitting with some of the supervisors' wives two tables away. Sister Ana was the youngest of the three Oblate Sisters. She would celebrate her twenty-third birthday in October, having been professed as a Sister for barely two years. One of her distant relatives lived in Milbuk and Sister Ana stayed with them for two months before entering the convent. She was fluent in Cebuano & Tagalog and very adept at translating my sermons from English to Cebuano for the benefit of the ordinary people in the barrio.

Ana was always a pleasure to be with. All the people she met soon came to love her. She was easy to speak with and very approachable. Her pleasantness was contagious. It was not too surprising that this young, beautiful woman caught the attention of Mr. Woods. "Father", he said to me," do you see Sister Ana over there? Have you ever seen such a beautiful smile?" I glanced up from my plate and observed Sister Ana speaking to the other women with some animation, smiling that "Cheshire cat" smile of hers. I nodded my head in agreement. And Mr. Woods repeated again, "She has the most beautiful smile that I've ever seen." I stored this observation within my mind for further reference.

There, over at the table of Mr. Roberts sat Colonel Laraya. I noticed that one of the other officers had just left the side of the Colonel to return to the command post. This was my opportunity to give a report of the events at Malisbong. I turned to Jim Woods, "Jim, I need to speak with Colonel Laraya. Could you please excuse me? It was good talking with you. We got to do this more often."

"It's my pleasure, Father", Jim said graciously.

I approached the Colonel. "Colonel, could I speak with you for a few moments please?"

"Of course, Father. Here, have a seat. So, did anything happen at Malisbong? How did you find Colonel Molina? Were you able to speak with him?"

"Oh yes I did. Let me tell you what happened." I narrated all that had occurred at Malisbong. I placed special emphasis on my conversation with the Colonel and the remark he made... "Is it better to feed them or to kill them." I described the scene at the Mosque and the number of Muslim men detained there. Then I related the event when eight of the Muslim prisoners were gunned down along the shore.

Colonel Laraya listened passively. There was no emotion shown on his face. His whole affect was flat as if I were reading to him from the phone book. I then ended my story by exclaiming in frustration, "What can you do to put a stop to this impending massacre?"

The Colonel's reply came slowly, deliberately with a coldness that sent a shiver through my body. "There is nothing I can do." He then went on to explain. "Colonel Molina has complete jurisdiction over that whole area. He has permission from the highest authorities to do whatever he considers necessary to put down this insurgency."

I was amazed at the seeming complacency and candor with which Colonel Laraya spoke to me concerning the plight of the Muslim detainees, imprisoned in the Mosque. There was no apology for this government policy. Terrorism by the Muslims would be dealt with by use of absolute suppression. Insurgency would be put down hard. There would be "no mercy".

I believed that Colonel Laraya was not only intelligent but also a man of integrity. Nevertheless, he too had sold out to the government's policy in its "total war" initiative against its Muslim minority. Whenever these armed groups of rebels commit an act of terrorism against the Armed Forces of the Philippines and its people, then there would be retaliation and attrition against the non-combatants...against the Muslim civilians. As someone once observed when questioned why the "Geneva Accords" were not being followed concerning the harsh treatment of prisoners and civilians, the reply came back, "During war, we are not concerned about following the rules but only about winning!"

Though Colonel Laraya may have avoided placing himself in the position of carrying out these macabre duties, he was nevertheless complicit in its execution. The dozen or so Muslim men, whom I "guarded" on the loading dock on Sunday, had been taken away to be interrogated by the intelligence operatives under the command of Colonel Molina. These prisoners, allegedly, were all subsequently executed. No trace of their whereabouts ever surfaced. They were among the several hundred men who went "missing".

Though it appeared that Colonel Molina enjoyed his role as chief executioner, it was evident that Colonel Laraya avoided the opportunity to be involved in such actions. You could say that the hands of Colonel Laraya were tied. It must have been hard on his conscience to follow orders with which he did not agree. If he refused to go along, there was the real possibility that he would be removed from his position and possibly court-martialed and imprisoned.

It became clearly evident to me, after my conversation with Laraya that I would need to travel to Manila. I must let someone know what took place here. Everyone else was either too afraid or simply didn't care about what was happening to the Muslims. President Marcos had effectively blocked-out all news reports from the areas of the civil war. This news blackout affected all media. It discouraged foreign news services from even sending journalists to report on the fighting in the Southern Philippines. The world needed to know so that the government would responsibly call a halt to this "genocide".

The moment became awkward for me as I continued to sit next to the Colonel, who now was ignoring me, turning his body slightly away from me and engaging several of the other guests in trivial conversation. I felt a surge of anger rise within me. A rush of blood warmed my face and colored it with a blush of red. It was time to leave. I rose from the table and headed directly toward the manager's table. "Mr. Roberts! Thanks for inviting me. It was a nice party."

"You have to leave so soon?" he replied.

"Yes, there are still evacuees over at the high school that I must attend to. Also, I need to make plans for the 1500 Muslim women and children who will be detained over at Kulong-Kulong by tomorrow. Let me ask you now, would it be possible for me to take a ride to Davao on the company plane next Monday? I will need to travel to Manila to obtain contributions of food and clothing for the evacuees."

"Yes, of course. Speak with Buddy. Tell him to make room for you on the plane. Tell him I sent you."

"Thank you again. I really appreciate all your help." With that, I turned and left the celebration to return to the convento.

Shortly thereafter, I rode the trail bike to Buddy's home. There was no one there. Buddy's wife was managing the birthday affair. So I continued on toward the airstrip in the hope of contacting him. Luckily, he had just returned from Davao and was instructing the mechanic concerning some repair problem that needed fixing. I hung around until Buddy completed his conversation and then approached him with my request.

"Hey Buddy; I spoke with Mr. Roberts about flying with you to Davao next Monday morning. Can you make room for me on the plane?"

"I'll make sure that you get on the plane, Father. Just be here at the airstrip by 5:45 A.M."

"Thanks again, Buddy. I'll see you on Monday. Oh, by the way! How is Nards doing? Is he in much pain?"

"He told me that there was a little pain and discomfort in the foot. The bullet went right through the fleshy part of his foot and only grazed the bone. Nothing was broken or shattered, thank God!"

Later that evening, I was called over to the medical clinic to attend to the sick and wounded. The doctor called my attention to a soldier who had been brought in from Malisbong. He had been shot and was now lying dead in the makeshift morgue at the end of the medical building. I entered the room and viewed the body lying on the table. The soldier was all dressed up in his army fatigues ready to be shipped north to Manila to be handed over to his family.

Whatever blood there may have been was already washed away. His face was unmarked. There was no sign of any serious trauma.

"Where was he shot"? I asked the attendant.

The attendant proceeded to demonstrate for me the circumstances of the soldier's death and related the following: "This soldier was guarding a group of rebels earlier in the day. His detachment was taking them to a secluded marsh half a kilometer down the beach from Malisbong. Some say that these rebels were to be executed for their involvement in the ambushes at Milbuk. This soldier was bringing up the rear of the rebel column. The last Muslim in the line was slowing down and not keeping up with the rest. This soldier began striking the man in the back with the butt of his rifle. After hitting the captive several times in the back, the Muslim rebel swung quickly around, grabbed the rifle in the soldier's hands and stuck the barrel under the soldier's chin, pulling the trigger at the same time. The bullet exited through the top of the soldier's skull and killed him instantly. Before the rebel could turn to face the other soldiers with the rifle, he, in turn, was shot down right where he stood. With that, all the other Muslim captives began running helter-skelter down the beach and into the water, but to no purpose."

I looked more closely at the soldier's head. There under his chin was a blackened round indentation where the bullet entered and at the very top of his head, I saw a jagged irregular hole surrounded by matted black hair. "This soldier's death will be the reason for some to seek revenge by killing the prisoners", I thought to myself.

# CHAPTER 24

# *Care of My Muslim Brethren*

## Wednesday, September the 18th...

As I was returning from the church after celebrating Mass, I noticed several of the teachers ascending the front steps of the high school leading to the principal's office. Out of curiosity, I followed them. As I approached Mrs. Gaviola's office, there she was with two of her senior members of the teaching staff heavy into some discussion.

"Good morning all. Does this mean that you're back to work?"

"Yes, Father," they all chimed in with laughter. We have one main problem though...there are still some families occupying the classrooms. We might need your help to encourage them to return home."

"Exactly how many people are we talking about?" I inquired.

"Maybe there are eight families...about 35 or 40 people in all" was the reply.

"Well let's see who among them are able to return home. If we can cut down the number to half, then we can use the economics classroom to house them for a few more days. So, you really think we can open the school tomorrow?"

"Yes, we can, Father," they all answered unanimously.

"Good, then. I'll send over my boys from the convento to help you clean and set up the classrooms. Call some of the senior students to help also and to spread the news throughout Milbuk that the High School will be open for class tomorrow morning. The sooner we return back to normalcy, the better."

After breakfast, I sat quietly with my breviary, silently praying the psalms of David, seeking solace in the comforting words, "The Lord is my shepherd, I shall not want..." This was one of the rare times that I took to my breviary for prayer, despite the fact that all priests were under the obligation to recite the hours...a task that could take an hour and a half on any given day. I always came up with the excuse that the work was so all consuming that there was hardly any time to pray. My life, after all was apostolic and active. My prayer life, apart from meditation before and after Mass, consisted of prayer on the run. How short-sighted I had been. I needed to stop, slow down and to focus on things that really mattered so that my choices and deliberations would be God-guided and not based on human emotion only. "Though I walk through the valley of death, I will not fear. You are there with your rod and your staff that comfort me." I read, prayed and meditated. Then slowly I placed the prayer book on the table next to me and closed my eyes, experiencing the peace of the moment.

"Father Art!" The call loudly echoed up the stairs and the noise jolted me from my serenity. "There's someone to see you in the front office."

Rising from the chair, I descended the stairs and entered the front office. There in the doorway was a young student who was one of the ten Muslim scholars who had started the school year back in June. She was the only female student to apply. She was housed with the Oblate Sisters in their convent and helped them with chores around the house. "Fatima", I exclaimed with surprise. "How are you?"

"I'm fine Father," she replied.

"Where did you come from," I questioned?

"My mother and aunt are waiting for me in a jeepney over there", she said, pointing to a small settlement, of a dozen homes or so, that butted up against the logging camp fence, just in back of the church. There was a large passageway through the fence that the local people

223

used as a short cut to the church, school and marketplace. The Company didn't seem to mind that the integrity of the camp was so compromised.

"I can't tell you how happy I am to see you. I'm so excited to tell you the news that we will hold classes again at the high school tomorrow morning. Will you be there?"

"No, Father. I'm afraid. So much has happened this past month. I'm afraid to return to classes."

"I understand. Keep the books that I gave you. Attend the high school in Palimbang, if that will make you feel safe. Complete your studies so that you can make a good life for yourself."

"Father, I need to ask you something very important", she nervously stammered.

"What is it", I asked with great curiosity.

"My father and brother were taken by the Army and put in the Mosque at Malisbong. Can you get them released? I'm afraid for them. Bad things might happen to them." She was almost in tears.

"Write down their names for me. I will speak with Colonel Laraya about this today. Is there anything else I can do for you? How is your mother and the other family members? Are they all well", I inquired.

"Yes, everyone else is fine; I just want my father and brother to return home to us."

"I'll take care of that. Right now, I want you to be careful and safe. I accompanied Fatima outside of the convento and bid her farewell, "God bless you and take care of yourself." Then, turning to Rudy, I said, "Go with her to the opening in the fence and make sure that nobody bothers her."

"Rudy", if anyone is looking for me, tell them I'm over at the Army command post speaking with Colonel Laraya."

After Fatima had left the area, I unlocked the garage and wheeled out the trail bike. It didn't take but 4 or 5 minutes to reach the outpost. "Is Colonel Laraya able to speak with me at this time", I asked the Sergeant at the desk.

"One moment, Father, let me ask him." The Sergeant rose from his chair and turned around to the door leading to the Colonel's office. He knocked twice and opened the door, closing it behind him as he entered. Within a minute, the Sergeant appeared in the open doorway, ushering me within, "The Colonel can see you now."

"Thank you very much", I replied as I entered the Colonel's office.

"Good morning, Colonel. How are you today?"

"Much better, thanks. What can I do for you, Father", he officiously answered.

"Well, first of all, my staff and I are ready to begin working with the Muslim evacuees at Kulong-Kulong. Can we begin tomorrow", I asked?

"Yes, of course you can. I'll draw up instructions for my staff to assist you in every way possible."

"Thank you. I couldn't ask for more. However, there's another issue that was just brought to my attention by one of my former Muslim students, a young woman by the name of Fatima Balitao. This young woman is a scholar at the High School and also an aide to the Oblate Sisters. Her family comes from the barrio of Wal. Fatima was able to visit me this morning at the convento and told me that both her father and brother were taken by the military and placed within the Mosque at Malisbong. I need a big favor from you. Would it be possible for you to speak with Colonel Molina to release this young woman's father and brother from the Mosque? I don't believe that these people have anything to do with this rebel group."

"Yes. I will speak with Colonel Molina today and hopefully get them released and returned to this girl's family."

"How can I thank you, Colonel? I am in your debt."

"Don't worry, Father, I'll take care of this personally myself."

## Thursday morning, September 19th...

"I wonder how much damage was done to Kulong-Kulong during the Navy bombardment", I thought to myself as I rode over to the home of the Manobo children. The next agenda on my calendar was to make plans for visiting Kulong-Kulong and assessing the needs of the Muslim women and children who would be living there.

"Knock, knock…anybody home?" I yelled, standing outside the Manobo house. There were no children in residence at this time. They were still with their families in the hills above Milbuk. Gradually, they would be filtering down to Milbuk once word reached them that classes were in session.

"Good morning, Father Art", the voices of the two teachers sang out in unison from within the house. "We'll be out in a minute."

I paced along the side of the outside kitchen area attached to the end of the building. I didn't have to wait long.

"We're ready now, Father", Cecilia and Lisa chimed in again. "Where are we going today?"

"You will be helping Mrs. Gaviola today prepare the school rooms for classes. But tomorrow, you will assist me in visiting the evacuees at Kulong-Kulong. We will leave early in the morning. We need to come up with a plan to help these people get settled. I don't know what their needs are yet. There are several things we need to examine carefully, namely, sanitation, clean water supply and available food. Not all the evacuees are from Kulong-Kulong. Most of the people are from Malisbong and five or six other small barrios. There could be a thousand or two thousand women and children living in this one village. We will leave for Kulong-Kulong at 8:00 A.M. from the back of the convento. Don't dress up too well. We will be there to work, not to sightsee."

The next day arrived without incident. We all assembled on the small beach behind the convento and boarded the banca for the Muslim refugee camp. The trip to Kulong-Kulong took barely twelve minutes. As the banca headed into shore, I could see a lot of activity taking place within the village. Women and children were moving along the "main street" that divided the barrio. Some stopped to gaze down at the new arrivals at their village. Several armed soldiers walked to the edge of the village and gave a cursory glance at the strangers and then they moved on too, obviously aware of our coming. It was low tide. My companions and I walked up the sloping beach and entered the bustling village. Children were running all over the place. The suspicious eyes of the women stared blankly at us.

I began my instruction to the two teachers: "I want the two of you to separate from me. Speak with the women. Find out who among the women are from this village. Seek out the leaders from among the women and we will speak with them privately. We need the people to help us. I'll just float around and smile at the children. When you find out who is in charge, call me." The teachers nodded their heads and went off together. It was not Muslim culture for a strange man to speak with any Muslim woman. I needed to deal with the situation at hand in an almost indirect way, using my teachers as intermediaries.

As I began to stroll through the village, a voice rang out, "Fr. Art". I turned around in surprise and there was Fatima Balitao, my Muslim student, with a shawl thrown over her shoulder, dressed in Muslim garb.

"My goodness, what are you doing here?"

"I came here with some of relatives to wait for the release of my father and brother. May I accompany you on your walk through the village?"

"Yes, of course. You can be my interpreter if I need to ask any questions from the people here", I answered gratefully.

I noticed the presence of the armed soldiers throughout. I greeted them as they passed by, making a mental note regarding their behavior in the village and how they treated the evacuees. A plan was slowly evolving in my mind as my time in the village reached an hour. "Sanitation is a must", I mumbled. "Slit trenches must be dug some distance from the village to take care of bodily functions and bamboo modesty screens erected for the women. The soldiers can be used to dig these trenches. We must safeguard the cleanliness of the drinking water from any contaminants. The last thing we need here is an outbreak of cholera. Disease is the greatest danger among so many people.

"Father Art", the teachers beckoned, "come over here, please." "We want you to meet some of these women who are willing to help us."

With a big smile, I greeted the women with "As-Salaam Alaikum". "Alaikum Asalaam", they replied.

"Tell the women that we want to help in whatever way we can. Both of you will be coming here every day to monitor the situation and to let me know what I can do to have the Army assist in this project. I will be leaving for Manila in a few days to obtain donations of food and clothing for them. In the meantime, there should be enough food to take care of their needs for at least two weeks."

It was almost noontime. The first day of assessment was completed. It was now up to me to speak with the Colonel and request the Army's help in constructing the slit trenches for the evacuees. We may need to truck safe drinking water into the village if the present spring or well has been contaminated. "What a mess!" I mumbled again, as the banca left the shore of Kulong-Kulong heading back to Milbuk. I did not know the whole of it.

My Muslim Brethren: This collage depicts the situation that developed in Kulong-Kulong when there was a violent outbreak of cholera. The Army (AFP) sent medical personnel into the evacuee camp in order to hold back the outbreak of this deadly disease. Over the next few weeks, dozens of sick women and children had to be evacuated to another village in order to isolate the infected from the healthy. Sanitary measures were put into operation and the people were educated about methods to prevent the further outbreak of this deadly disease. Over a hundred died needlessly from the outbreak.

# CHAPTER 25

# *The Sermon*

C olonel Laraya had requested the Logging Company manager to cut out a road from Milbuk to Kulong-Kulong across the marshy patches of land that divided the two communities. The Army wanted the road to continue through the interior of this coconut plantation to the other small villages and lastly to Malisbong itself. The road building began early in the morning on the day after the Army had invaded this coconut treed delta. It didn't take long for the loggers with all their heavy equipment to punch through a road to Kulong-Kulong. Two hundred or more loggers on bulldozers, graders and trucks made easy work of plowing away the undergrowth and small trees and to fill in the marshy spots of land with rocks and soil from the nearby hills. When the loggers reached Kulong-Kulong they found themselves in a deserted village. They went from house to house and store to store taking whatever was valuable. They snatched up the canned foods, sacks of grain, yards of cloth and even the goats and chickens running about the village. This was in revenge, they reasoned, for all that the rebels did to their brother loggers. These were spoils of war.

The loggers returned home happy that day with their ill-gotten goods. Even some of the Manobo men went along with this civilian crowd to loot and pillage. The loggers couldn't wait until the next day when they would "visit" the other abandoned villages, not as large and prosperous as Kulong-Kulong, but who knows what they would find. The Muslim evacuees had fled their villages with the clothes on their backs and little else. Such was their fear of the invading Army. When the evacuees from Kulong-Kulong returned to their village, there was nothing left of their belongings. All the food had been taken.

It took over two days before I became aware that the good Christians of Milbuk had looted the village of Kulong-Kulong. On Wednesday morning, just before Mass, I casually looked out my bedroom window and noticed several goats tethered in the yard of one of the logging supervisors, my closest neighbor. "Hmm", I thought, "where did the goats come from?" This didn't register with me at the time. It was only later in the morning, during a conversation I had with Sister Helen that I inquired, "By the way, where did 'Frank' get his goats? Is he raising goats now?"

Sister Helen laughed and then almost ashamedly began to tell me the whole story. "Two days ago, the loggers went to Kulong-Kulong and took everything they could find that belonged to the Muslims."

"They did what?" I growled angrily. "Where was the Army?"

"The Army was with them. They let them take whatever they wanted."

"Oh, my God," I exclaimed. I felt so badly. "Here I am traveling to Kulong-Kulong day after day to help the evacuees. And you're telling me that the people of Milbuk are stealing from them. What must they think of us?"

For four days, I held in my anger and disappointment. I would have an opportunity on Sunday to address this issue at Mass during the sermon. I also found out that even the Manobos had participated in the pillaging of the villages. I told my two teachers to speak with them and explain that God is not pleased with us when we steal from others. "Have you not received clothes and food from Father Art? You don't need to steal from others. We must all trust in God's love for us. God will provide all the things that we need."

## Sunday, September the 21st ...

I was up early to review in my mind the words I would use to teach the people. It was not my manner to scold people or to embarrass them. I could let the whole incident go without any comment, as if stealing from others didn't really matter. In such a small place, everyone knew by now how disappointed I was about the looting. Now the people were anticipating what I would tell them. As I opened the kitchen door at the side of the convento to walk the 100 meters or so to the Church, the door was blocked by bundles of clothing that had been placed on the small porch. "What are these, Rudy?"

"Oh, you mean the clothes? I saw a couple of Manobo men depositing the bundles on the back porch earlier this morning."

"Can you imagine," I marveled, "the Manobos returned the stolen clothing! Remarkable!"

As the time approached for the Mass, I peeked out from the sacristy and saw that the Church was nearly full. This was good. "I must mention the incident without condemning the people to the fires of hell", I reminded myself. I chose as the gospel reading the story of the Good Samaritan. The Samaritans, inhabitants of Samaria in Palestine, were a mixed race, descended from intermarriage of Israelites and Assyrian colonists. The hatred between the Jews and the Samaritans was so great that Jewish travelers going between Galilee and Judea often had to cross the Jordan into Perea for safety. In practice, the Samaritans worshiped the same God as the Jews, and in such matters as Sabbaths and feasts, circumcision and worship they were in full agreement. But though competing with the Jews in the strict observance of Mosaic regulations, they disowned the Jerusalem temple and priesthood. The rival sanctuary of Mt. Gerizim was revered as their holy place.

When the time came for the reading of the Gospel, all eyes were on me. "The Lord be with you," I greeted the congregation.

"And with you also", the people answered back.

*"A reading from the Holy Gospel according to Luke."*

"Glory to you, O Lord", the congregation replied back.

I then began the reading of the Gospel.

*"At that time, a lawyer stood up to pose this problem to Jesus: "Teacher, what must I do to inherit everlasting life?" Jesus answered him: "What is written in the law. How do you read it?" He replied: "You shall love the Lord your God with all your heart, with all your soul, with all your strength, and with your entire mind: and your neighbor as yourself."*

*Jesus said, "You have answered correctly. Do this and you shall live." But because he wished to justify himself he said to Jesus, "And who is my neighbor?"*

*Jesus replied: "There was a man going down from Jerusalem to Jericho who fell prey to robbers. They stripped him, beat him, and then went off leaving him half-dead. A priest happened to be going down the same road; he saw him but continued on. Likewise there was a Levite who came the same way; he saw him and went on. But a Samaritan who was journeying along came on him and was moved to pity at the sight. He approached him and dressed his wounds, pouring in oil and wine. He then hoisted him on his own beast and brought him to an inn, where he cared for him. The next day he took out two silver pieces and gave them to the innkeeper with the request: 'Look after him, and if there is any further expense I will repay you on my way back'.*

*Jesus then asked the lawyer, "Which of these three, in your opinion, was neighbor to the man who fell in with the robbers?"*

*The answer came, "The one who treated him with compassion."*

*Jesus said to him, "Then go and do the same."*

I raised the holy book high above my head and declared, ***"This is the Gospel of the Lord."***

And the people answered, "Praise to you, Lord Jesus Christ".

The congregation then sat down and waited attentively for my sermon. I began to teach the people.

*"There are three essential lessons in this Gospel reading that I really need to explain to you. The first lesson is this. Mercy to another person*

*is more important than any sacrifice we may offer to God. This is seen in the importance of the small details that Jesus mentions concerning the first two men who passed along the road and saw the wounded man but continued on.*

*People traveled to Jerusalem either for business or for worship. Both the Priest and the Levite had gone to Jerusalem for the purpose of worshipping God in the Holy Temple. They were servants in the Temple, assisting the people in their worship of God. Now they were just returning from the Temple where they had prayed and offered sacrifice in fulfillment of the law. And yet, as religious as they pretended to be on the outside, they failed to fulfill the law of God by not coming to the aid of the wounded man. These two men, officials in the Temple, should have been the very ones to show mercy.*

*The second essential lesson people forget in this story is why Jesus uses the example of a hated Samaritan as the third character in the story. Samaritans were cousins to the Jews. They worshipped the same God but on a different mountain. The Jews worshipped God on Mt. Zion in Jerusalem, the Samaritans on Mt. Gerizim. These two people had been feuding with each other for centuries. The Jews hated and feared the Samaritans. The man who fell prey to robbers was obviously Jewish and must have been returning home after worshipping at the Temple or doing business.*

*Jesus uses this example to teach us that we must overcome our hatred and prejudice to others by acts of mercy and forgiveness. This is what justifies us in the presence of God. The Samaritan did not see a hated Jew but a wounded human being, a man like himself, who was in need of his help.*

*The third lesson so overlooked by most of us is contained in the question Jesus asks the lawyer after he had told his story. "Which of these three, in your opinion, was neighbor to the man who fell in with the robbers?"*

*"The one who treated him with compassion", was the lawyer's answer. Yes, it was the hated Samaritan, the non-Jew, who went to the aid of the wounded man. And yet we forget that the question the lawyer first asked Jesus was: "...and who is my neighbor?"*

*Jesus is teaching us to have compassion on all men and women, regardless. Everyone is our neighbor. Yes, even the Muslims that you say you hate." This morning we are all here to worship God our Father through the Holy Sacrifice of His Son Jesus. We remember how Jesus in his love for you and me and for all humanity sacrificed Himself upon the Cross. And Jesus said, "Father, forgive them for they know not what they do."*

*If we have sinned against our neighbor in any way, let us come before this throne of mercy and ask our loving Savior to wash us clean with his sacred blood. And when we leave here, let us make atonement for any offense we have committed against our neighbors. Jesus reminds us also that when we come before God the Father to offer our worship and there remember that we have sinned against our neighbor, we are to leave our gift at the altar and first go and be reconciled with our neighbor and then come and offer our sacrifice.*

*Forgiveness, mercy, compassion…these are the gifts we bring before God, our Father."*

*"What has happened during the past week concerning the looting and pillaging of the Muslim villages is a shame upon this community. The evidence of what you've done stares me in the face. Since when have the people of Milbuk begun to raise goats in the camp? Yesterday, my teachers spoke with the Manobos whom you took with you on your trips to the Muslim villages. They instructed them that God is not pleased with this theft of someone else's clothing. 'You must trust in God alone to provide for you', they told them. This morning as I was about to leave the convento for Mass, my back door was blocked by the bundles of clothes taken from the Muslims. The Manobos had returned these ill-gotten goods and they are not even baptized Christians."*

*"I know that all of you have suffered much during the last two months. You have lost husbands, sons, brothers and friends. But you have judged an entire people for the crimes and evil deeds of a few. Those Muslim evacuees are victims like you. And we as Christians, true followers of Christ must show mercy and compassion on them. We must begin to forgive from our hearts. Will God continue to bless us if we remain hard-hearted and cold to Him?" "How can you say that you love God, if you do not love your*

*neighbor? For how can you love God whom you do not see, if you cannot love your neighbor whom you do see?"*

I dropped my eyes from the assembly and slowly turned from the pulpit and walked to the middle of the altar. Only the sound of small children could be heard. Nobody else stirred in their seats. The words embedded themselves deep into their minds. How would they respond? With a loud voice, I exclaimed, "Let us proclaim our faith…" The congregation all stood and in unison prayed, "We believe in One God, the Father Almighty…"

No one approached me after Mass. Most of the people hurried back to their homes, exchanging thoughts and comments about the sermon. Within two days, all the goats were gone from Milbuk. Some were killed, cooked and eaten. Others were sold to people who lived outside the camp, excited to purchase such delicacies at a bargain. It was never the same after that. I could never get close to my people as before. They felt ashamed that maybe I knew that they had participated in the looting or had accepted the stolen articles. They were friendly toward me, but guarded. I, on the other hand, felt a bit betrayed. It would take a while for me to forgive and forget as well. I needed to follow the Lord's advice. "And who proved himself to be a neighbor to the man who fell among robbers?" The answer was, "The one who treated him with compassion". And Jesus said, "Go and do likewise".

Wounds come in many forms and shapes, colors and sizes. People's wounds may not be all that visible but sensitivity to a person and their situation will invariably bring forth a clearer vision of their condition. I left Milbuk before I had a chance and the time to bring resolution to my relationship with this community.

# CHAPTER 26

# *The World Is Watching*

**Monday, September the 23rd …**

I arrived at the airstrip at exactly 5:45 A.M. The men at the airfield were busy loading two fifty gallon barrels of aviation fuel, a highly flammable liquid. Both barrels were being lashed to the inside of the eight passenger Beechcraft, a twin engine plane that the Company used for transporting large pieces of machinery and engine parts, as well as important visitors. I walked up to Buddy as he was directing the men in securing the barrels to the inside of the plane.

"We won't be flying to Davao today, Father. I've been ordered to fly these two fifty gallon barrels of aviation fuel to one of our logging affiliates at Butuan in Agusan. Their supply of fuel never arrived at their camp. The planes sit empty on the airstrip. But we will continue on to Manila after we drop off the fuel."

"Well, that's lucky. I hope you don't mind if I tag along with you to Butuan and Manila?"

"No, not at all…as long as you don't mind riding next to two fifty gallon barrels of aviation fuel."

"I don't mind at all. You're a good pilot. I have faith in you."

The fuel was delivered to the logging company in Butuan. We all had a quick snack and boarded the Beechcraft for Manila, arriving at the airport about 1:00 P.M. A company vehicle picked up Buddy and his brother. I took a taxi to Quezon City, to the housing compound owned by the Passionist Congregation to conduct their business affairs. There was a small guest house within the compound to handle the continual flow of missionaries and visitors to the Philippines.

That night at supper, I was the center of attention as I narrated the events of the past month to five of my fellow missionaries. I told them in detail of my encounter with the Army Colonel at Malisbong and the fear I had that many of the captured Muslims would be killed. One of the priests sitting around the dinner table that night was a middle-aged man who had worked with the Muslims in his parish for many years. Fr. Frank Hanlon was among the first band of missionary priests to staff the parishes of the diocese of South Cotabato in the latter part of 1958. His long term assignment was in the parish of Santo Nino in the town of Surallah, situated in an area called the Allah Valley.

The Christian settlements in the Allah Valley were made up of farmers who had migrated here from various parts of the Philippines. Their lives would be forever linked to their Muslim neighbors whose residence in this fertile land went back for hundreds of years. These migrating peasants from Luzon and the Bisayas had been clamoring for land reform and a share of the huge land holdings of the rich oligarchs, who treated these tenants as so many medieval serfs. The rise of Communist inspired armed groups had worsened this conflict and brought the whole issue into an active rebellion against the government. The government sponsored a migration to Mindanao in the late 1930's to open up the resources of this rich land by promising each family a homestead of eight hectares of land. This offer was just too tempting to pass up. Thousands boarded ships with all their belongings and headed with their families to this vast undeveloped land. It was only with the planned migration of these Christian farmers to Mindanao from the troubled provinces of Luzon in the Northern Philippines, that the government was able at the same time to ease the tensions of these tenant farmers.

Many of the first settlers in this region were especially expert in designing and plotting out farmlands out of all shapes and contours of land. The Muslims were not noted for their agricultural skills.

Mindanao during the late thirties through the early sixties was a vast region of truly virgin soil made fertile by centuries of volcanic activity. The soil of Mindanao lay ready to energize the seeds of the farmers and produce abundant crops of rice, soy, corn and other cereals to feed not only the people of Mindanao but to become the "bread basket" for the whole of the Philippines.

The Muslim inhabitants looked on in envy. Never did they suspect that their lands were so valuable. Now that the Christian farmers had shown them the way to prosperity, they too wanted to share in the abundance. Whatever price had been paid to the Muslim owners of these lands, it was now evident that the price was much, much too low. You could say that the confiscation of lands from the Muslims by the government was a steal, similar to the handing over of the vast areas of land belonging to the Native Americans.

Dissension broke out in the mixed communities. Former Muslim owners were now demanding more money in compensation for such valuable land. The Christian farmers refused. There were burning of crops, random killings and kidnappings for ransom. The settlers responded with a vengeance of their own. They would not be moved or intimidated. The stronger the Muslims pushed, the stronger the settlers pushed back. Vigilante groups of farmers and villagers began to be organized to protect both the homesteads and towns. It was a lawless time. Each group established their own type of justice. Suspects in land grabbing, kidnapping and murder were judged guilty and summarily executed. In response, the Muslims organized their own roving gangs of vigilantes, who in the name of Allah initiated a jihad against these offending infidels. Civil war broke out among peoples who previously had got along quite well. If not for the greed and avarice of a few, and the incompetence of the government in settling matters justly, the communities may have come to some compromise in order to continue to live amicably with one another.

Father Frank Hanlon spent over fifteen years working in this area of Mindanao. This short, stocky man of Irish descent was a happy-go-lucky person. With every project he undertook for his people, he radiated enthusiasm from every pore of his being. His friendly, smiling face belied a certain intensity that lay beneath the surface. The goal of his mission was the promotion of justice and harmony among the people he served.

Frank considered himself a father not just to the Christians of his parish but to the Muslims as well. Not intent on converting the Muslims to Christianity, he reached out to them to create a relationship of friendship, understanding and cooperation. His Christian parishioners couldn't understand why he trusted the Muslims at all. They only shook their heads in disbelief when he encouraged them to enter into dialogue with the Muslims. "Seek a compromise. Resolve your differences amicably. Above all, never stop from communicating with each other."

Some considered Father Frank more as a Muslim Imam than a Catholic Priest. What was he doing, spending so much time among these people? He doesn't know them as well as we do. Muslims can't be trusted. Over the course of fifteen years, this tension weighed heavily on Fr. Frank. He needed to free himself from parish work and devote himself entirely to a more effective dialogue with the Muslim leadership in Mindanao. Maybe his willingness to listen to their complaints and aspirations would enable him to be an interpreter and mediator with his Christian brothers. Harmony, understanding, cooperation and forgiveness were all necessary to bridge the gap that was widening each year as the conflict heated up to the waging of a civil war. Frank was anxious to hear my experience. He was only too glad to assist me in telling the world of the government's "total war" policy and the planned ethnic cleansing in Malisbong.

The person whom Father Frank contacted to hear my story was a member of the Egyptian delegation to the Philippines. This person, whose name has been lost to memory, was described as the religious liaison to the various Filipino-Muslim communities. The Egyptian was a tall, handsome man whose command of English was impeccable. His speech was so clear that there was hardly a trace of an accent. Evidently, he was quite educated. He listened intently to every word, recording my narration of events to memory. I could be sure that the world would know of the threatened massacre.

"When will you be returning to the States, Father Art?" he asked.

"I still have a year left on my tour of duty."

The Egyptian Imam smiled at me and added, "Whenever you do return, think of traveling to Egypt. It would be my honor and pleasure to have you as my guest in Cairo."

I was surprised and speechless for a moment. "Thank you very much for the wonderful invitation. I have always desired to visit Egypt. The history of your great nation intrigues me."

I was perceptively aware that I might be placing myself in a rather compromising position of being set up as a political ploy in this international game of power. I couldn't wait for the slow pace of diplomatic talks when the lives of so many were at stake. I then phoned the office of the Associated Press International in Manila. The Bureau Chief, a certain Mr. Arnold Zeitlin, answered the phone himself. He was the only foreign correspondent stationed in Manila. The other news services employed Filipino newsmen to cover this beat.

President Marcos had placed a complete news blackout on what the newspapers could report on the raging conflict in the Southern Philippines. The Philippine Government had censored Mr. Zeitlin back in February of this year for writing a story about the Armed Forces of the Philippines and their military engagement with Muslim secessionist forces in the city of Jolo. Mr. Zeitlin claimed in his first hand story that up to 10,000 Muslims had been killed by the military in their efforts to prevent the town of Jolo from being taken over by the rebels. Jolo was razed to the ground by a fire storm. The majority of the dead were innocent civilians caught up in the cross-fire and bombardment of the city. Tens of thousands of Muslims fled the area and were displaced for months. After the conflagration of the town, only 5,000 people remained to sift through the burnt wreckage of their homes to recover the bodies of their loved ones.

When Arnold Zeitlin heard in brief, the story that I wanted to tell, he immediately came to the Passionists' housing compound in Quezon City to speak with me in person. Mr. Zeitlin spent over an hour with me, asking me many questions and writing down all the information. Finally, he inquired, "When do you plan to return to Milbuk?"

I replied, "I still need to speak with the director of the Catholic Relief Services here in Manila in order to obtain food and clothing for the evacuees. I plan to fly to Davao city the day after tomorrow, early in the morning. Hopefully, I can catch a ride on the Logging Company plane back to Milbuk."

"Can I come with you? I would like to visit your place and see for myself the village where the Muslim evacuees are being held."

"That would be great! It would be my pleasure to have you as my guest. Shall we meet at the Manila International Airport on Thursday morning? My plane leaves at 7:15 A.M."

On the following day, I traveled to Manila to the office of the Catholic Relief Services. The Director of C.R.S. was available to see me. I told him my story and he patiently listened. I could tell that he heard similar stories like this before and recently. There were so many areas in the southern Philippines that were affected by this conflict between the Muslim secessionist movement and the government. The needs of the people in Jolo and Zamboanga were horrific. The sheer number of homeless and displaced families was truly staggering. So when the Director told me that the "cupboard was bare", I knew exactly what he meant. The C.R.S. warehouses were empty. The only thing he could offer me was powdered chocolate milk and bales of clothing. I accepted his offer with gratitude and asked him to keep me in mind when new supplies of food arrive.

I felt quite dejected at not receiving the supplies of food that the people needed. However, this trip was not a complete failure. I was able to publish the news of the massacre and to make known the plight of the Muslim people. Upon my arrival at the Passionist compound, I settled in for an evening of conversation with my associate missionaries and a good night's sleep. I would be leaving early the next morning for the airport. Only heaven would know what problems would be facing me upon my return to Milbuk.

# Thursday, September the 26th...

The driver for the Passionist Religious Superior was up early, dusting the car and washing the windows. I threw my small suitcase in the back seat of the car and sat next to him. Leo had worked as driver and handy man for the Passionists during the past eight years. He lived in a small house within the compound together with his wife and small son. His wife was the lavandera or washer woman for the small community. It was 5:30 A.M. We needed to leave early in order to avoid the crush of traffic along the main highway. An hour and fifteen minutes later, Leo dropped me off at the main entrance to the airport. I already had my ticket in hand and so I proceeded directly to the boarding terminal and registered for the flight. The passenger lounge or waiting area was almost full. Luckily, there was an empty seat right next to Mr. Zeitlin, who had arrived almost fifteen minutes before.

"Good morning, Mr. Zeitlin. It looks like we have good flying weather."

"Good morning, Father Art. Did you get all your work done?"

"Yes, Catholic Relief Services will be sending clothes and powdered chocolate milk for the refugees. The demand at this time is so great. There must be dozens of communities like Milbuk, with similar problems."

"Yes, you're right. No matter what war-torn country you're in, the suffering is the same. Ordinary people, especially the women and children, all experience the hunger, disease, displacement and death brought on by man's greed and avarice. It's discouraging."

"Do you ever get discouraged at seeing the same old scenes time after time, country after country?" I asked.

"Sometimes I need to break away from these scenes of human tragedy...but I can't seem to stay away long. I feel guilty when I am able to get up and leave with my photos and story. At times I feel a compulsion to view again the human face of misery through my camera lens."

"You're doing a great service to these innocent people by recording their suffering and telling their story. The government officials must be made accountable for their misdeeds and held responsible for creating these situations among their people. After all, the whole world is watching. Maybe someday, some group of people will have the power, courage and ability to say, "No more! Enough is enough!" and be able to exert such influence on these countries and political systems that change will begin to take place. The peoples of the world need to have these events recorded. We must remember the past so that we don't repeat its mistakes."

"That was quite a sermon, Father. I joke with you, of course. Everything you say is true. I know that I've embarrassed some politicians to the point where my life was in danger. And it is so easy to lose your life in covering one of these stories. You simply become another casualty of war…collateral damage."

I continued, "I remember each day the friends that I've lost and the senseless brutality of this war. Someone needs to know what's happening in Malisbong. If the unjust and cruel actions of the military go unchecked and unchallenged, then they will be free to continue their unbridled violence on every barrio in the Philippines, whether Muslim or Christian. Democracy is dead in the Philippines as we speak. That's why the military feel that they are in charge of the Republic under their Commander and Chief, Marcos. I'd better be silent lest someone overhears my comments and I find myself on the next plane to the States. …Well, it looks as though all is ready to board the plane. The trip is not that long, maybe two hours. We should be in Davao by 9:30 A.M."

## CHAPTER 27

# *Reporting a Massacre*

The flight was uneventful. We arrived on time, grabbed our luggage from the overhead racks and headed to the end of the terminal where the hangars for the private planes were situated. There on the tarmac was the Weyerhaeuser Beechcraft. We went into the hangar and saw Buddy and the co-pilot talking to employees of the airport, giving them instructions concerning the fueling of the airplane and other essential information. Buddy greeted me as I entered the building. I introduced him to Mr. Zeitlin and told him about our plans of traveling back to Milbuk. Buddy said that he wouldn't be returning to Milbuk until the afternoon, about 2:00 P.M. He would be able to accommodate us on the flight back. We made plans to meet him here at the plane by 1:30 P.M. In the meantime, Mr. Zeitlin and I took a taxi into Davao to eat a good breakfast and talk some more.

All went according to plan. Upon arriving at Milbuk, we were dropped off at my convento. I showed Mr. Zeitlin to his room and gave him a quick tour of the house. We then boarded my jeep and headed off to the command post to speak with Colonel Laraya, seeking permission for Arnold Zeitlin to tour the refugee camp at Kulong-Kulong.

Arnold and I rode quickly through the camp, out the main gate and onto the road to the Command Post. Groups of soldiers were milling here and there waiting for some order to proceed to their

245

next assignment. I parked the jeep off the side of the road and the two of us ascended the small incline to the flight of stairs leading to the main offices of the Battalion. I was greeted by Sergeant Romero, who rose from the desk and approached us.

"Good afternoon, Father."

"Good afternoon, Sarge. Sergeant Romero, I want to introduce you to Mr. Arnold Zeitlin, Bureau Chief of the Associated Press in Manila. He's here to do a story on our relief efforts on behalf of the Muslim evacuees at Kulong-Kulong. We would like to speak with Colonel Laraya. Is he available?"

Sergeant Romero stretched out his hand to Mr. Zeitlin and said politely, "Nice to meet you, sir. Let me inform the Colonel that you're here."

Within a minute, the Colonel's office door opened and the two of us were ushered in. Colonel Laraya stood behind his desk, hand outstretched as I entered the room. "Good morning, Father Art."

"Good Morning, Colonel. I have the pleasure of introducing you to Mr. Arnold Zeitlin, Bureau Chief of the Associated Press in Manila."

"Yes, of course. Good morning, Mr. Zeitlin."

"Good morning, Colonel."

Over to the Colonel's right stood an officer whom I had met briefly. Colonel Laraya turned to the two men and introduced the officer." "I want you to meet my adjutant, Major Jose Bernardo."

"Major, it's good to meet you again," I said as I turned to greet him. Mr. Zeitlin also acknowledged the Major.

"What are your plans for tomorrow, Father Art?" the Colonel inquired?

"Well, I plan to leave for Kulong-Kulong by 8:30 A.M. I would like to ask your permission for Mr. Zeitlin to accompany me to the village and see the work that is being done for the refugees."

"That will be fine, Father. Major Bernardo will accompany you," Colonel Laraya instructed us. "And when you return from Kulong-Kulong, please come back and let me know how everything went."

Turning to Major Bernardo I said, "We'll meet at my convento inside the camp by 8:30 A.M. tomorrow morning. Is that a convenient time for you, sir?"

"Yes, the time is good," he replied.

"We'll be riding in my banca. It will not take us but fifteen minutes to reach the village. My house is not difficult to find. It's the only two-story building in the camp, except for the High School next door."

"I'm sure that my driver will be able to find it," the Major added flatly.

"Thank you, Colonel, for all your assistance."

"Don't forget to come and see me after your visit," the Colonel added as we departed his office.

As we rode back to the convento, I remarked to Mr. Zeitlin, "That Major has the personality of an ice cube. He may cause us trouble during our trip tomorrow. I can see that he already is suspicious of me in bringing you all the way from Manila."

"Yes, I've seen soldiers like him before. He will be all over us," Arnold commented. "He doesn't want the Colonel to be embarrassed by anything we may find out."

"Let me take care of the Major. I'll find something to distract him."

I took Mr. Zeitlin on a brief tour of Milbuk. The best way to see the whole complex was to climb the small mountain overlooking the logging camp. It was late in the afternoon and the view was spectacular. The haze of the day had lifted and a cool breeze drifted in from the sea. The camp area, the veneer mill complex and the sprawling barrios of San Roque and Santo Nino were bustling with life. Workers from the mill were returning home. Children were running through the streets, playing their games. The basketball court played host to a make-up game of teenage students who laughed and joked around. And there in the distance hidden beneath the canopy of coconut trees lay the refugee center of Kulong-Kulong, 4-5 kilometers away.

We soon returned to the convento to share a San Miguel and to relax before the panorama of the Celebes Sea. The twilight of the afternoon soon gave way to darkness. Dinner was brought to us and we feasted on fried chicken, steamed rice and string beans. It was simple fare, nothing like the gourmet foods of the Apo View Hotel.

For the next two hours, we sat talking quietly about home and family. Mostly it was I who did the talking, taking advantage of a captive audience. Usually, my evenings were spent alone, in silence, not hearing the voice of another human. Arnold did share when I let him. But he was too gracious a guest to let me know how bored he must have been, listening to my ravings. The one statement I remember him making was the observation of how lonely and isolated I must be living here alone by myself. He said, "If I were assigned here for a long time, I would need a trunk full of books to keep me occupied." I laughed at his remark and pointed to a steamer trunk of my belongings sitting in the living room, along the side of the wall… "See that trunk there…it's full of books." He laughed and shook his head in acknowledgement. "Yes," I replied. That's what keeps me sane".

All in all, it was a very pleasant evening. It was almost 9:00 P.M. when I bid good night to my special visitor and retired to my room. It was years later that I began to realize how deeply regarded Arnold Zeitlin was as a journalist and foreign correspondent. "I didn't know how famous you were, Mr. Zeitlin."

## Friday, September the 27th …

Morning arrived quickly. I was up and out of bed early, showering, shaving and preparing myself mentally for the hours ahead. I made sure that hot water for coffee and a good breakfast would be ready for me and Mr. Zeitlin upon my return from celebrating Mass at the Church. I spent but a minute or two in thanksgiving after Mass and hurriedly headed toward the convento for breakfast. When I ascended the stairs to the living/dining room area, I could see that Mr. Zeitlin was already awake and ready for the day's work.

"How did you sleep last night, Mr. Zeitlin?"

"Well, I lay awake reading and taking notes for about an hour or two. I probably slept for four or five hours. I feel pretty good."

"I see you found the hot water and coffee. Come on let's eat."

After breakfast, Arnold and I descended the stairs and went to the back of the convento. There we met Major Bernardo who had just arrived by jeep from the command post. Within minutes, all three of us were boarding the banca. Cecilia and Lisa and another teacher, were already patiently sitting within the boat waiting for us. The two boatmen pushed the banca out into deeper waters and started the engines. It was a pleasant day with hardly a breeze. The sea was calm. The banca cleanly cut through the water and made quick time to the sandy shores of Kulong-Kulong. The tide had gone out so that the banca was a good forty yards from the village. The five of us disembarked from the boat and walked up the steep, sandy incline to the edge of the village. People had gathered in small knots within the alleys separating the houses to eye the six of us walking into their midst. These people were all women with groups of small children running here and there excitedly. I smiled at the women. They knew me when I first came among them almost two weeks ago to set up the relief activities. The teachers were very familiar with the women, visiting them daily, whenever they could get a ride from the Army. The teachers circulated among the women immediately, inquiring about their needs and anything that may have occurred over the last two days.

Arnold and I slowly walked through the refugee village, past crowded houses and sad faced but stoic women. As Zeitlin made his way down the main street, he would see a scene that caught his eye and would politely ask the people if he could take their picture. No one refused. Arnold didn't waste his time on photographing things... it was the people that told the story.

"This is so reminiscent of the many other places I've been in Southeast Asia and elsewhere," Arnold commented to me as he placed the camera to his face and took another picture. "I feel that I've taken these pictures a hundred times before, same scene, different country, same suffering but different village."

Cecilia Ramos, one of the teachers, approached me and quietly whispered, "Colonel Molina ordered the release yesterday of the remaining men from the mosque at Malisbong. This is the second day that they've been free. The men are living in the next village up the beach toward Milbuk, about a half kilometer away."

I was surprised at this news and asked impatiently, "How many men are in the village? What did the women tell you?"

"They said that many of the men are missing. Not all of the men who were captured and placed within the mosque have returned. There are less than 200 men living in the next barrio."

I walked up to Arnold Zeitlin and waited while he finished shooting a picture of two young Muslim women, teenagers, who managed a slight smile for the camera.

"Mr. Zeitlin, the men I told you about who had been captured and placed within the Mosque at Malisbong...well, the survivors have been released and are living in a small village up the beach from here. One of the teachers told me that less than 200 men were returned. I wonder where the other three hundred men are. Come on, we'll walk up the beach and speak with these men. They should be able to tell us what happened at Malisbong during the past two weeks."

Arnold's face lit up with this news. I went over to Major Bernardo and informed him that it was necessary for us to visit the men at the other village to assess their needs and how we can help them. The Major thought about the request for a moment or two and finally acceded to the request. The whole retinue headed up the beach including Julio, the boatman.

I turned to Julio, "Tell your cousin to bring the banca up the beach to the other barrio. I want you to remain with Mr. Zeitlin and be his interpreter. Tell the men in their language what Mr. Zeitlin asks them and give the answer back to Mr. Zeitlin...O.K.?"

I then turned to Arnold and whispered, "Julio will be your interpreter. He's a High School graduate and understands and speaks

English well. He also is conversant in Maguindanao...the language the Muslims use. I will run interference for you and take care of our Major here so that he doesn't become a problem. The men will feel more comfortable without Major Bernardo looking on when you question them."

"That's a great idea. Thanks."

"I see that you have a tape recorder with you, I observed. Is that to check out the accuracy of the answers you receive?"

"Yes. And also to help me remember all that what said and how it was said. I want to be as accurate as possible."

As we approached the village of thatched, wooden and bamboo huts, the men of the village all came out to greet us. Silently they came and quickly surrounded us. Major Bernardo stood a short distance away observing the scene. I greeted the men in Maguindanao... "As-Salam Alaikum"..."Wa Alaikum Assalam," they replied. Then in Tagalog, I asked one of the men who seemed to be their leader, "Where did you come from?"

"We came from Malisbong yesterday morning", he answered.

"Are you the men who were kept by the Army in the Mosque for the past two weeks", I replied.

"Yes we are the men."

"Were there not five hundred of you? Where are the other men", I inquired respectfully?

"We are the only ones left. The other men are dead."

The Major started to approach closer so that he could hear what was going on. I whispered to Arnold, "Go with the men into the village. I will stay back here with the Major."

I separated myself from Zeitlin and faced the Major. "Major, there's a serious problem over at Kulong-Kulong that I want you to see. Maybe you could help me solve this." The Major hesitated and looked over my shoulder as Zeitlin moved into the middle of the village. The crowd of Muslim refugees encircled him and he disappeared into their midst.

The Major and I stood alone on the beach. "This way, Major. It's only a short distance."

I showed the Major the terrible condition of the latrines that the Army had built for the women evacuees. "These latrines need to be moved farther from the village and dug much deeper than this. If the latrines are not moved and deepened, then you can expect many of these people to become sick. Disease is not the problem we want to deal with." The Major shook his head in agreement and promised to take it up with the Colonel.

After about a half hour later, the Major and I walked back to the other village and met up with Arnold, Julio and the teachers. Julio's cousin had already brought the banca up the beach to the second village. We all boarded the boat and returned to Milbuk. I refrained from asking Arnold any questions about his interview with the men from the Mosque. I didn't want the Major to know about whatever information Arnold had gathered from the men.

I left Arnold at the convento while I returned the Major to the Command Post in my jeep. I reported all that I saw at Kulong-Kulong to the Colonel, leaving out of course my little deception with the Major. On my way back from speaking with the Colonel, I stopped by the Company's office and spoke with the Business Manager who was in charge whenever the Logging Manager was away from Milbuk. I arranged for Mr. Zeitlin to be flown to Davao and as luck would have it, the plane was scheduled to leave Milbuk by noon time. It was already 11:15 A.M. I hurried back to the convento and told Arnold that the plane for Davao was leaving in forty minutes. Arnold was very happy. He quickly gathered up all his belongings and placed them in his bag.

We boarded my jeep and in a short while arrived at the airstrip. I sighted the plane parked just off the apron, about thirty feet away. Arnold Zeitlin shook my hand and thanked me, saying, "As much as I would like to stay here for a while to keep you company, I really need to return to Manila and get this article written for New York. I'm a little pessimistic that the whole story will be accepted for publication by the Associated Press' main office in New York. The Article details all that the men told me about the mass execution of the Muslim detainees at Malisbong by the Army. Such a story could

252

incite the Muslim oil producing countries to place an embargo on shipments of oil to the Philippines. Such an event could cause untold economic crisis in the country. I'll write to you and let you know what happens…and I'll send you some of the photos I took. Thanks for your hospitality. You made everything work so nicely."

The Cessna took off on time. Buddy told me that Mr. Zeitlin was able to catch a late afternoon flight to Manila. It would be a couple of weeks before I would be receiving a letter from Mr. Zeitlin. In the meantime, I simply had to wait.

Arnold was able to tell me some of the startling things that the Muslim men evacuees had told him in their village. My conversation with him was for no more than fifteen minutes or so, from the time I returned from the Company's office until Arnold's departure on the Cessna for Davao. But I had another source that I could depend on for more information. Julio, my boatman, would be able to tell me all that the men had said about the execution of their Muslim brothers. Presently, he was at home having lunch. I dropped by and asked him to return to the convento when he finished eating.

When Julio returned, both of us went upstairs to the living room and sat at the dining room table. For over an hour, I interrogated Julio concerning the questions that were asked and the answers that the men gave to Mr. Zeitlin. Julio then went further and described even more information which the men had told him as they walked about with him in the village. This is the gist of the story as told to me by Julio on that Friday afternoon.

Julio explained to me that the Army imprisoned only those men in the Mosque whom they considered able-bodied enough to carry and shoot a gun. There were some young boys as old as 14 years who were also included, as well as men in their late forties. By their own count, there were more than 500 men placed within the Mosque under guard. All their names had been taken down on the very first day. Later that afternoon, ten of their number had been taken out and bound. They were placed in a special house overnight so that they could be interrogated early the next morning.

Within the next few days, almost fifty of the men had been taken out for questioning. None of them returned. Some of the prisoners were able to strike up a conversation with the more friendly guards. These soldiers encouraged the men to be truthful and to give up those Muslims in the village who were rebels or rebel sympathizers; otherwise they would die like the others.

"Do you mean that those who were taken from the Mosque during the last few days are now dead?" asked one of the prisoners.

"All that I'm saying is this," the soldier continued…"If you don't tell the truth about your involvement with the rebels or give the names of those who are rebels, then you will be considered a rebel yourself. Others will take you down the beach and you will be shot."

These words of the soldiers brought terror to the hearts of the captives. They complained among themselves, "We are not rebels. We cannot lie about others to save ourselves."

Fifteen to twenty men were taken out for interrogation during the morning and another fifteen in the afternoon. None of these men returned to the Mosque. The remaining captives were now sensitive to every sound that came into earshot. Yes, they could hear volleys of gunshots echo in the distance once or twice each day. Now they knew what these sounds meant. Where were they taking these prisoners? Those men who lived in Malisbong knew the area well. One of them offered this explanation.

"If you go up the beach about half a kilometer away," he said, "you will see a small creek emptying into the sea. During the rainy season and when there are rain storms in the mountains, a river is created that runs between the hills and empties out into the sea at this point. There's a large basin of water that lies a short distance inland from the mouth of the creek. Here the water lies stagnant, forming a watery marsh or swamp for most of the year. I believe this is the place where the soldiers are killing our brothers."

When Julio had asked the returned prisoners why they were so fortunate to have been released, one of their spokesmen explained it this way, "Look at us. Are we fit to be soldiers in a rebellion? We are old. We have wives and many children who themselves are married.

Our sons are the ones they questioned. And they were never returned to us. Maybe they just got tired of killing so many of us. It seems that the soldiers were calling out names from a list. They seemed to know whom they wanted to interrogate."

Julio also added that there were only about one-hundred and eighty men released from the Mosque. It seems that over three hundred Muslim men from the Mosque had been executed over a period of ten days on charges that they were rebels.

Reporting a Massacre: (Top) Arnold Zeitlin, Bureau Chief in Manila for the Associated Press, had asked to accompany me back to Milbuk after I had reported to him all that had happened in Malisbong the day after our arrival at Milbuk, we were permitted by Colonel Laraya to visit the evacuees at Kulong-Kulong. These photos were taken by him. (Top) In this photo, I am being guided by my former Muslim student (whom I named Fatima in the book) to view the condition of the village and the people. (Lower left) People love to have their photo taken and so we convinced these two young women to pose for such a shot, with their permission of course and the permission of the older woman in the background. (Lower right) These are a few survivors from the Mosque at Malisbong. As I stated in the book, only less than 100 men returned to their families from the disastrous happenings at the Mosque.

# CHAPTER 28

# *The Numbers Game*

## Tuesday, October the 1st ...

The soldiers under Colonel Molina had settled down as an army of occupation throughout the five villages spread over the area. I had already visited Kulong-Kulong on several other occasions, sometimes making the trip riding high in the cab of a logging dump truck over the road constructed by the Company. On such occasions my mind would fantasize on being shot by a sniper, attacked by some invisible rebel in a coconut tree or hidden within a clump of bamboos. All I could think of was the prospect of getting shot in the face similar to what happened to those two friends of mine in the Toyota pickup during the second ambush.

At this time, however, I received a request from Colonel Molina's office to celebrate Mass for a group of thirty soldiers stationed in an encampment at a small Muslim village within the interior of this coastal delta. The village lay off the beaten path, almost a kilometer west of Kulong-Kulong, hidden beneath the canopy of never ending coconut trees. I decided to use my trail bike for the trip since part of the area was impassable to the jeep. I placed all my Mass supplies neatly within a knapsack and strapped it to my back. Mounting the motor cycle, I left the camp and took the road by the airstrip heading toward Kulong-Kulong over the new road constructed by the Company over three weeks ago. As I approached within half

257

a kilometer of Kulong-Kulong, I turned sharply off the main road across a sandy stretch of land and into the maze of coconut trees. The bright, sunlit road running parallel to the sea gave way to a darkened, twisted corridor of trees as I traveled deeper and deeper into the center of the plantation hoping to see some signs of life.

"Am I heading in the right direction?" I thought. "How convenient it would be to kill me in this lonely place and dump my body in one of the nearby swamps running along the perimeter of the plantation." I was more afraid of being assassinated by the military rather than by some wandering rebel band. I knew that my action in bringing the A.P. Bureau Chief to Milbuk would stir up a lot of resentment within the government and military leadership once the story of the massacre reached the front pages of the world press. I had compromised my neutrality and yet what were my alternatives? Could I live with myself and keep secret the terrible slaughter of the Muslim detainees by the military? Hardly! I always spoke up for injustice wherever I found it. This did not always make me popular. I began to realize that pleasing everyone was not possible, especially in my line of work.

The first five minutes within the darkened maze of trees was without incident until I found myself surrounded by a large patch of swampy ground that made my passage hard and difficult. I had truly painted myself into a corner. There was no turning back. I had to muscle the trail bike through this muddy morass and onto more solid ground. The bike strained in its efforts to plow through the mud and water, slipping and bucking as it went, sending up sprays of brown liquid. Even though the trail bike was light weight, its hundred plus pounds gave me a hard workout. My shoes were wet and muddy within and without, with moisture and mud stretching half way up both legs.

The errant trip through the patch of muddy swamp had delayed me by fifteen minutes or more. I had planned to be at the Muslim village for Mass by 10:00 A.M. and it was already five minutes before the hour. Once on dry land, I rested for a minute or two, surveying the area and preparing my next move. With the bike's engine running quietly, I could hear no other sound nor see any other living creature. There were neither birds nor chirping insects, only the wind gently rustling the palm fronds fifty and sixty feet above the ground. However, there was a smell, a strange, pungent smell as when an animal has died in the forest or woods and left to rot. Where was this smell coming from? Was there something or someone dead in the swamps nearby? I feared to linger longer than necessary. I revved the motor cycle to life, moving smartly through the labyrinth of trees heading once again toward my destination.

Continuing west by north west, I finally sighted two men in the distance, each walking separately from each other by 20 meters or so but headed in the same direction. My intention was to approach one of these men and ask for directions. To my surprise, I came upon a well beaten path, maybe five to six meters wide that appeared to serve as a highway for pedestrians traveling between Kulong-Kulong and the villages in the interior. I didn't need to ask for directions after all. It was evident that this road would lead to the village of my appointment.

Upon arrival at the village, several older Muslim men were walking by the dozen or so homes that made up this small community. I smiled at them as I stopped and dismounted from the trail bike. "Assalam alaikum", I greeted them. "Alaikum assalam," they replied shyly and shuffled off down the road. Several soldiers approached and welcomed me. One of the soldiers led me to a covered structure that was attached to another building. It was open on three sides and probably served as a makeshift store on market day for selling vegetables, meat and "batik" for making dresses. This was the place where I would be celebrating the Mass for the soldiers. I searched about and found a small table which I checked for sturdiness. Cleaning off the top of the table, I brought out the implements for Mass, first spreading a small white cloth over the table and placing the chalice, paten, water and wine cruets upon the make-shift altar. I donned my white cassock, placing my head and arms through the garment letting it fall down over my shirt and muddy pants. I took the stole from one of the pockets in the knapsack and placed it over the back of my neck, bringing both ends to rest against the front of the cassock. Finally, I took out the Mass book containing the scripture readings and Mass prayers, laying it upon the altar.

There were only three soldiers present upon my arrival at the small village. Except for the two old Muslim men wandering about, the village was deserted. Nevertheless, it felt strange celebrating Mass in a Muslim village. What must the old Muslim men have been thinking at this strange turn of events? After about fifteen minutes, a group of about a dozen soldiers showed up to attend the Mass. Where were the other two dozen?

I began the Mass with a penitential service, reminding the soldiers that Christ suffered and died on the cross to forgive sin. I prepared them to examine their consciences and to bring to mind the sins they may have committed, placing themselves in the loving mercy of Jesus, speaking from the heart of their sorrow for having offended God, and promising to change their lives, avoiding these sins in the future. If there were any sins so grave that the soldiers felt necessary to confess to a priest, they should do so at their earliest convenience. Then, I gave general absolution to all the soldiers in attendance, encouraging them to receive the Lord Jesus in Holy Communion for the strength that His love and presence within them would give.

The Mass concluded within thirty minutes and the soldiers returned to their posts. I gathered up the Mass equipment and slung the knapsack over my back, strapped it and mounted the trail bike. Saying goodbye to the two remaining soldiers, I wished them and their companions the protection of the Lord for their safety. Not wanting to end up in the swamp again, I used the pedestrian highway which led directly to Kulong-Kulong and then took the new road for Milbuk. All in all, the trip went well.

## Thursday, October the 3rd ...

It was almost a week since Arnold Zeitlin departed for Manila. I had been pondering how I could document the fact that over 300 Muslim men, who had been detained in the mosque at Malisbong were still not accounted for. According to the survivors, the men who were detained with them never returned after their interrogations. I knew that I needed to put faces on these missing men and give them names. Who among the two thousand refugees at Kulong-Kulong had male relatives detained at the mosque, relatives who never returned? So I devised a form that would enable me to document in some way a list of the "missing".

That afternoon, the two teachers came to the convento in the afternoon to meet with me concerning their efforts in helping the people at Kulong-Kulong. They told me that they had no more food to distribute and that the people's rice supply was quickly dwindling. Supplies had arrived the day before from Manila in the form of powdered chocolate milk. I had stored the cartons of powdered milk in the vacant room in the downstairs convento. I told them that they could bring these boxes with them on Saturday, when they returned to Kulong-Kulong. The bales of clothes that Catholic Charities had promised me were still impounded at the warehouse in General Santos City and would not be released until I could personally sign for them and have them shipped up to Milbuk. I explained all this to Lisa and Cecilia.

Then, I spoke with them about my plan to document the "missing" Muslim men detained in the mosque at Malisbong who had not been returned to their families. The Army had the full list of all the men whom they had detained. However, the Colonel was not about to turn over this list to me, so I had to make up my own list from the information that their relatives would give to my teachers. I showed the teachers the forms that I had typed up. I wanted them to use these forms while passing out the powdered chocolate milk to the women adults in the village. The form looked like this:

### Men Detained at the Mosque in Malisbong

| Relative's Name | Detainee Name | Relationship | Released? Y/N | Signature |
|---|---|---|---|---|
| | | | | |
| | | | | |
| | | | | |
| | | | | |

I explained to the teachers how to question the Muslim women at Kulong-Kulong. First ask them if any of their male relatives had been detained at the mosque in Malisbong. If one or more of their male relatives were taken by the Army and placed within the mosque then ask them for the name or names of these men. List all the names in the column, and then ask them what relation she has to each man. Is this man your father, husband, son, or uncle? Next, is the most important question you will ask? Was this man released by the Army? Is he among the men in the neighboring village? Or is he still missing? Under Released you will write either yes or no. Finally, it is important to write down the name of the woman giving the information. If she can write her name, let her sign the document, if not then let her mark an (X) next to her name. After explaining the procedure to Lisa and Cecilia, I told them to be ready by 8:30 A.M. We would be taking the banca to Kulong-Kulong and bring along with us the boxes of powdered chocolate milk.

On the following morning, we all gathered at the back of the convento and boarded the boat. Julio and his cousin had already loaded the boxes of powdered milk into the banca. Upon arrival at Kulong-Kulong, the teachers moved quickly to set up a table and chair to begin the process of registering the women and taking down the information on the forms. Lisa walked through the village informing the people that there would be a distribution of food. Once the women were assembled, she began to explain to them that the main purpose was to gather information on the men in their families who had not yet returned from Malisbong.

"We want to help you find out what really happened to your relatives", she said.

Lisa emphasized the importance in obtaining this information. Several women in the village who had the opportunity of some high school education were able to translate the instructions into their native dialect. These women stood by the teachers at the desk. As each adult woman in the village approached, the Muslim woman translator would assist in the questioning, insuring that the name of each man "missing" would be spelled correctly and encouraging each of the women to cooperate.

I went along to oversee the entire operation. But I kept discretely away in order not to compromise the efforts of the teachers and their Muslim translators. It was fortunate that I went along with the teachers. A half hour into the "registration", a jeep roared into the village from Milbuk. Major Bernardo was sitting majestically in the passenger's seat. He raised his hand and ordered his driver to stop. He slowly exited the jeep and stood at full height, smoothing down the front of his army uniform and looking about with an air of superiority. We both eyed each other at the same time. I smiled and called out my greeting as I paraded myself down the street to meet him. He had stopped his jeep only ten meters from the line of women waiting to "register".

"Major, I'm so happy to see you. What brings you here?"

"I'm on my daily rounds. I want to be sure that everything is running properly. Oh, by the way, we will be having the services of an Army doctor in a few days. It seems that there is a bit of illness among some of the people. There's nothing to worry about though. How are you, Father?"

"I'm doing just fine."

"What are your teachers doing there? What's this line all about?"

"Well, we just received cartons of powdered chocolate milk. We're distributing packets to each family. We're registering the women of the village, the heads of households, to be sure that everyone receives their fair share of the food. We expect a large shipment of clothes by next week, courtesy of Catholic Relief Services in Manila."

"Sure. That makes sense", the Major muttered. "Well, I have to leave you now and tour the other villages. Take care."

"Thank you, Major. Have a pleasant day."

The Major seemed satisfied at my explanation. It was a lie of course, something that I preferred not to do. I am not going to justify my deviousness. Needless to say, the Major was unaware of our real intentions. And I was determined that nothing or nobody would jeopardize this "registration".

Once the "registration" was completed, I took the filled out forms and carefully placed them within a folder. It had taken us four hours to record all the information onto 12 sheets of paper.

Some women of the village had prepared a large platter of rice for us, together with some dried fish. We sat down to eat about 1:15 P.M. in the afternoon. I could hardly wait to return to the convento to review all the information with the teachers. This was not the place to do this. After eating, we boarded the banca and returned to Milbuk. Once at the convento, I invited the two teachers upstairs to the living room where we went over the forms, counting the number of men whose names appeared under the first heading. Now the "missing" will have names and faces. They are real after all. These are the men whose families knew them well. These men did live and laugh. They worked and cared for their loved ones but were present to them no more except in memory. But they did live, no matter how strongly the government denied their existence. The names of the "missing" never reached 300. We counted a total of 218 names of men whom the women swore were taken by the Army, placed in the mosque at Malisbong and were never returned to their families.

If the "registration" had been taken a week earlier, there would have been more names added to the list. Not all of the women were present at this time in the village. The Mayor of Palimbang, Datu Druz Ali, had arranged with the military commanders to release the women of certain families with whom he was acquainted. The Army acceded to his request to lessen the burden of caring for so many refugees. Nevertheless, now there was a documented list of 218 names of "missing" Muslim men not accounted by the Army.

## Friday, October the 4th...

The news of the incident was out. Even though Arnold Zeitlin's news story, detailing the massacre of the Muslim detainees by the Army had been censored and cut out by the A.P. editors in New York…a story like this was hard to keep secret. The story now became a humanitarian piece about the assistance given to the refugees by the Philippine Army... leaving out any details or references to the massacre/executions. The Philippine Government knew that such news would eventually resurrect and return to haunt them. President Marcos was fully aware that less than a year ago, in November of 1973, that the OPEC Nations placed an embargo on the United States on all oil shipments from these countries because of America's policy of favoring Israel over the Palestinians. This embargo lasted four months and had far reaching consequences on the American economy. If word leaked out that the Philippine Government was promoting or even tolerating such harsh measures against its Muslim population, then similar action by the Muslim oil producing nations could be expected. The evidence of such atrocity had to be removed.

The Navy Commander of the Philippine Destroyer was still patrolling this area of the Celebes Sea and sent a patrol boat to Kulong-Kulong for the purpose of transporting Colonel Molina to his ship in order to speak with the Commanding General by phone about a very important matter. When Molina arrived, he was quickly escorted to the Communications Room. There, he was handed a secure phone and the door to the room was closed. The voice at the other end simply identified himself and quickly went right to the matter of this call.

"Where are the bodies now?" the General inquired of Colonel Molina.

"They were all dumped in a swamp," he responded in a matter of fact way.

"Can they be recovered?" the General countered with some annoyance.

"Why? "What would be the purpose of that?" Molina retorted.

"We must destroy all evidence that this thing ever happened. Do you understand?" the General bellowed over the phone in exasperation.

"Yes sir", replied the Colonel. "I'll take care of the problem right away."

"You had better make sure of that, Colonel. This matter is of the utmost importance," the General added. "Get it done today! The

Commander will assist you in whatever you need to take care of this problem."

With those few words, the Colonel hung up and quickly left the ship after conferring with the Destroyer's Commander about all that he would need to complete this dastardly deed.

The Colonel called his officers together upon his arrival and instructed them, "We need to recover every body that lies in the swamp. Instruct your men to bring the bodies to that large open field near the village. We will incinerate the cadavers with kerosene and whatever other fuel we have and bury the bones and ashes of the remains at sea."

The Colonel was able to obtain a couple of flatbed trucks from the Company, the very same kind of truck that hauled the bloodied, bullet pierced bodies of the loggers down from the mountains almost two months ago during the first ambush. The trucks approached the swamp as close as possible to enable the soldiers to load the corpses more conveniently. It was a ghoulish scene. Many of the bodies had lain there for over three weeks. When first killed, the dead bodies would float but eventually sink beneath the waters to the bottom of the three foot deep swamp. But after putrefaction sets in, there's a natural buildup of gases within the cavities of the body, which after a few days in this hot humid climate causes the body to float to the surface.

The ½ hectare of swamp was glutted with the floating bodies of the murdered Muslim detainees. The soldiers were horrified. Nevertheless, they were under orders to remove each and every body from this marsh of death. The soldiers waded into the swamp, their mouths and noses covered with handkerchiefs to ward off the horrible stench of the bloated bodies. In pairs, they dragged the bodies through the water to the edge of the swamp and then carried the dripping corpses to the truck, lifting the heavy water soaked flesh onto the bed of the truck.

For hours, they performed this onerous task, stopping only to retch and vomit. When the last of the floating murdered Muslims had been retrieved, the soldiers formed a line across the swamp and walked slowly through the contaminated waters feeling the bottom of the marsh for any other body that may still lie hidden beneath. Several more bodies were recovered in this process. With that, the soldiers left the area quickly to remove their clothing and bathe themselves in the sea in the attempt to wash away the stink and filth of the swamp.

The trucks labored slowly down the sandy beach with its load of putrid flesh. It would take several trips up and down the beach before the last of the bodies reached the clearing. On the other end, other soldiers were assigned to unload the bodies from the trucks and to place them like cords of wood prepared for a bonfire in the field adjoining the village of Malisbong. The village was completely empty of any civilians. The hundred and eighty survivors from the mosque had already been sent to the small village next to Kulong-Kulong. Only Colonel Molina's battalion would be witnesses to this whole affair. The stench of death filled the air and caused quite a few of the soldiers to spew up the contents of their stomachs in nauseous disagreement with this activity.

Once the last body was piled upon the funeral pyre, the soldiers began to pour gallons of kerosene and other fuels upon the three hundred corpses. It took close to an hour before the task was completed. Then with the whole corps of soldiers assembled around the fleshly bonfire, the funeral pyre was ignited. The flames exploded in a bright orange ball. Smoke belched upward to five or six hundred feet and drifted out over the plantation. As quickly as the flames ignited, so also did the intensity of the fire. The kerosene proved to be a poor fuel for destroying this mountain of water-logged bodies. The heat produced by the kerosene and other fuels lacked the degree of intensity needed to set the bodies aflame with their own fuel. So now the Colonel was left with a mound of blackened bodies. What to do next?

The Colonel then called upon the Navy. "We have a problem". He then began to explain to the Commander in charge of the small fleet of Frigates and Fast Boats that he needed some of the Landing Crafts (L.S.T.) to dispose of some bodies. The Commander had obliged the Army on other occasions when circumstances like these arose. Fortunately, the Celebes Sea is very, very deep with the bottom reaching to four miles. It will serve well as a watery grave for all those corpses. Early the next morning, when the fire had cooled down over the night, the soldiers once again were loading the now burnt cadavers onto the landing craft which was able to maneuver across the sandy beach close to the field where the mountain of corpses had been burnt.

Now, added to the smell of rotting, putrid flesh was the unmistakable aroma of burnt bodies. All through the morning, the soldiers grabbed one corpse after another and carried them onto the deck of the landing craft until there were none left remaining. The ramp of the LST was raised and the amphibian backed down the beach with its cargo of death, into the water and out into the bay for a two hour trip to the middle of the Celebes Sea. There the mutilated and desecrated bodies of these nameless, faceless men would be thrown overboard into some of the deepest waters in the world, some to be eaten by scavengers, others to sink slowly to the bottom, the final rest of the forgotten.

# CHAPTER 29

# *Casualties Come in All Forms*

**Sunday, October the 6ᵗʰ...**

After celebrating Mass on Sunday and baptizing several children, I returned to the convento for lunch. The weather was pleasant, neither too hot nor too cold. Yet I could feel a warmth building up within me. I was perspiring more than usual and my body ached at the joints. I had a vague feeling of weightlessness in my head. Maybe I had let myself get run down. It seemed the right course for me was to take off the rest of the day and just rest. I called out for Rudy and told him to inform the Sisters and any other prospective visitors that I was not feeling well and would be unavailable for any meetings. Please extend my apologies.

When I awoke from my fitful sleep at 4:00 P.M., my head was ablaze with fever. I didn't have a thermometer since I hardly ever became ill. I asked Rudy to check the hospital and see if Dr. Domingo was available. After several minutes, Rudy returned and informed me that the Doctor would be in the hospital at 6:00 P.M. for his final rounds. I sat in my living room and made some hot tea for myself, waiting for the hour of six so that I could have the doctor examine me. At 6:00 P.M. I slowly rose from my chair. My head began to ache and my body felt so frail and weak. I was able to reach the hospital as Dr. Domingo was arriving by jeep.

"Good evening, Doctor", I called out weakly.

"Good evening, Father. What are you doing here at this hour?"

"I'm not feeling very well. Could you please examine me? I don't know what's wrong with me."

"Sure, come into my office."

After a few minutes in his office, Dr. Domingo mumbled, "Let see…your blood pressure is normal to low…yes, you do have a fever…102.8 degrees. I'm going to give you some aspirin to take right now for your fever and some more for later. You know, Father, you might have malaria. There are no signs of congestion or any indications that you might have cholera. I don't know. I am going to treat you for malaria and help you get that fever down. You must rest. Stay in bed until you feel better and drink a lot of water. Is there someone who can care for you?"

"Yes. I'll speak with Sister Helen. She's had some training in this area."

"I will be visiting you now and again to monitor your condition. You don't appear to need hospitalization at this time. I want you to take these pills for malaria in the morning and evening. Drink plenty of liquids. Don't dehydrate yourself." Do you need any help in returning to the convento?"

"No, doctor, I can manage. Thank you for your help."

My fever persisted day after day until that Friday when it finally broke. Sweat flowed from every pore in my body, inundating me in a bath of perspiration. Then I began to cool down. A chill ran through my body. The wet, soggy clothes made me so uncomfortable. As weak as I felt, I needed to change my pajamas and the bed clothes thoroughly soaked by my sweat. I rose from my bed, a bit dizzy, and was able to peel off the wet pajamas from my body. I pulled the bed apart and threw the dampened sheets into the corner of the room, returning to bed, clothed in a t-shirt and shorts, enwrapped in clean, dry, crisp sheets. I fell deeply to sleep, awakening several hours later feeling well rested.

My energy was returning. I felt ravenously hungry. After shaving my stubble face and dressing myself in fresh clothes, I descended the stairs of the convento and entered the kitchen where Rudy and the three boys were seated, eating their supper. It was about 5:15 P.M. and the sun was just dipping below the horizon. For five days I had been a prisoner in my room, bound to my bed by a mysterious fever. Only Sister Helen came to minister to me, making sure that I was drinking plenty of fluids and getting the proper nourishment to sustain my energy. Five times a day she would visit me, checking my temperature, administering the medication and feeding me. She would sit by my bed and watch over me as I slept. Each day she would keep me updated on the events at Milbuk. Today she would be surprised when I would knock at her door.

Sister Ana opened the door to the sister's house. "Father, what are you doing out of bed?"

"My fever broke. I'm feeling much better now."

Sister Helen was preparing my tray of food and was also startled at my presence. "Father, you shouldn't be out of bed. You might have a relapse."

"I'm really feeling much better now. May I join you for supper?"

"Why, of course you may. Here sit over here. We are almost ready to eat."

"So, tell us...what are your plans now?" Sister Helen questioned me as she spooned several lumps of rice onto my plate.

"I'll remain in Milbuk until Sunday and then fly to General Santos City on Monday. I plan to be examined by my friend, Dr. Ibanez, who specializes in Internal Medicine and is American-trained. He'll know what I should do next."

"How long will you be gone this time?"

"I don't know...probably a week or more. I might need to travel to Manila and be seen by our Congregation's doctor. I know that all of you can carry on well without me."

"We will miss you, Father Art", they all chimed into together. "The people will miss you."

"I'll return as soon as possible. You don't think that I like being away from here, do you?"

"We know how much you have done for these people, Father. You have become so much a part of all our lives."

"Well, thank you. I wasn't really looking for compliments…but I'll accept this one. Tomorrow, I will ask the manager for a ride to General Santos with Buddy. He has never let me down yet".

I remained at Milbuk for that weekend, celebrating Mass for the people and taking the time to speak with Mrs. Gaviola and the two Manobo teachers, Lisa and Cecilia. After Mass on Sunday, many people approached me and asked about my health. I told them that I was much better but that I needed to see my Doctor in Dadiangas and maybe even travel to Manila for tests.

## Monday, October the 7th…

While Colonel Molina was busy disposing of the evidence that would implicate him in the massacre at Malisbong, the battalion doctor returned from Davao to attend to the needs of the soldiers under both Colonel Molina and Col. Laraya. Many of the soldiers had diarrhea and were vomiting. The doctor was alarmed that these young men had contracted cholera from unsafe drinking water. The soldiers were all well-educated to this serious problem during their training, but there are always some who become careless. The Manobo teachers approached Colonel Laraya in Milbuk, requesting the assistance of the doctor for the refugees in Kulong-Kulong. So many of them had become sick during the past week and they didn't know what to do about it. When the doctor held sick call later that morning he was shocked to find many people sick with cholera. Several hundred people stood patiently in line under the blistering sun waiting for their turn. After examining the first dozen or so, the doctor rose from his chair and called the two teachers over to the examining table.

"We have an epidemic on our hands", the doctor announced to the teachers. "The present latrines must be covered over and new ones dug back away from the village and far away from any source of water. How many people have died so far from this disease?"

"Some of the people tell us that maybe eight or nine have died so far, young children mostly", one of the teachers replied.

"Well I can tell you now," the doctor cautioned, "that many more will die if we do not separate the sick from the healthy and provide care to those who are ill. These people contracted cholera by drinking contaminated water and eating food containing the cholera bacterium."

*(Cholera is an infection of the intestine and produces diarrhea. Approximately one in 20 infected persons has severe disease characterized by profuse watery diarrhea, vomiting, and leg cramps. In these persons, rapid loss of body fluids leads to dehydration and shock. Without treatment, death can occur within hours. The very young and the very old are especially vulnerable to this disease.)*

It didn't take long for the disease to creep into the inhabitants of Kulong-Kulong. The old people and the very young were the first casualties of the epidemic that quickly spread through the refugee camp. Unable to retain food and drinking contaminated water again and again, the people began to die. My pleas to Major Bernardo to instruct the soldiers to build the latrines far from the village and to insure that clean water was provided to the people obviously fell on deaf ears. There was only a half-hearted effort on the part of the military. The soldiers made sure that the water they drank was from a safe source and boiled. They even added special pills to purify the water they drank.

Lisa and Cecilia were beside themselves with grief and worry. "Father, we must isolate the sick from the general population if they are to survive."

"Let me speak with Colonel Laraya", I answered, "so that we can get help from the soldiers and transportation to bring the sick to another place."

A makeshift hospital was set up at the deserted Moslem village of Sinangkangan, two kilometers north of Milbuk. There were two "Marcos-type" school rooms in the village, built of hollow brick walls and G.I. roofing. Both "rooms" were attached to one another and made up the village school. This would become the "hospital" where the sick from Kulong-Kulong would be brought by company trucks to stay until well. The teachers and the Moslem women volunteers would care for the patients. Here there was a well with "safe water". There were no crowds of people here and so the hygiene of the place could be monitored more strictly. The emergency lasted almost a month and during that period of time, over one hundred of the evacuees died from the cholera. Most were the very young and the elderly, whose immune systems could not bear the ravages of the disease. This, of course, was more "collateral damage" as a direct result of the conflict.

I had been sick for a week, but I felt strong enough to leave Milbuk once more, this time to be checked out by a doctor friend in General Santos City. There was a general feeling of weakness throughout my whole body. I knew that I was not fully recuperated but was strong enough to travel by plane. I needed to get at the root of this illness.

## Monday, October the 14th...

I stood at the maintenance shack alongside the airfield and watched as Buddy Capacite walked meticulously around the Cessna, checking out the wings and ailerons for any damage. He waved his hand to me to board the aircraft. Buddy revved up the Cessna and headed down the runway, picking up air speed as we approached the front apron of the strip. The plane shot skyward, borne aloft by the strong breeze that blew in from the sea. We continued straight out over the Celebes Sea for several miles, and then Buddy sharply banked the plane left. We swung back toward land, still climbing steeply till we reached several thousand feet. We were heading south, following the coastline along this western part of Mindanao. As we entered the air space above the north western sector of South Cotabato Province, there below us was the still pristine jungle and deep green mountains of the rain forest. Now we were heading inland, South by Southeast across the still untouched forests of mahogany and hardwoods. From the coast, the outlines of roads were slowly snaking their way up to the precious treasure of wood. It wouldn't be long before huge swatches of mountain would be laid bare of its green foliage and stand nude and brown in the sun, unable to protect the nutrients of its soil from the ravages of torrential downpours. The soil would be rendered useless, changing the ecosystem forever.

Thirty-five minutes later, Buddy was circling the airport at Lagao making sure that no stray carabao was munching on grass in the middle of the runway. As usual, Buddy brought the plane to a smooth, flawless landing and dropped me off fifty feet from the main terminal. Bidding him my heartfelt thanks, I yelled a blessing to him for a safe journey to Davao. He was already in the air before I had even time to board the jeepney to Dadiangas.

Upon my arrival in the city, I struggled to free myself from the packed jeepney, apologizing to my fellow passengers for taking up so much room. I had been let off in front of the Parish Church convento where my good friend, Father Albinus was just finishing daily Mass. We sat around the breakfast table and ate pan de sal, coffee and cold fried eggs that had been cooked a half hour before. No matter where in the Philippines I found myself, I can't ever remember eating hot fried eggs. It was some kind of a custom that I could never get used to.

I told Father Albinus all about my illness and how I still felt rather weak and run down. He suggested that I spend a day or two in the hospital for observation. He would notify the superior at Calumpang of my condition. We boarded his jeep and he drove me to the Doctor's Hospital of General Santos City, along the main highway to Lagao. This hospital was run by a group of Religious Sisters, most of whom were nurses. They made sure that I would get the best of care. The first thing that the doctor did was to hook me up to an intravenous and begin pumping fluid into my body to re-hydrate me. For three days I rested, slept and ate. I couldn't stay much longer. I was becoming impatient with this long delay and guilty of the wonderful care that was given me by the Sisters. I signed myself out on the third day and went directly to Calumpang where I met with my Superior. He decided that the best course of action would be to have me checked out thoroughly by the Congregation doctor in Manila.

Several days later, I was undergoing extensive blood tests. The doctor suggested that I submit to a liver scan, a non-intrusive, low level x-ray. The results of the scan indicated that there was evidence of temporary damage to the liver from a source still unknown. The doctor in charge of the tests questioned me at length concerning whether or not I drank alcohol. I assured him that the only alcohol that I drank was during the celebration of Mass and an occasional glass of wine at bedtime. Other than that, I was not a drinker.

The tests were inconclusive. Several months later, I had another liver scan and all was normal. Whatever passed through my system did only temporary damage to the liver. The liver has remarkable restorative powers and apparently healed itself or so I thought.

It was 20 years later that I was able to find out what really attacked my liver. During one of my annual check-ups, a blood test indicated that my liver enzymes were quite elevated. I was tested for exposure to Hepatitis A and B but all tests came back negative. A new test for the Hepatitis virus had been invented to detect what medical doctors referred to as Hepatitis neither A nor B. They called the virus, Hepatitis C. I tested positive for this virus, the most virulent of its strain and underwent treatment for a year, having only temporary remission. Now twenty years later, my liver is still functioning, though irreparably scarred and damaged by the virus. Cirrhosis has not yet set in.

Evidently, I had contracted the virus while assisting the doctor in the operating room at the hospital clinic of Milbuk during the conflict. I recall holding forceps to hold back a section of a young man's chest while the doctor stitched up damaged tissue from a bullet wound he suffered during a battle. There were no latex gloves to use on my hands as a barrier to any bacteria or virus. My hands were awash in blood for at least thirty minutes at a time. Then I would wash them off and begin again to assist the doctor with the next patient. I thought I was invincible and impervious to any disease. Yet sickness and death were realities that showed no favoritism.

Death was everywhere and the prospect of my own death was always a reality. Though I never obsessed about the possibility that

I might also die because of these hostilities, yet the thought was never far from my consciousness. After all, wasn't this the allure of the missionary life…to give of oneself for the sake of the Gospel and the salvation of souls even to the point of dying in the process? Yet how I died was very important. Some deaths of missionaries seem to be truly heroic, choreographed, as it were, by some great Heavenly Hollywood director, but others not so.

My trip to Manila would not be complete until I handed over the "list of the disappeared"…the names of the 218 men detained at the Mosque in Malisbong, who had not returned to their families. I took this "list of the disappeared" to the Ateneo University in Quezon City and presented it to Rev. Pedro Laurente, a Jesuit priest, one of the members of the Peace and Justice Commission, headed by Cardinal Jaime Sin. This Committee was formed by the Philippine Catholic Hierarchy as a clearing house for any martial law abuses that might occur throughout the county. This committee had its hands quite full almost immediately at its inception.

At the outset of martial law, declared by President Marcos on September 23, 1972, the 'writ of habeas corpus' was suspended and mass arrests of suspected terrorists, insurgents and political enemies was initiated. Now there was no need of any proof of a crime only suspicion. No evidence was required to charge individuals with subverting the Philippine government other than the suspicion, bias or prejudice of the individual placing the claim. Fear swept the country. Demonstrations were forbidden. Military commanders were appointed governors in some provinces and a total ban on all firearms was promulgated. Failure to surrender arms could lead to the death penalty.

The leaders of the Catholic Church from almost every province banded together. The Bishops of the Philippines, led by Cardinal Jaime Sin, Archbishop of Manila, together with their priests and laity, began to hold regional meetings to provide education and morale support to the people. One of the key developments arising from these meetings was the establishment of the Commission for Peace and Justice. Its main goal was to end martial law and re-institute the democratic process in government. The immediate goal was to handle justice issue complaints such as unlawful arrest, imprisonment, torture, and extra-judicial killings. It was to a member of the Commission that I showed the more than 12 pages of signatures (Arts) and the names of the two hundred men missing from the Mosque at Malisbong.

I had hoped that this list would give further credence to the news story of Arnold Zeitlin. Maybe the Peace and Justice Commission could influence President Marcos and compel the military to find other means of securing the peace and unity of the country. How naïve I was. The government only answered these accusations by saying, "Where is the evidence?" The only action that they took was to destroy whatever and whoever might implicate them in such atrocities.

Seven years later, members of the Commission had contacted me through a friend. It seems that they were interested in interviewing me concerning the allegations that I had made so many years before. By this time, I was already living in the United States and could only answer their type written inquiries on a tape recorder. I never kept a copy of the tape nor heard again from the Commission. What the results of my deposition were I do not know.

There was no reason for me to remain in Manila. After all, I felt really fine now. There was so much to do in Milbuk. I had been away far too long with all this testing.

# CHAPTER 30

# *Lies, Lies, Lies!*

**Monday, October the 21ˢᵗ...**

I left Manila early in the morning by plane and arrived in Davao before 11:00 P.M. The distance from the main terminal to the series of hangars where Weyerhaeuser kept their planes over night was less than a quarter-mile away. Hoping to catch a quick flight back to Milbuk, I hurriedly walked to that part of the air strip where I knew the plane would be parked. Sure enough, there was activity near the hangar. I spied Buddy talking to one of the mechanics. It appeared that he was ready to leave. He saw me approaching and his face lit up with surprise, "Where did you come from Father?" "I just flew in from Manila. I was hoping that you might have room on the Cessna to take me to Milbuk" "Well, you're in luck. There is an empty seat. We will be leaving in about twenty minutes", Buddy replied. "Well, thank God. I didn't want to spend the night in Davao. Thanks Buddy. I'm forever in your debt." I found a chair inside the hangar where I could sit out of the heat of the noon-day sun and wondered what else would happen to me when I returned.

The plane trip turned out to be a scenic tour of the rain forest. The clouds were at 3-4,000 feet elevation and so we could fly just below them and admire this pristine forest. Buddy again brought the plane down low enough so that we could maneuver within the valleys that snaked through the mountain ranges and fly below their peaks. Below us were several falls, ribbons of crystal pure water cascading down a thousand feet to the mountain floor. My attempts at conversation with Buddy didn't yield much news about what had transpired in Milbuk during the ten days that I was gone from the parish. Soon we were at the grass air-strip and within ten minutes I was walking through the kitchen door of the convento. The sisters were all-a-flutter with the news that top Philippine Army Officers wanted to question me about the alleged massacre of Muslim detainees at Malisbong. After a quick lunch, I drove over to Colonel Laraya's command post to speak with him about the whole affair.

As I entered his office, the Colonel stood up and greeted me with the news, "Good morning, Father. Well it looks like you stirred up a hornets' nest. A certain Major Pedro Montenegro arrived here by Army plane from Cotabato City three days ago just to interview you. I didn't realize that you were in Manila, so that when I inquired from the Sisters concerning your whereabouts, they didn't know where you were or when you would arrive back in Milbuk. The Major was a bit disappointed but did get the opportunity to speak to a few people and even to visit the barrio of Kulong-Kulong."

"Well, I'm back now", I said and with a bit of bravado, "I would be only too happy to oblige the Army, even if I have to travel to Cotabato City."

Inwardly, I was more than a bit nervous about the whole business. I was suspicious of the government's intentions to know the truth. Was this going to be a "palabas"? Did the government intend to put on a show for the world, to prove that they truly had the interests of the Muslim people at heart?

The Colonel radioed the information to Central Command in Cotabato City and received the reply that a plane would be sent to Milbuk to transport the priest to the hearing. The Army plane arrived early on Wednesday morning, October the 23rd. One of the Company's jeeps swung by the convento and informed me that the pilot was waiting for me. I grabbed my satchel of clothes and quickly boarded the jeep, thanking the driver for such kind service.

The Army plane was no Cessna but a military version of the Piper J3 "Cub" Trainer. If I'm right, it was probably the L-4A liaison aircraft, a gift from the U.S. Army. It was shaped like a box...not like the trim, aerodynamic lines of other small planes. There was room for only three passengers with little room for cargo. This type of plane was often used by the military as an observation plane to determine rebel positions and movements. Needless to say, each trip that the plane took into hostile area was extremely dangerous. The plane had no armor or weapons system. Its maximum speed was barely 85 miles an hour. It was ideal for ferrying officers from camp to camp, since the plane needed little or no runway to land and take off.

When we were ready to depart, the pilot took the plane to the far end of the air strip and revving the engine several times, released the brakes and headed down the runway. We barely reached the midpoint of the strip when the plane slowly lifted into the air heading out to sea. The pilot banked the plane right, heading northward toward Cotabato City. When we reached an altitude of 3500 feet, we headed inland, riding the ridge of mountains that stretched all the way to our destination. The trip was smooth and the weather clear and cloudless. Reaching the mountain overlooking the coastal valley that ran along the Celebes Sea, we descended rapidly into the valley and circled the airport that was located just four or five kilometers outside the city.

All along the perimeter of the airport, gun emplacements were strategically placed. Off to the north eastern section of the airport a battalion of soldiers were encamped to safeguard this important facility. Cotabato City was embroiled in frequent attacks by the rebels who were trying to wrest control of this important Muslim town from these infidels. The importance of Cotabato City as a center of Muslim culture and commerce went back for over four centuries, even pre-dating the coming of the Spanish. Cotabato was once the seat of the Sultanate and this held an important place in the minds of the Muslim rebels.

Disembarking from the plane, I was led by one of the soldiers to a waiting jeep. I instructed the driver to stop by the Oblate Sisters of Notre Dame in Tamontaka so that I could inquire if Sister Ana Codilla was present at the convent so that she might accompany me to the deposition hearing at the Army Command Post. Sister Ana had left Milbuk several weeks after the 1st ambush in a military helicopter with one of the visiting Colonels. Their helicopter was ambushed by MNLF troops, in the hills overlooking the Cotabato City airport as the aircraft was making its final approach. Luckily, the pilot was able to maneuver the helicopter and avoid the bullets of the terrorists. Sister Ana had been witness to the aftermath of the massacre of the loggers.

When I knocked on the door of the convent and inquired about Sister Ana, the attending Sister, simply called out her name and there she was, already to go with me as if she knew that I was coming. The Army jeep sped quickly through the several check points leading to the city. Parts of the city were built on a plain bordering the Polangi River. The larger administrative buildings, hospitals and schools, including the Army Central Command Center for the Mindanao Region were built on one of the surrounding hills, some of which rose several hundred feet. The name "Cotabato" signified the place of the "stone caves", since there were many caves in the area, most of the larger ones sealed up. These caves were often the hiding places of smugglers, robbers and brigands who used to prey upon unsuspecting travelers.

We entered the Army command complex, driving up a steep winding road to one of the outlying buildings. Here I was led upstairs to the second floor. The building was all made from wood. It had previously been painted in drab olive colored paint. The sun had bleached out the sheen of the paint and made the whole building a faded, bilious green. The inside of the building had that worn and tired look. The hundreds of soldiers, whose boots and careless manner had reduced these offices to almost slum-like conditions, were probably oblivious to the finer things of life. They were used to camping out in the jungles and barrios of the far-flung provinces. Only those soldiers assigned permanently to office duty would appreciate a clean and orderly place in which to conduct their business. This was not the place.

The soldier brought me into a non-descript room with a table in the middle, surrounded by six chairs. Soldiers were going in and out of the room, passing through it to other parts of the building. An officer entered the room with a briefcase under his arm and a warm, disarming smile on his face.

"Father, how are you? I am Major Pedro Montenegro, a lawyer with the Army's Legal Section. I am here to take your deposition concerning the events that allegedly took place near Milbuk."

"Good morning, Major. I am Father Art Amaral, the parish priest of Milbuk, and this is Sister Ana Codilla, an Oblate Sister assigned to Milbuk. I am happy to meet you, sir."

"Good. Let's be seated and begin the interview. Don't be too distracted by the coming and goings of the soldiers. I told them to keep access to this room closed, unless absolutely necessary."

"How long have you been in Milbuk, Father?"

"I arrived in Milbuk sometime in July of 1972.

"Could you describe for me the events leading up to the alleged killing of the Muslim detainees as reported by a newsman who allegedly was in the area? It was said that you were the source of these reports."

The Major measured his words well. He didn't mention anything about a "massacre" and called the missing Muslim men detainees not prisoners. There was no reference to these men as combatants or rebels. And so I began my story.

It was almost noontime, and the deposition was winding to an end. As the Major was about to conclude the interview, a Sergeant entered the room with a copy of the Manila Times newspaper just newly arrived from Manila by commercial plane.

"You'd better look at this, Major", the Sergeant said in a stage whisper.

Major Montenegro took the newspaper in hand and held it out in front of him as he scanned the front page. "Ah, here it", he exclaimed loudly. "You'll want to read this, Father! It's all about yesterday's press conference for all members of the foreign news services and local news outlets. It was held by Defense Minister, Ponce Enrile."

The Defense Minister had called this "special" press conference to answer questions concerning a story that had circulated about a massacre of Filipino Muslims in Southern Mindanao. For this purpose, Defense Minister Enrile had ordered that all the important public officials from the town of Palimbang, including Mayor Druz Ali, the Vice Mayor, Colonel Laraya and supervisors from the Weyerhaeuser Logging Company, be brought to Manila to testify to the falsity of such charges. The Defense Minister had interviewed all these people and they knew of no such massacre. In fact, the Army was doing a wonderful job of assisting the evacuees with food and medical care. In effect, this "story" of the massacre never happened. It was merely a rumor instigated by the parish priest of Milbuk to discredit the Army. The priest was a liar.

Yes, this news story highlighted the fact that none of the" important" people of the township were aware of any massacre in the area. The people welcomed the Army and were more than satisfied with the security they brought to the community and the good behavior they showed in relating to the people. When the newspaper arrived, the Major went immediately to the front page and found exactly what he was looking for. The Major suspected that the results of the press conference would be exactly this...that the massacre never happened. So why have this deposition?

What a marked difference in attitude the Major displayed with the arrival of the newspaper. There was nothing else he needed to hear from me now. For the past three hours, the Major had listened intently and respectfully to everything I said, taking notes and asking relevant questions.

Then he said, as a matter of fact, "Well, it's all here. The story of the massacre has been dealt with as regards the government. The report of this interview will be brought to Manila. Don't expect anything to be done about it."

I stared at him in disbelief. "You mean to tell me that the whole incident has been white-washed…it never happened? And they called me a liar." With those words, the interview was over.

The Major turned toward me as he was leaving and said with a bit of compassion, "Father, for what it's worth, I believe everything you've told me, but there is nothing I can do but to submit the report of this deposition for all the good it will do."

The Major closed his writing pad, placed all his paperwork into his briefcase, closed it and slowly rose to his feet.

"Father, I'm sorry that all this has happened. It's been a pleasure speaking with you. Thank you for traveling all the way here for this interview. I appreciate all that you have done to make this right. Have a safe journey back home."

With that, I shook his hand and left the Army compound. Sister Ana and I walked to the main road to take the next jeepney to the Bishop's house. There I would tell my story and spend the night. The next morning I took the bus to Davao and later that afternoon another bus to General Santos City.

# CHAPTER 31

# *The Anatomy of a Massacre*

**Sunday, November 10ᵗʰ ...**

When weeks, months or years have elapsed after the event of some catastrophe, people will ask, "Have things returned to normal?" My question is what "things" are they speaking about and more importantly, what is "normal"? It's true that the Notre Dame High School was now open for classes and the sound of children's laughter could be heard on the playing field. You can also hear the blaring of bus horns on the main road as the loggers returned from the mountains, an indication that the men were now back to work and able to feed their families. Even today, the Church was well attended for Sunday Mass and the people sang well. But something was amiss. Why did I feel so empty?

Here I was, all alone, sitting at the window on the second floor of the convento, with book in hand, gazing out at the Celebes Sea. I had just returned from the Church after baptizing several infants. Each family had invited me to join them for the celebration of their child's Baptism. To each one I graciously declined, offering some lame excuse. To all outward appearances everything looked "normal".

Rudy walked half-way up the flight of stairs and called out my name, "Father, the Sisters are inviting you for a 'merienda' at their house".

"O.K., Rudy. Tell them that I'll be there in a couple of minutes", I called back.

I closed the book on my lap and rose from the chair that I had placed before the screened window. Enough of my reveries! I can't stay mired in the darkness and sorrow of my thoughts. I need to be with people.

I was invited for a Sunday afternoon snack at the Sisters' house...a 'merienda' they called it. The 'merienda' consisted of a variety of delicacies such as rice cakes, suman, bibingka, assorted cookies or sweet breads coated with sugar. My favorite snacks were "suman"... a rice delicacy cooked with coconut milk, salt and sugar, boiled in hot water and rolled up within a banana leaf; and "bibingka"... a white powered rice, steam-cooked with sugar, coconut milk and "tuba", used as a yeast to raise the sticky, sweet mass into a delicious treat. And of course, there were the assorted drinks of coffee, tea or cola. The merienda was an opportunity to stop the business of the day and take the time to be with friends... to converse, laugh and cry. This snack time would last from 15 minutes to an hour in length.

When I arrived at the Sisters' house, I knocked at the main door situated on a small porch overlooking the sea. The door swung open at my first knock as if the person was holding the knob waiting for my rap. Sister Helen stood there with a wide cheerful smile on her face and welcomed me into the small "sala" or living room where Sister Josephine was already seated together with a tall handsome man dressed in Army boots and pants and wearing a non-descript short sleeved shirt, definitely not Army-issue. "I've seen this man before", I thought. Today he was not wearing his sidearm. I recognized him as one of the two Army intelligence men who were attached to the battalion of Colonel Molina over at Malisbong. The young man rose respectfully from his seat and held out his hand in greeting. "Good afternoon, Father! I'm glad to meet you."

Sister Helen intervened and said, "Father, this is Sergeant Nestor Mangubat. He's from my home town."

"Yes, I've seen you around the Command Post several times with the other Army gentleman. I'm happy to meet you."

287

"That other man...well, he's my boss. His name is Captain Ben Tesoro," Sergeant Mangubat volunteered.

These two Army intelligence men stood out from the other soldiers by the way they dressed and the manner in which they conducted themselves. I never saw them in complete Army issued clothes. Apart from the boots and khaki pants, they wore different colored t-shirts or short sleeved shirts worn over the pants. The shirts did not cover the .45 caliber sidearm that each wore strapped along the right side of the hip. The older man, late twenties or early thirties, was resolute and intent in his looks. His stride was purposeful and he was always in the lead with the younger Sergeant following along behind him. These two men headed up the intense interrogations that followed the invasion of the delta. They employed some very nasty tactics in forcing the detained Muslim men to provide information concerning rebel activity in the area. We would call these tactics TORTURE! But, what the hell! It's been almost two months since all that happened and here we all are sitting in the living room and eating suman and bibingka.

The conversation was light and cheerful. Topics such as "where do you come from?" and "do you enjoy being in the Army?" were interspersed with stories of people they knew and places they visited. I was in the conversation as it flowed from Tagalog to English and back again to a combination of both. I let the Sisters dominate the conversation until the point where I felt that Sergeant Mangubat was right at home and comfortable with our non-threatening inquiries.

"Sergeant, can I ask you a question about something that's been bothering me for almost two months now", I said to him almost apologetically.

"Sure, Father! Go ahead."

"Well, when I was over in Kulong-Kulong supervising the relief efforts with my teachers, the Muslim women were complaining about the disappearance of their husbands and sons. These were the men who had been detained in the Mosque immediately following the invasion. Colonel Molina had told me that there were about 500 men detained within the Mosque. Now some of the men had been released three weeks or so later, but they numbered only 180 men of the original 500. Now my question is this. What happened to the other three hundred Muslim men who had been detained in the Mosque?"

Nestor was silent. I had cornered him and he was becoming a bit nervous. I continued my soliloquy. "I saw eight of the prisoners shot along the beach. Was it the policy of Colonel Molina to execute these so-called rebels? I heard that as many as 25 or 30 detainees were executed and dumped in the swamps each day."

Nestor listened to me uncomfortably and then as if in a confessional, he blurted out, "I only killed one man. The other intelligence officer killed many of the prisoners. He was the one in charge of the interrogations. He gave the orders to execute the prisoners."

Nestor needed to unburden himself of the memories of these terrible deeds. He was a decent man but involved with people whose orders he must follow. Then, Nestor volunteered information of which I was completely unaware.

"Father, a list was made of all the Muslim men who were detained in the Mosque. This list was shown to Mayor Druz Ali who was asked by the Army to identify those men whom he believed were associated with the rebel insurgency. As the Mayor went down the list, he marked off the names of those men he thought were rebels or supported the rebel movement."

"You mean to tell me", I excitedly replied, "that the Mayor was involved in determining who the rebels were?" And he shook his head affirmatively.

Most of the people from Kulong-Kulong, Malisbong and the other neighboring barrios were politically opposed to the Mayor. They voted against him in the last election. What the Mayor did was evident. He accused his political rivals of belonging to the secessionist rebel group. Eliminating these men would insure the Mayor's victory in the next mayoral election and all this in the name of democracy. How fortunate it was for him that the Army actually believed him. After all, how could Imam Druz Ali, a Muslim Mayor betray his own people if they were not truly rebels? So the military reasoned. Like the Scribes and Pharisees before Pontius Pilate, the accusation of the Mayor compelled the military to lead the detainees of the Mosque down the beach in groups to be executed.

I was shocked at all that Sergeant Nestor Mangubat told us. He was relating to us damaging information that could possibly endanger his own life. Was his candor the response of an upright man unburdening himself of these awful events or the naiveté of a fool? I chose to believe in the former, that his very presence in the house of the Sisters was providential.

Mayor Druz Ali, like the Sultans of former years, was always intent in achieving the goal of expanding his circle of followers and accumulating wealth and power in the process. He proved himself to be unscrupulous in his efforts. Secretly, he was the number two leader of the Muslim paramilitary group of "black shirts" in the township of Palimbang. They were his private army.

He had shown cooperation with the various commanders of the MNLF in their campaign to unite the various factions of Muslim militants under the banner of their leader Nur Misuari. But the Mayor, like others of his kind, was reluctant to declare enthusiastic allegiance to such a group lest he find himself on the losing end of the conflict, becoming an enemy of the State. Druz Ali's betting money was placed on the power and wealth of the Philippine government. He understood how to manipulate and prosper under the auspices of the Marcos administration. Outwardly, the Mayor played the patriot and swore his loyalty to Manila. He was also the model of cooperation with the AFP soldiers that were sent into his township.

The Mayor likewise ingratiated himself to the Weyerhaeuser Logging Company, smoothing the way for the construction of the roads and the logging of timber in these Muslim regions. The Company was all too grateful to him for providing such safe access that they made his assistance worthwhile monetarily. Yes, he and his fellow "datus" received a "tong" for their cooperation.

Only few knew of Mayor Ali's clandestine meetings with the commander of the MNLF rebels before and after the massacre in

Kalibuhan. He had prior knowledge that the Christian loggers of Milbuk would soon be under attack by these same rebels and he did nothing to stop the slaughter of the first ambush in the mountains and was a bit late in informing the logging management of the impending ambush near the village of Wal.

During the four week lull after the first ambush, Mayor Druz Ali had met again with the rebel commander, Dimalub Maulana, concerning plans to entice the loggers out of the armed Milbuk camp and back to the mountains. By false assurances, the Mayor guaranteed safe passage for the loggers to return to work. The Company believed him, through the voice of the Vice Mayor, his mouthpiece, who was a Christian after all. Why would the Vice Mayor lie and jeopardize his friendship with the very people with whom he lived.

The trap was set for another slaughter. The defenses of Milbuk would be weakened. To allay suspicion that there was any danger of ambush, the Mayor arranged a small fiesta type meal to celebrate the loggers' return to the mountains. But for the foresight of the logging manager, Mr. Roberts a terrible massacre was avoided that could have numbered over sixty slain. Still nine men did die at Wal in the second ambush. And the Mayor knew all about it. In fact, there was little that went on in the township of which he was unaware.

When the AFP Army and Navy invaded the coasts of Kulong-Kulong and Malisbong, the Mayor knew about it before it even happened. He heartily supported the military with his own pleas that peace be restored to his town so that the commerce of the township may return to full operation. This was necessary for the welfare of his people and for his own monetary gain.

And on the other hand, he informed the commander of the rebel MNLF group of the time and place of the invasion. Thus, it was not surprising that there was no opposition at all when the amphibious troops stormed the beaches and invaded the villages of the delta. No weapons, ammunition or military supplies were found. The rebels had either mysteriously disappeared into the sheltering trees and jungles of the mountains or simply returned to their villages and appeared as the farmers, fishermen and coconut gathers they were.

Druz Ali wove a delicate web of deception that would play off the antipathy of the two combatants, the MNLF and the AFP. He wanted to rid his town of these rebels who were interfering in his affairs. If they took over power in the township, then he would lose his followers and the opportunities to increase his wealth and power. The MNLF dominance over his town would spell the end of his reign.

Yes there were rebels and rebel sympathizers among the captured men at Malisbong. The MNLF had strong sympathizers among the people of the Malisbong area, many of whom joined the rebel commander for training and combat exercises in the mountains. Some joined Commander Dimalub in the two ambushes of the loggers. Many others participated in the siege of Milbuk. But above all, these people from Malisbong swore allegiance to their own datu. When the opportunity arose to examine the list of men detained in the Mosque, the Mayor was only too happy to accommodate the Army. Mayor Druz Ali checked off the names of those whom he knew and suspected of being rebels from the list of the 500. This was just too easy. The Mayor knew that with one fell swoop, he would be able to eliminate his political rivals and weaken the control of the MNLF in the township by the killing of these men.

There had been times when the Mayor overplayed his hand. The few attempts on his life were indications on how evil this man was. He had proven to be quit adept at deception. Even though Druz Ali was an Imam, he could find no contradiction in the Koran concerning his actions. The loggers who were massacred were of no account... they were infidels after all and obstacles in his way. The death of his brother Muslims at Malisbong were really not by his own hand, but by the hands of the military. Besides, their deaths were sanctioned by the fact that these were his political enemies who had injured his pride and honor. He had a right to seek revenge - "maratabat".

When occupation by the military set in, after the routing of the rebels and their subsequent executions, the Mayor began to visit the delta area of Kulong-Kulong and Malisbong with some frequency. He befriended the Army officers and set before them a plan to make the occupation profitable for them. Here before them was a plantation of coconuts, thousands of trees, many of which had to be harvested. The "owners" of the plantation were either dead or missing and their relatives too frightened to protest any takeover of the fruits of the harvest. Thus, in collusion with the military officers, the Mayor shared the proceeds from the sale of copra harvested in the occupied areas. What a wonderful windfall for the Mayor.

# CHAPTER 32

# *The Tragedy of Forgetting –*
# *A Comparison of Events*

*'Those who cannot remember the past are condemned to repeat it.'*
- George Santayana -

President Marcos had given a privileged position to the military so that initiatives shown by its officers in putting down insurgencies by any means necessary was never subject to much scrutiny, if any at all. The military exercised a 'total war' approach to put down the dissidents despite the danger of violating citizens' human rights. This approach and attitude was in direct opposition to the tenets of democracy. The Philippines under the dictatorship of Marcos had become a police state. Not only did the military arbitrarily arrest and imprison its citizens, it also engaged in various methods of torture and in a ghastly practice call 'salvaging'.

'Salvaging' or extra judicial killing was a practice of the military in eliminating real or suspected rebels, dissenters and insurgents, or any 'enemy' of the state. The military held the belief that death was a better form of justice than to allow a suspect the right to a trial and the presumption of innocence. Such democratic practices were after all, weak, slow and costly. "We are at war", the military believed, "and there is no time for such niceties". If some of the 'suspects' die unjustly, then that can be attributed to the 'collateral damage' that every war produces. There are always innocent civilians who die in such conflicts. Such is the way of war. After all if there were a trial, a guilty person could possibly be set free to continue with his/her acts of insurgency. "Tell me, Father. Is it better to feed them or to kill them?"

Much of the 'salvaging' occurred in the conflict between the AFP military and the Muslim insurgents. There was a subculture in the military...a subculture of tyranny and oppression that ran rampant during this time of martial law. The practice of the military in relation to Muslim Filipinos was tantamount to genocide or as some would call it, 'ethnic cleansing'.

Torture was a common practice at this time. What the AFP military did in Jolo and Zamboanga, it continued to practice in Mindanao and at Malisbong. Operatives from the Central Intelligence Services (CIS) of the Philippines were already present at Malisbong working alongside the military. They would be interrogating the Muslim prisoners one by one. Their methods were time honored and tested by countless other intelligence services throughout the world. These methods were simple and uncomplicated, especially for countries of the Third World.

All that was occurring at Malisbong and elsewhere in the township of Palimbang reminded me of a particular incident that occurred only six years ago in South Vietnam during that horrible and devastating war. It was called the My Lai Massacre.

### Massacre at My Lai (Vietnam)

On March 16, 1968, US Army troops murdered several hundred Vietnamese civilians at the villages of My Lai and My Khe during the Vietnam War. This incident was one of the most horrifying incidents of violence against civilians during the war. The victims were mostly elderly men, women and children - all non-combatants. Many were also sexually assaulted, tortured, or mutilated in one of the most shocking atrocities of the entire bloody conflict. The official death toll, according to the US government, was 347. The

Vietnamese government, in contrast, asserts that 504 villagers were massacred.

The My Lai Massacre took place early in the Tet Offensive, (a major military drive by the Communist Viet Cong, (the National Front for the Liberation of South Vietnam ), to force out the South Vietnamese government troops and the US Army.

In response, the US Army initiated a program of attacking villages that were suspected of harboring (or sympathizing with) the Viet Cong. Their mandate was to burn houses, kill off livestock and spoil crops, and pollute wells, in order to deny food, water and shelter to the V.C. and their sympathizers.

The 1st Battalion, 20th Infantry Regiment, 11th Brigade of the 23rd Infantry Division, Charlie Company, had suffered almost 30 attacks via booby-trap or land mine, resulting in numerous injuries and five deaths. When Charlie Company received its orders to clear out possible V.C. sympathizers in My Lai, Colonel Oran Henderson authorized his officers to "go in there aggressively, close with the enemy and wipe them out for good." Army commanders had advised the soldiers of Charlie Company that all who were found in My Lai could be considered VC or active VC sympathizers, and ordered them to destroy the village.

When they arrived, the soldiers found no Viet Cong, but rounded up and murdered hundreds of civilians, mostly women, children and old men, in an extremely brutal fashion, including rape and torture. Lieutenant William L. Calley, leader of Charlie Company of the American Division's 11th Infantry Brigade, was reported to have dragged dozens of people, including young children, into a ditch before executing them with a machine gun. Not a single shot was fired against the men of Charlie Company at My Lai.

Whether the soldiers were ordered to kill women and children is a subject of dispute. Certainly, they were authorized to kill "suspects" as well as combatants. By this point in the war, Charlie Company evidently suspected all Vietnamese of collaborating with the rebel Viet Cong.

The My Lai massacre reportedly ended only after Warrant Officer Hugh Thompson, an Army helicopter pilot on a reconnaissance mission, landed his aircraft between the soldiers and the retreating villagers and threatened to open fire if they continued their attacks.

Knowing that news of the massacre would cause a scandal, officers higher up in command of Charlie Company and the 11th Brigade immediately made efforts to downplay the bloodshed. The cover-up continued until Ron Ridenhour, a soldier in the 11th Brigade, who had heard reports of the massacre but had not participated, began a campaign to bring the events to light. After writing letters to President Nixon, the Pentagon, State Department, Joint Chiefs of Staff and several congressmen, with no response, Ridenhour finally gave an interview to the investigative journalist Seymour Hersh, who broke the story in November 1969. This report subsequently led to a special investigation into the matter.

In 1970, a U.S. Army board charged 14 officers of crimes related to the events at My Lai. Only one was convicted. The brutality of the My Lai killings and the extent of the cover-up intensified growing antiwar sentiment on the home front in the United States and further divided the nation over the continuing American presence in Vietnam.

Why Did the US Army go out of control at My Lai? When the American troops entered My Lai, they did not find any Viet Cong soldiers or weapons. Nonetheless, the platoon led by Second Lieutenant William Calley began to fire at what they claimed was an enemy position. Soon, Charlie Company was shooting indiscriminately at any person or animal that moved. Villagers who tried to surrender were shot or bayoneted. A large group of people were herded to an irrigation ditch, and mowed down with automatic weapons fire. Women were gang-raped, babies shot at point-blank range, and some of the corpses had "C Company" carved into them with bayonets. When one soldier refused to kill the innocents, Lt. Calley took his weapon away and used it to massacre a group of 70-80 villagers. After the initial slaughter, the 3rd Platoon went out to conduct a mop-up operation, which meant killing any of the victims who were still moving amongst the piles of dead. The villages were then burned to the ground. The revelations of the My Lai massacre caused morale to plummet even further, as GIs wondered what other atrocities their superiors were concealing.

On the home front in the United States, the brutality of the My Lai massacre and the efforts made by higher-ranking officers to conceal it, intensified antiwar sentiment and increased the bitter divide among the population regarding the continuing U.S. presence in Vietnam. In November of 1970, the US Army began court-martial proceedings against 14 officers charged with participating in or covering up the My Lai Massacre. In the end, only Lt. William Calley was convicted and sentenced to life in prison for premeditated murder. Calley would serve only four and a half months in a military prison.

The My Lai Massacre is a chilling reminder of what can happen when soldiers cease to regard their opponents as human. It is one of the worst known atrocities of the war in Vietnam.

### *Massacre at Malisbong (Sultan Kudarat, Philippines)*

On September 9, 1974, elements of the Armed Forces of the Philippines executed several hundred Muslim civilians from the villages of Kulong-Kulong and Malisbong. The men were executed in a shallow pond, a short distance from the village of Malisbong and subsequently removed for the purpose of burning the bodies to remove any evidence of the massacre. The conditions were such that the bodies were not able to be consumed by the fire and so the remains were loaded onto amphibious craft to be deposited out at sea so that no trace could be found of the killings.

The Malisbong Massacre took place nine months after the invasion of Jolo City, during which the combined forces of the AFP, namely the Navy, Marines, Air Force, and Army clashed in a vicious battle with two thousand Muslim secessionists of the MNLF in an effort to force out elements of this rebel group from the city of Jolo and adjoining villages. Ten thousand civilians were reported to have been killed by the vicious bombardment of the naval ships and the bombing of the Philippine Air Force, which caused a mass conflagration of this crowded and tightly built city of almost a 100,000 people. Ten years later, after much research, it was determined that 20,000 civilians were killed in one night by the incessant shelling from naval ships and the bombing from aircraft. The inferno that consumed Jolo created such a wall of fire that only ash was left in its wake. It is estimated that 60,000 people were made homeless during the battle. 40,000 or more settled in Zamboanga and thousands fled to the island of Sabah.

What happened in Jolo does not justify the fact that more than 40 people from the village of Milbuk had been viciously ambushed and brutally killed by a group of Muslim rebels of the MNLF out of revenge. There was a real need for military assistance to protect the more than 4,000 Christian civilians of Milbuk and the surrounding villages from continued rebel attacks. The request for military help was strongly answered with a joint invasion by forces of Naval and Army personnel in September of 1974. The villages of Kulong-Kulong and Malisbong were bombarded by the shelling of a Navy cruiser sitting off shore. Almost immediately following the bombardment, elements of an Army Strike Force were ferried in by amphibious naval craft and proceeded to invade the aforementioned villages. Not a shot was fired against the invading army. The civilian population were herded together and obediently obeyed the commands of the military invaders. Houses were searched for weapons and ammunition but none was found, except for an old rifle that had been buried beneath a house and given to the soldiers upon their request.

The parish priest of Milbuk was asked by the Commanding Officer in Milbuk, the day after the invasion, to visit the Colonel in charge of the invading forces in Malisbong to ascertain his plans for the Muslim refugees. He wanted the Catholic priest to manage the refugee center and organize the people. This is the conversation that took place in the morning at Malisbong, the day after the invasion when the priest arrived for his conference with Colonel Molina.

"Colonel, where do you intend to set up the refugee camp for the evacuees?" the priest inquired.

"The women and children will be sent to Kulong-Kulong" he replied. "You can take care of them over there. The men remain here with me," replied the Colonel.

Then the Colonel's face grew dark and his eyes stared at the priest as he said, "Let me ask you, Father...is it better to feed them or to kill them?" (The Colonel was speaking of the 500 Muslim men that he had imprisoned in the Mosque under heavy guard.)

The priest was visibly shocked at these words...words that seemed unbelievable from a responsible Officer of the Army of the Philippines.

The priest began his defense of the detainees by stammering out... "Of course it's better to feed them than to kill them."

The Colonel replied..."If we feed them, then we will have to fight them another day."

"And if you kill them," the priest strongly countered, "you will have their sons growing up to hate you. They will fight you and the violence will continue out of revenge. It is better to feed them and win them over to your side in the hope that one day they will see themselves as true Filipinos and not demand secession."

After this interaction with the Colonel, the priest asked permission to see the Muslim men imprisoned in the Mosque. The priest was led by a Lieutenant to the side door of the Mosque. The sun was high and the brightness of the day made it difficult for the priest to see inside this almost windowless building. No noise or sound could be heard within, only the voices of the soldiers outside as they patrolled the village and kept order. Then slowly, as the eyes of the priest became accustomed to the darkness of the room, shadowed images began to appear from across the expanse of floor. From the front of the large prayer area and all the way to the back of the Mosque, the floor was covered with the squat figures of 500 men huddled together, and cramped into this tight space.

Fifteen minutes later, the priest would witness the beginning of the slaughter when a group of eight Muslim detainees were being marched along the beach, away from the village. Suddenly, a gunshot rang out, and the eight Muslim prisoners ran in panic and were gunned down.

Upon returning to Milbuk, the parish priest contacted Colonel Laraya and narrated all that had occurred at Malisbong, mentioning his belief that Colonel Molina was about to execute the imprisoned men at the Mosque until they were all dead. Could the Colonel intercede for the detainees and prevent this massacre? His reply was a definite NO! Colonel Molina had been given full control of the situation from the highest authorities and was at liberty to do what he thought was best for the situation. Three weeks later, only a 180 men, formerly detained in the Malisbong Mosque, were set free and sent to a small village close by Kulong-Kulong. They were interviewed a few days later by the Bureau Chief of the Associated Press, a certain Arnold Zeitlin, an American journalist. He wrote up the particulars of the events that occurred at Malisbong and in Kulong-Kulong. However, the New York office of the Associated Press did not publish the story of the massacre of those Muslim men detainees in the Mosque, but only the story of the refugees and the aid that they were receiving from the Army. There was the fear that any mention of such an atrocious slaughter of Muslims by the Philippine Military could bring down the wrath of those Muslim countries and result in an embargo of oil to the Philippines, resulting in catastrophic economic hardship.

As news of the alleged massacre began to filter through the media, government officials were being asked to respond to the allegations. Defense Minister, Ponce Enrile called together the local and foreign media to a news conference to answer questions concerning an alleged massacre by AFP military. Also present at the news conference were the military commanders of Milbuk and Malisbong together with Mayor Druz Ali and his Vice Mayor Rolando Abary, as well as officials from the Weyerhaeuser Logging Company. Mayor Druz Ali strongly supported all their assertions that there had never been any mass executions or massacre of the Muslim people in the area of Malisbong. Such stories were the fabrications of the American missionary priest. Why he should promote such lies is anyone's guess. If Muslim civilians were killed unjustly, wouldn't the Muslim mayor complain of such an atrocity perpetrated against his own people? There is no doubt. The accusations of the priest are lies!

The world had its answer. The government of the Philippines was in the midst of civil unrest because of communist ideology. This was not a religious war. Muslims were not being targeted as a people. There were some among them who were bandits and traitors to the country. These people would be dealt with according to the just laws of the Philippines. It was the same in the Northern provinces of Luzon where there were cadres of communist rebels among the Christian Filipinos. The Armed Forces of the Philippines were called upon to crush any movement that was causing harm to the country, no matter where they found it. The discussion was over! There was nothing that anyone could say or do to make any difference. The massacre never happened. There were no missing people...only the forgotten. IT WAS ALL A WHITEWASH!

# CHAPTER 33

## *Farewell & Repentance*

**Tuesday, February the 4ᵗʰ ...**

The last few months went by rather quickly. It was now 1975, a new year. I had performed all my duties with diligence but like a person sleep walking. The excitement and joy of my work was gone. I felt numb most of the time. I remember one time in particular when my anger and depression got the best of me. I was conducting a meeting with the High School staff to explain to them some new policies I wanted to implement. Some of the teachers began to object that the former policies worked just fine. Why did we have to change now? And here I thought that I was doing all this for their benefit and not mine. How ungrateful these people were, I thought. I burst out in anger and scolded them. I knew right away that I had hurt their sensibilities. I stormed out of the meeting embarrassed at what I had said and went directly to the convento where I could brood in peace.

I felt so guilty and sad. My scolding of these teachers was highly inappropriate. They did not deserve such treatment. The next day, I was able to apologize for my outburst. I assured them that nothing would be changed. Everything would be as it was. I knew then that my stay in Milbuk would be short-lived. I really needed to leave this place and return "home" where I could regain my balance and peace.

It was Valentine's Day, February the 14<sup>th</sup>, my last day in the logging camp of Milbuk. I rose early that morning to prepare for my departure. I sat quietly by myself in the large open area that was the living room. This room on the second floor of the priest's house had ten connecting windows, screened, and with louvered glass that faced out toward the sea. There were two other double windows, each on either side of the edge of the building. The two-story wooden building was situated only 40 yards from the edge of the shore. This gave me an unobstructed, panoramic view of the vastness of the Celebes Sea that lay before me. This room had been my sanctuary for the last three years.

The sun was about to rise and the soft early light of day slowly illuminated the sky. The deep waters of the sea were placid and appeared like a sheet of glass. I stared straight ahead toward the horizon as the mantle of darkness lifted. How much I loved this time of day with the sweetness of the cool breeze and the flocks of birds in the mangrove trees awakened by the sun, filling the air with their song. All this I will sorely miss.

There was still time for me to sit here quietly so that I could think, pray and remember. Tears welled up in my eyes. I cradled my head between my hands, as troubling thoughts raced through my mind. "Where did the past three years go?" I mumbled to myself. The time in Milbuk all seemed like a series of fleeting dreams. As in most dreams, there were pleasant scenes, visions that were rudely interrupted as when awakened from sleep; moments that enticed me to return to sleep once again to continue and hold on to the joy. And then there were the nightmares with all their chaos and fright. Most disturbing of all was the question these "hellish dreams" presented to me in my waking moments. "What good have I done here?"

The beauty of the place had blinded me to the cauldron of chaos that lay beneath the thin veneer of harmony and peace that once was Milbuk. Like the inner growling of a volcano, Milbuk appeared dormant, incapable of any violence. Yet there were the tell-tale wisps of smoke rising from the crater which I ignored. Rumblings could be felt, even though at times imperceptible, but present nevertheless. It was easy to ignore the signs. However, the collective consciousness of the people knew that danger was not far away. How could I have been so unaware? I felt helpless in the face of those events...events that were beyond my control. What a failure I had been. I was ready now...ready to leave this place forever.

There was no going away party to celebrate my time among these people. None of them would be gathering at the airport to say goodbye. Someone else would come and take my place in time and I would be forgotten. My face was now a mask of intense foreboding. I shook my head and thought to myself, "My desire to live the rest of my life in the Philippines is gone. Now there is only emptiness within me. What a fool I had been to think that any place is a paradise."

I arrived in Manila in the early evening of February the 14th and began to make preparations for my departure to the States. My old friend, Father Jim Walsh was also in Manila, having just completed retreats for two communities of religious Sisters in northern Luzon. Father Jim had been my confessor for almost five years now. He knew me as no other person did. My soul and heart was an open book to him. He was the one person to whom I could confess not only my qualms of conscience but even the very real sins and temptations that could destroy my very soul. Father Jim had the knack and talent for pulling me up from the muck and mire of depression and despair.

I approached him one evening after supper and asked if he had a few moments to hear my confession. We made an appointment for 7:30 P.M. in the compound's chapel. I sat quietly in the small chapel for half an hour examining my conscience. A fan stood to the side of the altar creating a breeze of warm air that hardly relieved the heat and humidity of the stifling room. Small beads of sweat spread evenly across my forehead and upper lip. Every now and again, I would apply a small tissue I held to brush away the layer of moisture. Father Jim soon arrived and sat in the chair opposite me.

"Bless me, Father, for I have sinned...", thus, I began my confession. "I confess to Almighty God and to you, Father that I have grievously sinned in my thoughts and in my words, in what I have done and in what I have failed to do. Through my fault, through my fault, through my most grievous fault."

Then, one by one I enumerated my sins, faults, failings and omissions. It was such a long category of weaknesses. Was I merely scrupulous or really sinful? Yes, I did despair at times, failing to fully trust God's presence in moments of crisis. I thought that I was in control. I knew what had to be done or so I thought...so why didn't the people listen to me? What pride! Yes, I harbored anger and resentment toward others. Though I never killed anyone nor struck out at anyone in anger, I did threaten a supervisor during the height of the conflict, saying that I would kill him if he didn't make provisions for all the women and children to be first among those to be evacuated. How stupid of me! This event occurred after the second ambush when the whole community was in great panic and chaos... including me. And I fantasized about killing the Mayor because of the evil he brought down on these people. Who was I anyway...the avenging angel? How foolish I had become to think that I was so spiritual, so justified in my actions that I could rightly lead these people in the footsteps of Jesus.

With all the temptations, with my outbursts of anger, with my failing hope and weakness in faith, God was never absent from me. The Lord Jesus gave me the grace not to surrender to the promptings of my feelings. Having gone through it all, I never lost faith or gave up hope. It didn't look pretty, but I was able to forgive others and myself as well and to overcome despair with God's help. There it was...all my sins laid out in graphic form, calling out for judgment. Silence came before Father Jim spoke to me. It was a silence not of fear of condemnation but a silence of peace.

*"Art, your confession seems to be complete and sincere", Father Jim began his counseling. "We are all fools at times, saying and doing what we later regret. The result of all that you worked for was truly disappointing and definitely not what you wished it to be. But this does not reflect on what you did or didn't do. Oftentimes events shape our lives and those of others. It is all out of our control at times. You need to accept life's circumstances,*

*knowing that you can change some but not others. And we pray to God, our Father, for the wisdom to know the difference."*

*"Remember that any success that you enjoyed from your work among the people was not because of you, but through the power, love and grace that Jesus gave. The same Holy Spirit that filled the life and actions of Jesus on earth, had been given to you as a Gift. The Lord made you realize that your ministry was not only among the baptized Christians of the parish, but also included the Manobos and the Muslim Maguindanao. All are His people. The Lord heard the cries of His people and heard your cries as well, because He was always present even in the most tragic of events. Jesus did not forget the people. In His time he will bring true joy and happiness to all because their lives mirrored His. Yes, you and the people were given the opportunity to share in the sufferings of Jesus on the cross. There is great good coming to you all. Believe it. This is what we call the mystery of the cross. All things work out for good to those who believe."*

*"The courage and love that you brought in ministering to his people were all so many gifts from a merciful and forgiving Father. Jesus knows us all too well. He knows the inner workings of our mind, soul and heart… yes, He knows our every weakness. What did St. Paul say to the early Christians about how God works: "God chose the weak…to confound the strong, so that the power of God may be revealed?" All that we, as servants of God, working in his vineyard…all that we can say is…"We are useless servants. We have done no more than our duty." (Luke 17:10)*

My confessor then rose from his chair and left me in the silence of the chapel. I experienced a deep peace brought about by the forgiving grace of a merciful Savior. Now I would be able to return home to the States with some joy in my life. I would use that time on furlough to ponder my decision whether to return to the Philippines or not.

I left Manila sometime in early March of 1975. When I arrived in the States, I reported to my Religious Superior at Union City, New Jersey. I stayed at St. Michael's Passionist Monastery for about a week or so becoming acquainted with many of the other priests whom I hadn't seen in years. It was during this time that I had an extensive conversation with Fr. Gregory, one of the Provincial consultors about my future as a missionary. I told him that I would like to join the U.S.

Army as a Chaplain. I was still young enough to join at 38 years of age. Many Army chaplains would be leaving the Armed Forces, since the war in Vietnam had come to an inglorious end.

Within a few days the answer came. NO! The Provincial Council had decided not to give me the permission to join the U.S. Army as a military chaplain. I didn't feel particularly sad over the decision and so I simply replied, "Well, I guess that I will return to the Philippines." That was it! By the third week of June, 1975, I was back on a plane heading for Manila.

Shortly after I arrived in Manila, I reported to the Religious Superior in Quezon City for my new assignment. "You will take over the parish in Marikina while Fr. Edgar, the pastor, is on leave." That was fine for me. I had never visited that parish and so didn't know what to expect. I only knew that Marikina was famous for the manufacture of shoes. That was it.

The Church was beautiful. The whole parish consisted mostly of pre-fabricated homes, a large housing development for Philippine Government workers. These people were the middle class of the Philippines, hardworking and religious. It strongly resembled the suburban developments that are so common outside large American cities. This assignment would be a "piece of cake", that is easy. I had a problem trying to keep myself busy each day. All the inhabitants, except for the very young children, the child care workers and maids, were all gone to work. The only time I saw most of the parishioners was at the Sunday Masses. This gave me a lot of time to think ... to think about my future ... to think about my life as a Priest. I stayed in Marikina for about nine months until the regular parish priest returned from the States. For the next two months, I prepared myself to return to the United States for the last time or so I thought. I left Manila for San Francisco on June 3, 1976. It was a new day. Another series of adventures awaited me, far different than any I had experienced in the past. But that's a story for another day.

# CHAPTER 34

# *Like the Phoenix out of the Ashes*

It has now been more than forty years since I left Milbuk in the quiet of the morning. I felt so sad of heart during those days because of all the death and destruction that I had witnessed. Even though no bullet had touched me, I still felt deeply wounded. For over six years, I really could not readily laugh and enjoy the company of people as I once did. I had not cried for those who died, nor for the families, torn apart by the terrible events of those days in 1974. I felt empty of any emotion except anger and distress. It would take six and a half years for me to experience emotionally the grief and the sorrow that lay beneath the surface. And it all happened during an *EST* seminar in Philadelphia, of all places, with almost a hundred other people in attendance. Here the façade hiding my emotions cracked and crumbled unexpectedly.

I had entered into a public dialogue with the facilitator of the seminar concerning the subject of living in the present moment and permitting ourselves to experience feelings, no matter how painful. Somehow the discussion began to focus on my past life in the Philippines. Why I brought up the subject is beyond me...but it was very appropriate.

The facilitator made the comment, *"See this man. He's not here in the present moment. He's somewhere in the Philippines."* I didn't get it at first! But as we talked, the questions he asked me and my response to them suddenly brought me face to face with all that happened in

Milbuk and Malisbong. I cannot tell you how surprised I was when torrents of tears flowed from my eyes. I heaved uncontrollably as the sorrow of those days gripped me violently. For fifteen minutes or more I cried bitterly for all that I had seen and felt during those difficult days and in grief over the people who had died. The disappointment in myself and the shame I felt welled up within me after all these years.

The people around tried to console me. Some placed their arms about me and held me as I wept. But I didn't need consolation...I needed to cry...to grieve and to cry again for all the forgotten ones...I needed to cry for myself as well.

The tears continued off and on for almost an hour. And toward the end of this period there arose within me such a joy and happiness. I surprisingly began to laugh...truly to laugh as the tears continued to roll down my face. How strange! And then there was this enormous feeling of relief that spread through my body as if a crushing weight had been lifted from me. Laughter, joy and an appreciation of all that I did accomplish rose to the forefront of my consciousness. The feelings of shame, disappointment and grief, once accepted and experienced, led to tears of laughter and the joy of remembering. I didn't run away after all. I accomplished what was intended for me to accomplish and no more. And the people would somehow survive and live on with their children...with the memories and with the feelings.

It took over 30 years to put pen to paper and narrate those experiences as best I could remember, in the book, *"On the Palms of My Hands"*. Never did I anticipate what the publishing of that book would accomplish. Here the story of the massacres ends but new chapters in the on-going story of the people of Milbuk and Malisbong need to be written.

"Palms", did not have *a happy ending*. The book seemed so incomplete without telling the story of ... "so whatever happened to" ...? This question and more, will be answered in this and the following chapters by the very same people of whom I wrote. The passing away of many of the pioneers, those who contributed so much to the community of Milbuk, will be remembered in these pages by the precious stories and memories brought to mind, spoken on lips, and written down on paper by the sons and daughters, and by the teachers, students and friends. I feel obliged to share their experiences in writing and to establish an historical document to attest to the power of community.

*The writing of "**In the Palms of My Hands**" was initially an exercise in catharsis. The dictionary defines this word as a feeling of spiritual release and purification brought about by an intense emotional experience. I think that the definition is accurate and speaks to the reality of why I wrote this story. There is no doubt that the happenings in Milbuk and Malisbong during the months of August and September of 1974 were truly traumatic. I experienced distress from those frightening and shocking events, as did the hundreds of other people living at that time. Writing the book released the pent up emotions and enabled me to speak of my experiences and the feelings behind them.*

*As I wrote, I could feel the pressure release. But what really freed me from my distress were the love, admiration and gratitude of the people of Milbuk who responded so positively to the writing of the book. People reading this book will experience much different emotions than I did in writing it. Each one who was touched by the events of those times were affected in some way in their lives and as a result made decisions in response to these feelings.*

Sometime during the month of February, 2007, after the publication of *"On the Palms of My Hands"*, I was surfing the web and came across a site called "WIKIMAPIA". Similar to its sister site, "WIKIPEDIA", (which is a free encyclopedia that accepts contributions from the public on all manner of subjects). "WIKIMAPIA" lets the public describe the world in which they live. It is an online editable map allowing everyone the opportunity to add information to any city, town or other location on the globe. And so I typed in the words, "MILBUK, PALIMBANG, SULTAN KUDARAT". To my amazement, a satellite photo of the coastline of Palimbang from Wasag to Malisbong popped up on the screen.

There in the middle of the photo was the unmistakable outline of Milbuk. As I magnified the satellite image, I could clearly see the rice fields of Sinangkangan.

The website then invited me to write something about the place and post some photos. Until then, nothing had been written. The site was blank except for the name MILBUK. I then uploaded four photos of Milbuk, which I personally took of the town in August of 1974. I also wrote a short paragraph that said: *"The four photos above were taken in August, 1974 during the first conflict with the MNLF in Milbuk. I'm sure that the present site of Milbuk is quite different today. There's a new book on the market that describes the events that led up to the massacre of more than 45 people from Milbuk and over 300 killed in Malisbong. The title is "On the Palms of My Hands" by A.E. Amaral, ISBN: 978-1-4259-8500-4 (sc). Author may be contacted at: aamaral11@ comcast.net".*

*A few weeks later, I received an E-mail from Australia. That's strange, I thought. I don't know anyone in Australia. The woman's name was Margaret. She was asking how she might be able to obtain a copy of my book. I immediately went to the "WIKIMAPIA" site to see if anyone had added some new information or comment on the photos. To my surprise, there was one entry. It was the person who had sent me the E-mail. She simply wrote:*

"I miss Milbuk. My family left Milbuk in 1972. I was only in Grade 2 in the elementary school when we all moved to Cebu due to the conflict between the Ilaga and Blackshirts. We used to live near the veneer mill (plywood factory), only a walking distance to the sea, church and elementary school. Each week my mama would take me food shopping at the market in Sinangkangan. I still remember the names of the few kids I used to play with: Florian, Bong, Nestor, and Emelia. My mama was an active member of the CWL (Catholic Women's League) in Milbuk. My late tatay worked in logging. I wish I could see the latest photos of Milbuk." -Margaret-

*In her second e-mail, Margaret wrote:*

"Hello Art. I want to order a copy of your book. Just tell me how much and how I can pay you. Now I have a story to tell my mum that you know Mrs. Capacite. I'm looking forward to see more photos of Milbuk. The photos you sent me by email, I was not able to print. If possible, could you send me another set of copies, please? Thank you.                                                                                          - Margaret –

G'day Margaret", I replied. Of course, I'll send you a copy of my book, "On the Palms of My Hands". I just ordered 100 copies for my friends and family. I expect delivery from my publisher within the next ten days. If you wish, you can give me your address in Australia and I will send you a copy. I remember Mrs. Capacite well. She was the president of the CWL. I'll send you some more pictures of the people of Milbuk. You may remember somebody in the photos."                                                                                               -Art –

*Checking the Milbuk site on Wikimapia was now my daily duty. I waited in expectation for more former students, teachers and residents of Milbuk to visit the site and comment on the photos and perhaps give their impressions of what Milbuk meant to them. I was also very interested in how the lives of the Milbuk people worked out since the events of 1974. Three months later there was this brief note from someone whom I still haven't met in person.*

"Please keep posting old photos of Milbuk." - Jerry Rocacurva-

*However unlike the former brief comment, Jerry Rocacurva followed up with a series of e-mails over a period of six months detailing his remembrances of Milbuk and the journey he undertook in life. This is what I meant when I voiced my desire to know more about what happened to the people after they left Milbuk. The e-mails read as follows:*

*07/10/2007–*

"I am so excited to read your book. I was about 10 years old when the ambush happened but the events are still very clear in my memory. Thanks for writing the book. I wish to own one. I have e-mailed all known Milbukians about your book and it stirred interest in everybody. I really need to read your book in order to give me further review. I studied at Notre Dame in 1977. It closed the next year due to the small number of enrollees. But it opened again 2 years later. The rest of my childhood was spent in that place and there are lots of good memories that I cannot forget. Like me, I know of some Milbukians who still harbor prejudice against the Muslims due to what had happened in the 70's. I hope your book gives us understanding and comfort so that there will be healing and reconciliation among the Christians and Muslims. God bless you."

*07/13/2007–*

"I can't express the joy in my heart upon reading your reply. I truly admire your intention in writing something that will remind us of our past and to understand the events that had happened. Hopefully this will lead to healing and understanding so that we may live in peace and with forgiveness in our hearts."

"My father worked as a Mechanic at the Veneer plant during the Weyerhaeuser days. Though my family attended Milbuk Evangelical Church, we still had great respect and admiration for any Parish Priest of Milbuk who celebrated the Catholic Mass. It was never a problem for us because of our affiliation with the Notre Dame of Milbuk High School."

"Right now, I work on the staff of the City Prosecutor's office, and do volunteer work for a non-government organization that caters to the educational needs of poor Filipino children and their families. I dream that someday I will go back to Milbuk and conduct a feeding clinic and send every poor child to school without them worrying where to get their school needs. It is true that our elementary education is free yet poor children could not come to school because the parents could not afford to buy basics such as school supplies, uniforms, shoes and other necessities. If they have money, they prefer to buy rice to fill their stomachs."

"When Weyerhaeuser left Milbuk we were as poor as everyone else. We did not have land to till. My father was dependent on his relatives so that we could have rice on the table. Going to school without shoes or 'tsinelas' was horrible, but we endured because our parents saw to it that we always put priority on education, even if we only have "lugaw" mixed with "banana" or "camote" on the table. The last time I visited Milbuk was in 2003 and the poverty of the people was apparent. My heart bled seeing those poor children experiencing poverty the way we used to. While I still have breath, my desire will always be to help the people remaining in Milbuk. Keep me in your prayers so that in God's time I can make this happen with the help of my family and some batch mates at Milbuk National High School."

### 08/08/2007–

"Greetings. I was so surprised to receive a copy of the book. I was expecting to receive the same in about 5 to 6 weeks, but lo and behold, it was already in my hand at exactly 3:00 p.m., August 8, 2007. I was still working at the prosecutor's office. I opened the package with excitement. I could not wait to arrive home to read it, and so I took a glimpse at the whole book. It was fascinating to read the word, MILBUK, in the text. I just finished reading chapter 7. The pump boat, docked behind the convent, which you mentioned was very familiar to me. I was in elementary school at the time when we played at the marshy area at the back of Notre Dame during low tide. It was fun to watch and catch the slow running mud crabs we call "Japon-Japon". After catching the crabs, we would go to your pump boat to play. I can still remember the caretaker warning us not to play inside the pump boat, telling us, "You don't want to play here because the Priest will be angry." I cannot wait to finish reading the book. The places you have mentioned in the early chapters were very familiar to me."

*01/25/2008-*

"Thanks for the invitation to visit you in New Jersey. Right now, I am here in Surrey, B.C. around 35 kilometers away from the City of Vancouver. I travel to Vancouver every Friday evening for my choir rehearsal and then again on Sunday morning for services at the Church. The leaders of this Church helped me come to Canada on a working Visa. As a gesture for their kindness, I volunteered to be their Choir Director. Every day I commute by bus to Langley about 15 kilometers from Surrey for my work. I work at Vitrum Industries, owned by an Italian immigrant. These people were so kind and generous to Filipinos. They are Catholics and I admire them for showing concern to the migrant Filipinos seeking employment here in Canada. God willing, I can apply for landed immigrant and bring my wife and two children here to experience how beautiful it is living in such a peaceful and abundant country where political turmoil, terrorism and poverty are not a daily experience."

"I feel blessed, knowing that God granted my prayers to leave the Philippines and find a job here in Canada. But I felt so sad leaving my family and friends in the Philippines, living in so much distress. I wish I could do much more in helping my poor countrymen, but I must care for my family first in the years to come. This is my dream and it will always be in my heart. I am still experiencing homesickness here. I feel so sad and lonely, but I have learned to stand firm for the sake of my family. Thanks again for the mail. I am encouraged by your friendship. I feel blessed to have a friend like you. Please extend my warm greetings to your wife and children. I am hoping and praying that someday I could visit you in New Jersey soon. God bless you."

-Jerry Rocacurva-

# CHAPTER 35

# *The Awakening*

*T*oward the end of 2007 and the beginning of 2008, there was a marked
increase in blogging activity on the Milbuk site of Wikimapia. About
a dozen participants during that period were engaged in a prolonged
conversation with one another that continued through the spring of 2008.
The conversations of six of those bloggers, frequent visitors to the web site,
were of such great consequence that it resulted in the creation of an "internet
social network" to rival that of Facebook. This social network enabled the
former residents of Milbuk, (loggers, homemakers, students and teachers) to
communicate with one another and renew old friendships. This is the story
of how it happened. The following are excerpts from their conversations
on Wikimapia.

*Oscar F. Carzada*

"Milbuk was home to my family and me for about 20 years.
This is where I spent my childhood, adolescence and the beginning
of my professional life as a young teacher at Notre Dame. We owe
Fr. Art gratitude for the writing and publishing of "On the Palm
of my Hands". This is one legacy I can leave to my children and
grandchildren, helping them trace my roots to a place that has been
and will continue to be a part of my life. I never returned to Milbuk
since I left in 1974."

*Amado 'Bong' Gonzales*

"Hello Mr. Oscar F. Carzada. I remember you very well, sir! You were my Algebra teacher in 3rd year at Notre Dame of Milbuk. We were neighbors as well in Campo #2. I met your brother Danny way back in the early 80's or late 70's in Agwood, Agusan del Sur and I knew your sister, Nang Estella very well. FYI, the most probable place to meet people from Milbuk is in Butuan City. Others, including some of my siblings, live in various places throughout the Philippines. The famous Art Labajo (the logging superintendent) in Milbuk was my brother-in-law and neighbor in Barangay Ambago. I also settled in that place with my family. At present I am an OFW (Overseas Filipino Worker) here in the Kingdom of Bahrain in the Persian Gulf, where I have lived for the past 17 years now."

"Well, as you said, I also miss Milbuk very much. We grew up there and enjoyed much fun with each other, as well as enduring the troubles affecting peace and order. I left Milbuk when I graduated in 1976, and went to ZAEC for college (Zamboanga) and never came back. So sad... but someday for sure, I'll be back to step foot on that memorable place once again. What about you and your family (your wife was also one of our teachers?). I'm not too sure but I am positive about that. I would be glad to hear from you soon. My best regards to all your family, and to the Milbukians."

*'Tita'*

My fellow Milbukians, I'm looking forward to the time when we can organize a caravan trip to our paradise called Milbuk. How I wish to go back to the log pond where I spent my spare time fishing and having fun by jumping and skipping on logs. I treasured those events all my life.

*Margaret*

Oh yeah! I remember that log pond. My brother used to swim there. He is a Notre Damean too (1974/75). I wish to visit Milbuk one day but it still sounds scary to me. Oh! The latest photo of the sunset and the birds flying out of the ocean trees (mangroves), looks like the back of Notre Dame High School. I went there one time to pick shells with my mother. Cheers!

*'Tita'*

Hi Margaret: I'm guessing that you are the sister of my classmate and best friend Jimmy. I remember how we used to hunt fruit-eating bats in your backyard until midnight. I'm sure that you are the sister of Estefa, whose house was near the elementary school. I was able to be present at the burial of our late brother, Erning Diaz. There were many others from Milbuk who attended the funeral.

*Amado 'Bong' Gonzales*

Hello Mr. Carzada, sir. I remember that your wife was my teacher as well. I also remember how she told us the story of her ordeal when the boat on which she was traveling was sinking. They were commuting to Basilan and she was saved by her acoustic guitar. It was sad to hear about the passing away of Mr. Erning Diaz. Please extend my condolences to his family. As I said before I am here in Bahrain for the past 16 years. I landed a good job here. Thanks to my solid foundation with NDM. It really helped a lot.

Currently, I am manager of the Design Department, a company owned by the Royal family. It took me guts, sacrifices and luck to get to the top. It was too bad that we were not able to meet each other here. Maybe there will be another time, so don't hesitate to contact me by phone. *What I don't like about this site is this: there are many restrictions. I am hesitant to give my e-mail address. How about creating another thread, exclusive for Milbukians on another site??? Is there anybody who might happen to have a handful of free time, lol! Sadly, I don't possess either the time or the expertise. Are there any volunteers?* Keep on posting. It's very touching to read those words. God bless you.

*Oscar F. Carzada*

Oh my God! Is this some kind of a reunion of Milbukians? This is getting to be a very interesting website? Who will ever forget the Larayas? The mother was a devout member of the CWL with Nitang Quingco, the businesswoman who sells goods on installment. I remember Vicky Laraya. Just to tell you, I remember her very well. I graduated ahead of Bob Aragon. We were together in the band under Mr. Fernandez. Bob was such a good trumpeter. Yes. My wife is beautiful as ever. We were blessed with 3 children who are grown-ups now and done with their studies. My eldest son is married to a Chinese woman and is staying in Florida.

*Margaret*

Hello Oca, you mention Villegas. Is that Fidelis Villegas? She's so pretty. We lived almost behind them. Hello Art. Thank you very much for this site. We Milbukians have communications here. I'm interested to know too the condition and situation of travel to Milbuk.

*Oscar F. Carzada*

Yes I know Fidelis Villegas, the one with long hair and the "crush ng bayan" when we were teenagers. But she is not the Villegas I mentioned who became the classmate of Madong Jorolan. He is the uncle Bonifacio who married another classmate Clarita Floreta. Miss Timbol was not one of those "girls I loved before". She was a close friend of my wife and was our bridge. She is now Mrs. Marcos and is a principal of a school in Antipolo. I met her a few years back. I am looking for the Dorotheo s. Vicente was my classmate as well as Amelia Santos, Gonzalo Ledesma and Jose Cahilog of Kanipaan. I am 57 years old now and some of the names sound familiar. But I am not too sure now which of them became my classmates. Besides, we are reminiscing events and names that were 35 years ago or more. But at any rate, anybody from Milbuk is close to my heart. I make it a point to talk to them if I can and introduce myself.

*The expression: "It's a small world" describes the experiences of many people who suddenly encounter one another under rather strange circumstances and discover, mostly to their delight, that they are related in some way to each* other. There is something in our lives' experience that creates a connection that binds us all together. Former friends, classmates, "kababayaan" from the same town are accidently thrown together by a twist of fate. The following exchange of blogs illustrates this very well.

*'Tita'*

Hi Margaret. I remember that I met your sister Bebie in 1987 at Rosario Pasig, Manila. I was on board a passenger jeepney and in front of me was a lady who looked familiar. Her face appeared to have the look of my best friend's face, Jimmy. The last time I saw Jimmy was in 1971 when I left Milbuk and never returned. Hesitantly, I asked her if she was from Milbuk. A shy smile flashed on her face and then a quick nod, yes. I asked her about Jimmy's and Benboy's whereabouts. She replied that Jimmy was working abroad somewhere in the Middle East and Benboy was at home sick. I had intended to ask more questions about your dad and mom, Nong Conie and Nang Melia, but I noticed that I was already in front of my job site near the Manggahan Bridge where I worked as a welder. And so we ended our short conversation with a goodbye and regards.

*Margaret*

Hello Nonie, what a small world. So you met my sister back in 1987 in Pasig. I was in Pasay that time staying with my brother Jimmy. Bebie is in Canada now. We had a one hour conversation this morning and I mentioned your name to her, telling her that you knew Jimmy well. I just texted my sister Liezle in Cebu and told her the story about how you met Manang Bebie in Pasig in 1987. She said it was her, Liezle, who was visiting me in Pasay. She said she just ignored you because she didn't know you. Ah! It's too bad, isn't it? What a shame.

*'Tita'*

Hi Margaret. Yes, it really is such a small world. Imagine meeting someone whom you haven't seen for the past twenty years from a very remote place in the southern Philippines. It was slightly mistaken identity. I really thought it was Bebie. I'm sorry for being wrong. The thing that I really remember about Jimmy's identity was the whisker below his ear. He said that it was his lucky charm. Margaret, the next time you contact Jimmy, please do me a favor and ask him about our childhood playmate, Nonoy whose house was just in front of yours. Could you please send me Jimmy's E-mail? Thanks.

*Oscar F. Carzada*

Today is Good Friday. I remember as a young boy in Milbuk how Holy Week was observed. We would have a procession or the "Santo Intiero" to commemorate the passion and death of Christ. Inside the Milbuk camp, altars were set up depicting the 14 Stations of the Cross. Fr. Henry Free, together with the CWL would head the procession and lead us in prayers. The amplifier was battery operated for the sound system. Vic Garayanala, a staff person at the convento was in charge. I recall this because it was in MILBUK, where I, as a young boy developed my own sense of religiosity. Later on, I would look forward to Easter Sunday because on Holy Saturday, I would sleep overnight in school, together with my fellow band members and get ready to play marching tunes during the "Domingo Encuentro", an Easter Sunday procession at dawn. How I miss those days in Milbuk.

*Amado 'Bong' Gonzales*

Hello everybody, I'm in the office today for a short period of overtime guiding some of my workforce for an urgent job to be done. When I was in Milbuk, I spent every Saturday and Sunday out to sea fishing and swimming. The result was blond hair and a dark brown skin like a "Samal".

It's a compliment being dubbed as one of the bright students during my time. The truth is I was one of the top five students from elementary to high school. Sadly I was deprived of being on the honor roll because I was very talkative in class and somewhat of a "bugoy" (disruptive, meddlesome) among my classmates. Despite these attitudes, I was able to maintain my high grades and sometimes topping some subjects. Sir Oca, it's too bad that we didn't meet each other in Bahrain. I could have offered you five star services. We could have driven in my new car and visit some night spots on the island. I hope and look forward to have that opportunity come again. Ahh! Milbuk.... how can we forget?

*For thirteen and a half months, a group of former residents of Milbuk spoke with each other from their hearts, expressing deep feelings of love and longing for friends, classmates, family members and neighbors. They spoke of a place where they all had lived, worked and studied...a place like no other. Something good happened to them in the town they called Milbuk. Now they were eager to re-connect and re-establish the bonds that were cruelly broken by war. There was a need to continue the dialogues and conversations of the last year and to expand this wonderful opportunity to the hundreds of other Milbukians that were far flung throughout the face of the globe. How to do this was the problem. The following excerpts tell of the creation of the Milbukians own website: Milbuklegacy.com.*

## Amado 'Bong' Gonzales

Hello once again, Sir Oca. That was a good proposal creating a new website for Milbukians. I mentioned this in my previous postings because of some restrictions on this site. However, I'm not knowledgeable enough when it comes to website creation. Secondly my time is limited for personal use since much of it is spent at work, (imagine in front of a computer 9 hours a day, 5 days a week). There are many websites we can mimic but someone has really to initiate this project, if it is to become a reality. I just hope somebody from Milbuk with that expertise comes to the aid of this site. Cross our fingers on that. "Insha Allah!" as they say it here.

## Oscar F. Carzada

Hello friends from Milbuk. I finally got in touch with Fidelis Villegas and we both thought of creating another site for all of us from Milbuk. Maybe there are others who would like to join us but cannot do so because of some "restrictions" on this site. Today

I received an E-mail from the son of the late Virgilio Jayme, from Cebu, a manager of a company, telling me the same thing. After comparing notes with Fidelis Villegas, I thought she would be in the best position to initiate this for us, since she has accessibility to IT facilities from where she works. And she is very familiar with IT. If there is extra cost for the new site, we can handle this on a shared basis. I personally feel that this minimal cost is well worth the price of getting connected with one another and preserving the glory and legacy of our dear Milbuk.

Thank you, kababayaan. We'll be expecting an update from you on this site. Watch for the launching of the new website for Milbuk, Palimbang, Sultan Kudarat. It will be more exciting, more spacious, with capabilities for uploading photos. Fidelis is now living in Oklahoma and will be kind enough to handle this for us. We are still doing a test run of the new site. I will keep you posted.

April 6, 2008 - Kababayan, I just sent an email to (Fr.) Art regarding the photos. I took the liberty of mentioning to Art about you and your role in setting up this new site. I thought it would be best if you can also get in touch with him through his e-mail at the Wikimapia website. Besides, I think the two of you are more familiar about copyright restrictions in the US.

*Fidelis Villegas*

Oscar, yes I agree. I will e-mail (Fr.) Art. Thanks again. By the way, I borrowed your word *"Milbuk Legacy"*. Please scroll down to bottom of this page. You've just given a name to our website. What do you think?

*Oscar F. Carzada*

I think "Milbuk Legacy" is very captivating. It connotes a "triumphalistic" and nostalgic review of the past. You and I, as well as many others belong to the second generation of Milbukians. It was your father and your mother that brought us all together to this website. I am sure that others will even belong to the third generation like Joey. This is what legacy is all about, namely, something valuable and important to hand down from one generation to another...and so forth and so on. Well chosen.

*Fidelis Villegas*

April 7, 2008 - Oscar, I need a brief write up about the book, "On the Palms of My Hands". Could you do that? I will copy and paste it on the Welcome page right next to the book cover. You may e-mail it to me or post it here, if you don't mind?

*Oscar F. Carzada*

Hello again. This is Amazing! I am very much captivated by your effort and the people behind you to create such a wonderful site. And this is a dream come true. You know what? It was eight years ago or so when I started surfing the internet and looking for some people from Milbuk. I began by typing some names that I knew, (most of them my classmates) but to no avail. Then I happened to stumble on a site called "Alumni" and there I found some familiar names. I tried to get in touch with them but nothing happened. It was very frustrating until our current communications on Wikimapia came to life. Now look at the fruit. We have our own site. Thanks and kudos to you.

*Fidelis Villegas*

**April 8, 2008** - Jun, I thought about your suggestion, but I am just throwing ideas out there for now. We'll sift it through as we go along. Your ideas are welcome. So whatever you and Sir Oca see that can be improved or entirely changed please do not hesitate to let me know. Currently we have a limited space but we can get those ideas in and see how it'll look. I am still working on the size of the objects and fonts. It's not very good when viewed in 800X600 especially this page. So you'll see some changes.

*Timothy 'Jun' Gonzales*

Kababayan, a pleasant day to you: You are "Ms. Beautiful" even now. No kidding! It's always a pleasure sharing things with you. If there is one person who merits all this praise, it must be you. Thanks for this wonderful site. The financial burden for this site should be shared in some way by us all. I hope more Milbukians will come and join us on the site.

*Fidelis Villegas*

Thanks for those kind words. Hey, I've visited that website *butuanon.org*. It's a good website as is expected of a big website. I believe it's professionally built. It appears to be an official website for a charity organization. This one that I've started is in its infancy. It's only four days old. Hey, if we cannot be trusted with small things how can we be trusted with bigger things? I don't have a formal training in web design. I just do this for fun even though it's laborious. But let's go forward with this for now. I am going to stick with it. Are you? God bless!

*Timothy 'Jun' Gonzales*

**April 10, 2008** - Dear kababayan, I didn't know that you're working on your own space for charity, I mean those religious deeds, God Bless you Sister! I am sorry if I ever offended you on my last posting. I didn't mean it. What I am trying to emphasize is this: I want us to get an idea of how things work better with expertise. Of course, I don't even possess those criteria. ("Sana nga may darating na taga Milbuk") Maybe someone from Milbuk will come to help us develop this site bigger and better. But for the time being this set-up looks great and I am very much satisfied with it. Thanks once again and more power to you on your good deeds.

*Fidelis Villegas*

Jun, please don't worry about it. I don't get easily offended rather I get challenged. Lol!!!! Thanks. We need a domain name. "Please read the postings I sent on Oscar Carzada's blog site.

I copy/pasted the document from the previous blog to this new one if you've noticed. In the next few days I will create more blogs on this page just to see how it looks. We can just grow it. And if we need more pages we can up-grade to the next plan with a click of a mouse. I also changed the template. See how it looks. However, the header photo no longer blends with the header color. Ay naku! I've not changed the colors of the rows just in case you like to keep the original template. Got to go now! Later Sir!

*Oscar F. Carzada*

Thank you for all that you have been doing for this site...for being ever "faithful". I wish I could be of help, but this 57 year old man is just beginning to find his place in cyberspace. Please be patient with me because of some of the bloopers I must have made in the process. I will be a little busy over the next weekend. My son and his wife will be here for a 15 day vacation. And I will be running two modules for a leadership seminar over the next 2 weeks also. I promise to check my mail and visit my blog site every day. Oops! I almost forgot the write-up on "The Palms". I am still working on it. Gracias Fidelis y vaya con Dios.

*April 13, 2008* - Hello and good day to all. The three of us actually had the same problem on Wikimapia. I thought I was barred from posting there. I thought that we must have consumed the limit measured out to us. Kababayaan, my choice for the website name is *"Milbuklegacy.com"*. The URL name is very unique. It all started from the people and events that we experienced in Milbuk and that we are remembering today. I was trying to inform the rest of the people about this site on Wikimapia, but unfortunately I was not able to post the announcement. Margaret, I know you are the only hope among the three of us. Please try your luck. God bless everybody, and peace to the world.

*Margaret*

Hello everybody. I thank all of you very much for making me confident. Ate, I agree. I also vote for the domain: *"Milbuklegacy.com"*.

*Fidelis Villegas*

Sorry folks about the changes. I am just not happy with this page. I think I like this format for now. If it lasts for a week, that's a record. I have very limited resources. It would really be nice if I could have a picture of yourself or your family. If you don't mind, it would be posted on this web page, not within the blog. But let me know what you all think? Teacher, the controversial texts have been removed. Thank you so much for your input. Please do not hesitate to point out anything that needs improvement or removal (including grammar and composition). Thank you. By the way, thanks to all for choosing *"Milbuklegacy.com"*. It's my #1 choice too. I got it from one of Oscar's e-mails. I give him the credit for naming this website.

*Oscar F. Carzada*

***April 14, 2008*** - Kababayaan, before anything else, when will you send us the bill? Remember we promised that the expense for this website will be handled on a shared basis. Thank you.

*On April 15, 2008, a short, concise message
from the Webmaster simply read:*

# *April 15, 2008, (U.S.A. – Eastern Standard Time: 04:08 A.M.)* We're officially on the Worldwide Net! *"Milbuklegacy.com"* Praise the Lord!

*Fidelis Villegas*

'Bong', could you tell the others through the Wiki forum about this new site. And remind Oscar F. Carzada about the other forums. You two know many more former Milbukians than I. Thanks for spreading the word. We need traffic for this new website. Thank you.

*Oscar F. Carzada*

Finally we reached our first goal, having our own unique website. Next, spread the news! Fide, I will inform all those whom I know through the internet about this site. I am pretty sure they will like it as much as we do. Thanks once again and have a nice day. Isn't it great! *"Milbuklegacy.com"* has come into existence??? I just can't believe it. How lucky we were to meet Fidelis on Wikimapia. God bless!

*Oscar F. Carzada*

*April 17, 2008* - Hi Letty! Things happened so fast. When I was at the wake of +Erning Diaz, this was not even a figment of my imagination. After some chatting and posting on the Milbuk Wikimapia website, we thought of creating this site because we did not know how far that website could go and besides it had so many other limitations to our free expression. When the IT Specialist joined the forum, we finally got what we had been praying for, namely, *"Milbuklegacy.com"*. This was a team effort, but most of the credit should go to Fidelis Villegas. Praise the Lord.

*Letty Orbigozo*

Hello! I am so happy to view this website. Presently I am residing here in Zamboanga. I hope to keep in touch and connected always. I'll invite some of the Milbukian friends to join this website.

*Art Amaral*

**April 28, 2008** – Dear Fidelis: I was so surprised and pleased at viewing the *"Milbuklegacy.com"* website. Thank you for the dedication. I just want to say that the website is not about me, nor about the book I wrote. *Milbuklegacy.com* is all about you, the Milbukians. All that I wrote was for one purpose, namely, to tell the world about the injustices done to the people of Milbuk and to the surrounding barrios. I was seeking to find an answer for myself. What I learned is compassion and forgiveness. Who was to blame? I don't really know. It's not that important anymore. What is important is what you all are doing in communicating with one another and renewing your old friendships. God had a plan in dispersing us throughout the world. Jesus wanted us to continue His work and spread His love to others. Now it is all coming back to us...as we return to the beginning. What can we do for those who are left in Milbuk? How can we leave our mark of compassion upon them? God bless all the Milbukians. Thank you.

*Henry E. Neibert III*

Dear Milbukians I was really surprised and impressed at the same time when I stumbled upon this amazing website, *Milbuklegacy.com*. Can you believe it? … A website about a place that I thought wasn't known by the world. Like everybody who blogs on this website, I am a Milbukian, and a very proud one, I must say. I graduated from Notre Dame of Milbuk. I am the son of the late H.E. Neibert Jr. It was really nice knowing that the place I lived in wasn't unknown and there are some people out there who know how to "tumingin sa pinanggalingan". I'm really thankful for that. Now I'm really proud to be a Milbukian, (though I always was). Thanks to everyone who have helped to create this website, especially the Memorial Section. Now

I always have the opportunity to see dad again whenever I wish. I would like to thank the Teacher from Zamboanga for the scholarship he has offered at Notre Dame because he will be fulfilling many students' dreams. More power and God Bless!!!!

*A month had hardly passed since the birth of the new Milbuklegacy. com website, when the bloggers began to look beyond the euphoria of new found encounters with their "kababayaans", teachers, classmates, families and friends. The conversations of the founders and pioneers of the website focused on the reality of today's Milbuk. Questions were asked. What does the place look like now? How many people and families that we knew still live in the township of Palimbang? Is the Notre Dame of Milbuk still in existence? What about the condition of the people living there…do they need our help and what can we do to assist them? And the call went out to the world…to the places where the former residents now live… a call to create something new again.*

# *Milbuklegacy.com*

*Over 500 people have registered on the Milbuklegacy.com website. Most are former residents of Milbuk and vicinity and others are the immediate family members. All of them call themselves "Milbukians". These are people who were forced to leave the area of Milbuk but have never forgotten their home town. They are dispersed throughout the Philippines and in a dozen foreign countries. They have all come back to Milbuk by way of this website to reconnect with long lost but not forgotten family, friends and classmates. Three grand reunions, one in Manila and two in General Santos City, have brought together many of these former residents of Milbuk. Each reunion has grown in attendance from 100 to 300 and then to 700 and more at the Global Grand Reunion in General Santos City in May, 2010. And also there are the small gatherings or mini- reunions that have popped up in various cities and towns throughout the Philippines and in other countries, like Bahrain, Canada and the USA. In the United States alone there have been over a dozen mini-reunions as documented on the website by the smiling faces of the Milbukians in the photos. California, Arizona, Chicago, New York, Oklahoma, New Jersey, Connecticut are some of the places where the events were held.*

# CHAPTER 36

# *Precious Memories*

*T*  *he energetic community that had once been Milbuk and the people who were forced to flee the area has not disappeared. Milbuk overcame the horrors of war and misfortune, creating meaningful, successful and productive communities, family by family, in the towns and cities in which they settled, whether in the Philippines or in other countries. There is a word to describe people like this who are forced out of their community to settle in other towns, provinces or countries. The people are known as the "diaspora". The word diaspora (in Greek, διασπορά – "a scattering of seeds") refers to the movement of any population sharing common racial, cultural or national identity who were either forced to leave or voluntarily left their settled territory, and became residents in areas often far remote from their distant hometowns. The term diaspora refers to a permanently displaced and relocated collection of people.*

*It is amazingly evident that "MILBUK" has become more than a geographical place. It was and still is essentially a loving community of people who never forgot who they are and from where they came. With these few thoughts in mind, I had proposed a "Story Book Project" to the Milbukians of the website over four years ago. I asked the members to search their past memories of the time during which they were still a resident of Milbuk and to write down the stories of their feelings and experiences.*

*A "Milbukian" is anyone who has lived, worked, studied or even visited for a while that blessed area of land we call Milbuk. The actual geographical area is not important, since "Milbuk" embraces all of the*

333

*surrounding barrios and sitios. "Milbuk" is both a "frame of mind" and an actual place on the map. And for most of the participants, Milbuk meant the experience of attending the Notre Dame of Milbuk High School.*

*The "Story Book Project" was to be completed by February, 2010. The plan was to publish the results in a small book that could be used as souvenirs at the General Santos Global Reunion in May, 2010 and as a way of raising funds to help the people of the Milbuk area who are still living there. However, none of this was realized to my regret. Nevertheless, the project is now completed, though not in published book form. It is still available on the Milbuklegacy.com website as a PDF document. As far as I am concerned, the "Story Book" document has fulfilled my wishes.*

*The following series of short stories from the "The Story Book Project", written by the people who lived them or who heard them from those who have passed on, has brought a wonderful conclusion to "Palms". It is important for me to acknowledge all those men and women who spent the time and dedication to write down the memories of their experiences in Milbuk. I know that many have avoided such a project because it was too painful. I hope that reading the stories of others may help us all cope with the trauma of past events and know that we have a community of support. As St. Paul reminds us, "…we know that God causes all things to work together for good to those who love God, to those who are called according to His purpose." (Rom. 8:28). Many wonderful events have entered our lives since 1974. We all have brought the story of Milbuk into the present so that all of us may journey together with confidence and joy into the future.*

"The memories of my childhood are moments that I will always cherish. I think that one of the greatest things about being "human" is that we have memories that are reasonably persistent throughout most of our lives. Our memories provide continuity between our experiences and the current moment. You can never really escape from your memories because those are the lenses, whether scratched or polished, which focus everything you now experience. How you see things is unique because the sum total of your experiences is unique. It is a fundamental characteristic of being human".

-Letty Orbigozo-

"Ok, I will try my best to recall the days in Milbuk: the events, people and places. We arrived together with other families, seven of them, in 1960 from Basilan Lumber Company (BLC). The new arrivals included the Macapili, Fabie, Concepcion, Javier, and Carzada families. We were not the original settlers because there were others who came ahead of us like the Villegas and Sarmiento families. We stayed in a row of 3 houses fronting the present boiler of the Veneer mill. Those houses belonged to the PTP, a logging company that operated in that area before Basilan Lumber Company came into the picture.

Life was so simple then. Nature endowed us richly and there was an abundance of food. The sea and white beach were almost pristine. As a young boy in grade 4, I was afraid to step on the sand because of the presence of sea water crabs (kasag). Artet day or "tabu" was on Saturday and with 10 centavos or "katap", the Manobo term for a 10 centavo coin, you could have a bundle of leafy onions, talong (eggplant) and tomatoes that would last a week. Other goods were brought into Milbuk.

Trading was common, especially among people who had little or no cash or coin. The "trading" area was then situated in front of the Malana residence. This canteen was privately owned by a Chinese from Cotabato, Lu Eia (pronounced Luya). When we arrived in Milbuk in 1960, the Notre Dame of Milbuk was already operational. I was subsequently impressed by the quality of instruction in the school as evidenced by the students' activities and performances.

At that time we had no TV, cell phones or video games to distract us. Most of the time was devoted to studying and household chores. The first Director of Notre Dame High School was Fr. Lawrence Mullin C.P. I heard he was very strict. Then several years later, he was followed by Fr, Cyprian Reagan C.P. Fr. Henry Free C.P. came next. When I reached High School in 1964, Fr. Henry was the Director and the Principal was Mr. Ladislao Gaston. He had an only son Xavier, after whom the name of the tailoring shop of the family was named (Xavier's Apparel). Social life in Milbuk included weekend picnics, jam sessions for the young (no disco yet) and occasional parties, if you were lucky enough to get invited. And, of course, there were the drinking sprees for some of the workers…beer for those whose budget allowed it and tuba when the budget was tight.

The company sponsored movies in the plaza were occasions never to be missed. The Company picked mostly English speaking films, but on special occasions they would show Tagalog movies. A big celebration in the community was the fiesta in honor of the Mother of Perpetual Help, the patroness of Milbuk.

When Weyerhaeuser took over from Basilan Lumber there were two logging camps set up. One camp was leading to Biao and the other was close by Kanipaan. The first ambush was in 1974 in the area of Biao where more than 20 loggers and 10 native Manobos were killed. I was a teacher then and helped unload the dead bodies at the company clinic. The following week was a horrible time in the camp. Imagine thirty dead people some of whom were my friends were gone. The whole camp was on full alert. At night we would sleep in the veneer mill. Logging operations stopped for about a month and later on resumed after a "peace talk" mediated by the mayor of Palimbang, Hadji Druz Ali. The peace quickly came to an end on the very first day that the loggers returned to the mountains. The rebel Muslims of the MNLF set up a second ambush close by the barrio of Wal. This was my first experience of the horrors of war. It was this experience that led me to leave Milbuk with my wife and to teach at the Ateneo. My wife is a professor at the Western Mindanao University in Zamboanga.

The Weyerhaeuser years in Milbuk put us on the map of the Philippines for the entire world to see. Production was good. I have never seen in my life such heavy equipment like the ones I saw in Milbuk. Huge dump trucks were driven by such men as Art Labajo. There were the latest "Peter Bilt" logging trucks, massive bulldozers and log movers whose rubber wheels reached a height of ten feet. Loggers were given a quota for production and were awarded bonuses. At times there would be up to 7 international cargo ships (e.g. Japan, Finland, and Greece) anchored at Milbuk harbor to load logs. Some called Milbuk a "loggers' paradise". Most of the workers were former employees of Basilan Lumber Co. Loggers would go "camping" sometimes. This meant that they would come home once a week from the concession area. This was due to the long distance from the main camp at Milbuk.

It was in Milbuk where I saw a real tropical rainforest. I went with my eldest brother, who was a scaler, to the concession area. Here was a real virgin forest in its entire splendor. After finishing high school at NDM in 1968, I went to Notre Dame University for my college degree. I was a working student recommended by my former high school teacher Mrs. Asencio who was a former professor at the University in Cotabato. I returned to Milbuk in 1973 as a fresh college graduate to teach at Notre Dame High School and the rest is history.                                      -Oscar F. Carzada -

*Morality is about what we do to one another and not about how we feel. Feelings, like the weather, changes…and changes. The following excerpt gives an example of such reactions, judgments and emotions. Remember there is no right or wrong in how you feel about something.*

"I belonged to the class of 1972 (NDM). I grew up under the pastoral care of Fr. Henry Free and Fr. Magbanua in Milbuk. I've read the book, "On the Palms of My Hands" and I am very thankful. I would say that I experienced only the beginnings of terror in Milbuk and was oblivious of the danger then. Like America that seemed invulnerable before 9/11, I saw Milbuk in the same way and I felt secure in living in the camp with my family. After high school I attended college in Manila and did not look back. In Manila I heard about the ambushes.

Mr. Will Ramchand who was one of the victims of the second ambush was my uncle by affinity. It was not until I read your book that I became aware of the horrors that took place in Milbuk and in Jolo and it drove me to tears. However, I was one of those who were prejudiced about Muslims. My uncle (my mother's brother), as told by my mother, was murdered by Muslims because he broke up with his Muslim girlfriend. This story built a wall of distrust toward the

Muslims in my heart since childhood and I felt there was no way that I could erase this prejudice or decide to wake up one morning with a changed heart. This malady became more evident after the 9/11 tragedy. Being trained in the Bible, I knew my prejudice was wrong. When I read the book, I saw your compassion and how you reached out to the victims on both sides, regardless of who they were. Your writing touched my heart. Your courage and your pursuit of social justice in the midst of the war torn people of Milbuk and the Muslims helped remove the veil that blinded me. Your book was an instrument used by the Lord to bring about the healing for my sick heart. I've been set free from that bondage now. Thank you so much."

- Fidelis Villegas -

"Many of us who witnessed the events in Milbuk during those trying times went through the painful process of soul searching, of trying to understand from the perspective of peace, reconciliation and interfaith dialogue what the implications of those events were. On a practical level we learned the bitter reality that war is divisive. It begets mistrust. But in the end, we remind ourselves what Jesus taught: "Love your neighbor as yourself." and "Whatever you did for one of the least of these brothers and sisters of mine, you did for me.'

"On the Palm of My Hands" has indeed unlocked some of the missing links that most of us were not aware of: the morbid recollection of the salvaging of the dead bodies of the Muslims at the swampy area in Malisbong: the "fiesta" tendered by the mayor; the Bureau Chief from the Associated Press who covered the story in Kulong-Kulong. This was the Martial Law regime at its worst. I found your book personally rewarding...It paved the way to an acceptable closure of the past in my personal life, the kind of closure viewed from the optic of compassion, charity and hope, a kind of hope that inspires us to move on despite the horrors of that bad dr eam."

- Oscar F. Carzada -

"My family and I lived in Tibulos with a handful of tenants to help my parents cultivate our land. They built our house near the sea.

The loud waves served as my lullaby every night. When I was small, I remembered how my mom would wake me at dawn, in preparation for attendance at the daily Mass. My mom, Herminigilda Garcia, was a former Catholic Women's League President and a teacher at Notre Dame High School during the 1960's. We would walk each day from Tibulos to the Notre Dame High School building where the parish priest would celebrate the Holy Mass on the first floor of the school. The Church of Our Lady of Perpetual Help had yet to be built. Milbuk was a serene, peaceful place to live. We felt secure in this community since we knew all the people. Trouble started in Milbuk when I was away at college. My parents bought an old but serviceable sari-sari (convenience) store just to be closer to some neighbors, since our home was somewhat isolated from the other houses.

During the second month of the crisis, September of 1974, there was an encounter between the rebels and elements of the Philippine Army at the airport. The rebels gutted our dear old house by the sea by fire. They also desecrated the burial site of my father. Most of our tenants left the land they tilled. My brother Nanding and sister Mediatrix transferred to General Santos City to live in peace. I visited Milbuk a short time ago (2010) and the place was not the Milbuk I used to know, sad to say."

-Evelyn Garcia-

*(Editor's Note :) A few days after the first ambush of loggers in the mountains, I was able to visit the Garcia home while blessing the gravesites of the deceased loggers. A small group of us held a burial and funeral service for the ten Manobos who had also lost their lives on the bus. We were only a short distance from the home of the Garcia's. I had never visited the home and so I was surprised when I viewed the house for the first time. The outside of the house was beautiful, distinctively clothed in the finest hardwood, stained dark brown. It showed a lot of character, hidden away among a grove of coconut trees. The inside of the two-story house appeared spacious and comfortable even though it lay empty of any furniture. No damage was evident to the house at that time. However,*

*when the hostilities heated up again and the rebels attempted to enter Milbuk by way of the airport, they laid waste to the house and the other dwellings in the area. I was probably the last person to see that handsome house before its destruction.*

"I belong to the younger generations who graduated from Notre Dame of Milbuk after the 1974 crisis. I grew up in Barangay Baranayan but I spent my teenage years in Milbuk. I finished my high school at Notre Dame of Milbuk (1985-1986) in the hard and trying times after the withdrawal of Weyerhauser. Nothing remained of Milbuk's former beauty but dilapidated bunkhouses. The power station lay in ruins and the veneer mill crumbled into decay. I started my freshman year at Notre Dame of Milbuk in 1982. My friends and I enjoyed swimming in the ball tank in Tibulos. We climbed the hill overlooking Milbuk elementary school and Notre Dame High School, and we cat-walked the winding pipeline going to the lighthouse.

The Greenbelt Wood Products Inc. operated the logging concession in the area during that time. The Greenbelt Company offered no improvements to the school because they did not feel obligated in anyway. In my short stay in Milbuk, I eagerly listened to the stories related to the dreadful events during the crisis days of 1974. Fronting Notre Dame High School was the Gothong Memorial Hospital that previously had been the Clinic/Hospital for the Weyerhaeuser Logging Company employees. There were plenty of stories about the truckloads of dead bodies dumped there during the time of the ambushes. Those were the accounts of the past.

The younger generation of Milbukians suffered so much because of the impact of the crises. During our time, (1982-1986), the power plant no longer provided 24 hours of electricity to the households of the camp and surrounding barrios. Whenever we had activities in Notre Dame, we had to use the petromax (hurricane or kerosene lamps) and hang those lamps on the posts of the stage with others scattered around the quadrangle. What was so painful to me was to experience the decaying state of the Notre Dame High School buildings and facilities. The beautiful abundant mangroves in the tidal basin fronting Notre Dame High School were gone, uprooted in 1974 to give clear view of the sea to warn the people of dangers from rebel attacks. In the years to come, the school became so vulnerable to the strong waves coming from the sea. I can well remember the day during one of our algebra lessons in sophomore year under Ms. Marietta Catadman, when a strong wave struck our classroom and half of my classmates became soaking wet from the crashing wave. Month by month, the classrooms were being slowly eaten away by the onrushing waves especially during the months of June, July and August.

Our family belonged to a farming clan in Baranayan, Palimbang. We all grew up in Baranayan but most of my siblings spent their secondary education at Notre Dame of Milbuk during the years 1979-1990. Three years before the crises of 1974, my father left Baranayan, Palimbang and joined the logging company of Perrett in Maguling, Maitum, South Cotabato. Our family moved to settle in Kiamba. While in Kiamba, the crises of 1974 broke out and some of our relatives evacuated to Kiamba and stayed with us for some time. With difficult times in Milbuk, my father decided to continue working at the logging company of Perret and later moved to Davao del Sur. Then in 1976, our family went back to Baranayan, Palimbang and settled for good. My grandmother had a homestead in Baranayan so my father tilled the land and earned a living as a farmer.

When Notre Dame of Milbuk reopened, my older sister (Imelda) was one of the first batch of students to graduate after the closure. She is now a Religious Sister with the Oblates Sisters of Notre Dame (OND). One of the most difficult things I had to do while pursuing my studies at Notre Dame was to hike all the way from Baranayan to Milbuk, a distance of more than fifteen kilometers. We had to pass by the area of Lopuken and Wal, Moslem barrios, near which the second ambush occurred.

I was very inspired by the warmth and hospitality of the people of Milbuk. During fiestas and religious events, the people were extremely hospitable and offered the best accommodations to everybody. In addition, there was the deep sense of religious piety among the people. A very important value that I learned in my stay at Notre Dame of Milbuk was the phrase "the Notre Dame Spirit." I am very sure that all who have passed under the portals of Notre Dame of Milbuk must have a large dose of this very potent spirit. For me, the "Notre Dame Spirit" encompasses everything for a Milbukian. This means excellence, integrity, camaraderie, love of God and country. This brings to mind someone who inspired me while I was a student there. I would like to pay homage to our very strict but good principal, Mr. Ricardo Tranco. May he rest in the eternal peace of his Lord and Savior, Jesus Christ.

Everything is totally different from the earlier accounts of the beautiful and vibrant Milbuk. Gone are any traces of what was a beautiful logging camp. The convento remains, having withstood the test of time and the strong waves that battered its foundation now and again. The church stands tall, in spite of the earthquakes that have shaken it. Moreover, the people of God in Milbuk continue to struggle to attain peace and prosperity. For all the Milbukians throughout the world, let us break the barriers of time and space. Let us once again be connected to the land that was Milbuk and let us give hope and inspiration to all the people of God who remain in Milbuk. This is the biggest challenge for all the Milbukians. May I call on the young professionals who are products of Notre Dame to extend a helping hand to the people of Milbuk?

Recently, I finished reading the book about those difficult times in Milbuk, "In the Palms of My Hands". The book contains very vivid memories of what had happened in the past. Tears roll from my eyes when I think of the title of the book. Truly you are right, "Milbuk is in the Palms of God's Hands." Presently, I'm working here in General Santos City as a public secondary school teacher. My family and siblings are settled here in the city. I have a twin brother, Fr. Reynaldo B. Mission, a Diocesan Priest of Marbel. He is presently on study leave at the Angelicum University in Rome taking up a Doctorate in Canon Law. I finished my degree, a Bachelor of

Secondary Education, at Notre Dame of Dadiangas University last 1993. Our youngest brother, Atty. Andres Mission, Jr. is currently the Clerk of Court of Regional Trial Court Branch 32 here in Gen. Santos City."

- Leonardo B. Mission -

"I was three years old when my family arrived in Milbuk (1959-1975). We lived in Campo Uno. I attended the Milbuk Elementary School from 1961-1968 and then entered Notre Dame, graduating in 1972. Before the coming of the Weyerhaeuser Logging Company, it seems that part of Milbuk were previously filled with saw dust. It may have been pArt of a larger mangrove swamp area. Thus, during the rainy season, the water would run knee deep and there were certain areas where the water lay underneath the saw dust. The old clinic was near our house, facing the shore line. In the morning, fishermen docked and brought their catch to the market. During Artet day, I used to watch farmers sell their goods. There were only two big acacia trees near the shore. This was our playhouse with friends. Since we were very near the coast, I could hear the waves as they crashed down the coast, especially at night.

I remember Amban, the Manobo. Early in the morning, he was outside our house. He would ask if he could chop firewood or clean our grasses. My mother would always cook one big kettle of rice, a really big kettle. Before lunch time, all of Amban's relatives would arrive and they would share their lunch together. Yes, there was nothing left in the kettle. My mother rarely went to church. But I saw she gave tithes. I never knew what the tithes were for at that time. She had this money well folded inside. I realize that she may not have been always active in the church's activities but she always gave her share, "kahit maliit" no matter how little.

I have no recollection of the massacre/ambushes until I read the book, "On the Palms of My Hands". I lost all memories of those incidents, that part of my life. All I remember was the time when I returned from college in Zamboanga for one semester (1973/1974). I was in Milbuk when Kulong-Kulong was bombed and attacked by

343

the naval ships. What I recall was a Cruiser of the Philippine Navy bombarding Kulong-Kulong on an early Sunday morning. I was at Elsie Bajada's place looking at the shelling through their binoculars. This was the only thing I remembered until now. I don't know why certain life experiences were erased. I only recalled some of them after I read your book. I watched the funeral of those many that died but I could not recall any faces or names, nor do I remember what I felt at the time. It took me sometime to remember the bits and pieces.

When we lived in Gen. Santos City, I would always remember the good times in Milbuk and longed to return once again. But it never came into my mind anything about the massacre, etc. I was still in high school when the Ilagas and the Philippine Military joined forces. The Ilagas ate and took their bath in our house. I saw one time their little bottle with roots. When Sinagkangan was burned down, we were left in school while the rest of the students ran home. I had to force my friend, Fidie, to walk with me. She seemed so frightened and nervous at the time. After supper, we would crawl beneath our house and sleep in the foxhole that my father had dug out for us. We wore black pants and dark jackets. My father who was a World War II veteran slept in the canal in front of our house. The canal, though was clean and without water.

In one of my travels, I met a military man who said he was one of those who entered Kulong- Kulong. He said, girls/women were raped and later thrown out in the sea with a sinker. He said that he ate the ears of his enemy (grilled) so it would make him brave during the encounter. I could not recall his name. I didn't know the true story of Kulong-Kulong until I read your book. It was only then that I remembered my conversation with this man in uniform. My family left Milbuk in 1977. The company closed down because of the conflict of 1974 and my father decided to go home to Basilan province. My parents travelled to Basilan with other Weyerhaeuser families on a barge. After leaving Milbuk, my father worked at the Alano hospital in Isabela, Basilan as part of the maintenance team. My mother had a store in the market. We had a small farm in Basilan. We tended our farm. We had coconuts and coffee as our main products.

I studied B.S. nursing in Ateneo de Zamboanga and I was supposed to go to Butuan Doctors' Hospital for my internship. I passed the examination but I did not push through because of the conflict in Milbuk. It had affected my studies due to limited finances. I shifted to Social Work and graduated from Western State University, Zamboanga City. I was hoping that by the time I finished social work, I could go back to nursing. However, due to the financial crisis, on leaving Milbuk, I did not have any choice. It took me three years after graduation to get my licensure. Our reviewers were from the Asian Social Institute. The former Dean of Social Work offered me a graduate assistant scholarship. What an opportunity. I resigned from work and went to ASI for my graduate studies. I now work on a project basis. I was a community organizer, among the fisher folk, the women, youth and children. Then later, I became part of a team of facilitators. We travelled from Aparri to Jolo but I was never able to return to Milbuk.

I wanted to go back to Milbuk but I did not know anybody. I thought all the people left Milbuk. I had visited General Santos City many times (almost every month) conducting trainings to church based leaders as far as Maitum. I never knew there were so many Milbukians around. The only person I met on my last training was Mrs. Lourdes Gaviola, the former principal of Notre Dame High School during the conflict.

When I was young, I had written on my bedroom wall long ago these words: *"the cruelty of mankind lies in the heart of every person"*. I never knew the reason why I had those thoughts until I read the book on Milbuk. The feelings that I am now experiencing were there all along, lost in my subconscious. Maybe that is why my life's work is in helping people. My life experiences in Milbuk have made me the person that I am today."

-Nelida Altibano Cayas-

# CHAPTER 37

# *About Heroes and Other Stories*

"We first arrived in Milbuk in the summer of 1965. My father (Capt. Vicente R. Dorotheo) was hired as the Chief of Security for Basilan Lumber Company (BLC) a year earlier (1964) and then he sent for us to live with him in Milbuk the following year. My first day in Milbuk was the happiest that I can remember, because it brought us all together again as a family after being away from my Dad for 3 years. I was only 9 years old at that time. There were six of us in the family. My father had been a captain in the Philippine military that fought against the Japanese during WWII under the USAFFE. After the war, he worked in odd jobs in Manila during the peacetime era and then my Mom and Dad stayed in Cotabato City where I was born on Oct. 16, 1954.

In Cotabato City he became a policeman in a predominantly Muslim city, which made him aware of the culture and the sentiments of the Muslim population. He spoke fluent English, Muslim and Chabacano so that he was able to effectively communicate with both Muslim and Christian. He had attended school in Manila and majored in law. His credentials as a law graduate, a local policeman in Cotabato City and a military man made him a perfect fit to head the security group of the BLC (Basilan Lumber Company) and eventually Weyerhaeuser Lumber. My mother worked as a company nurse in the medical clinic.

When we arrived in Cotabato City, we were picked up by the company plane piloted by Capt. Buddy Capacite and were brought to Milbuk. The flight from Cotabato City to Milbuk took less than 2 hours. We flew above vast areas of green virgin forest and beautiful coastal landscape along the way. It was a beautiful sight. On our approach to Milbuk, I had a bird's eye view of the whole town. I was awed by the sight of the green lush mountain in the background, the neat rows of houses in the two camps, the multitude of coconut trees, the log pond and the sandy beach nearby along the shore of the Celebes Sea. As we landed, I saw my father waiting for us at the airfield hangar and we were so excited to see him again. The very first thing that my siblings and I did as soon as we arrived at our house was to run immediately to the beach behind the house and take a dip in the clear sea. The water was so inviting that we did not care wetting our clothes. While we were enjoying ourselves in the water, we were immediately joined by many local kids of our age and we made instant friends with them from then on. This was by far the happiest day of my life. I remember in my years of living in Milbuk that the Muslim and Christian population coexisted in relative peace and harmony with one another. My dad knew a few Muslim families who lived in Kolong-Kolong and Baliango. Because of his friendship with them, two Muslim students lived with us in our house at the camp while they attended school at NDM. These two young men were Salem Kanda and Plun Piang. They were both bright students and studied under full scholarship. When they graduated high school and went to Manila for college, they lived with us in Sampaloc, Manila until they finished their college studies.

During my 1st year in high school, I remember attending a lavish Muslim wedding in. We were invited by Datu Piang (the father of Plun) and were treated like VIPs. We stayed with them for two days and were treated with the utmost respect by the local folks. We felt very safe and welcomed during that visit. The wedding celebration lasted 3 days. It was a very colorful spectacle especially on the final day of the celebration. The bridal party travelled from Palimbang to Kolong Kulong by way of a convoy of sailing vintas. In the evening, you could hear the sweet music of little gongs called "kulintang" for miles.

There were other significantly enjoyable moments that I remember about Milbuk. The plaza was a special place because it was the center of sports and entertainment events. Almost every weekend my dad and other company workers, staff members and the American manager, Mr. Lloyd Roberts, played tennis. After the game, they would order cases of cold San Miguel beer, Coke and fresh fish and partied right beside the tennis court. This was where I learned to play tennis and still played it until today. Another favorite sport enjoyed by the Milbukians was the annual basketball tournament among the different company departments including the NDM varsity basketball players. It was a very enjoyable event that brought out many people around the camp to watch. The month of December was a very special time for Notre Dame and the camp. NDM students would be busy setting up their booths for a fundraising Hawaiian party before the Christmas break. I remember going to the nearby mountain with my classmates to gather building materials such as bamboo, rattan and palms to build our booths. This event brought out the competitive spirit of each high school group. This event allowed the students to showcase their talents in booth building and decoration, food preparation and entertainment.

My young life in Milbuk evolved around my family, friends, school and religion. The physical isolation of Milbuk from major cities in Mindanao may have played a big role in the way we grew up. We did not have television then and the only way we got world news was by AM radio or the occasional newspaper brought back by the company plane. There was a handful of radio stations that could be received in Milbuk and most of them originated from Zamboanga. These factors provided us with an environment wherein we could focus our attention on our studies. We were also very lucky to have dedicated teachers who cared enough to provide us with the best possible education with the meager resources available.

I remember one particular Director of the NDM High School, Fr. Henry Free, who was also the parish priest. Fr. Henry took his job seriously and together with his dog Klim patrolled around the camp, after 7:00 PM, during school nights to discourage students from hanging out at the plaza. To me he was the original running priest because Fr. Henry could outrun the best of the student athletes and would always get his man. The following day those students would be carrying picks and shovels for yard duty after the flag ceremony at the end of classes.

My life in Milbuk was not always joy and happiness though. The first sad moment that I remember was when Mr. San Luis (a father of a friend) died from a logging operation accident. That incident brought the grim realization that the work in the mountain was back breaking and dangerous. Fortunately, accidental deaths from logging operation were few and far between.

I almost forgot Saturday nights. Most every Saturday night the company showed either a Filipino or American movie of a different genre for everyone. This gave the people in the camp and surrounding barrios a chance to come together with their families and enjoy the evening together. You just had to bring your own bench or chair (bangko) and your own baon (snack). Most of the movies that I remember were western cowboy movies starring John Wayne. I just loved how he portrayed his character as a brave good guy who could shoot straight. It reminded me of my dad who was also very brave and was very good with a gun. This was one of his talents that made him effective at his job. He used his ability to use a gun as a deterrent to bring peace among the people of Milbuk.

Let me tell you the story about my Dad who was also a gun enthusiast and an ex- military person. He was a sharp shooter both at long and short arms and he used the gun as a tool for peace. When he was the Chief of Security of Weyerhauser Logging Company in Milbuk, and as a policeman in Cotabato City, he used the gun as a deterrent against the local Muslim thugs. His ability to shoot straight and his courage to face the Muslims on their own turf earned him the respect (and possibly fear) from the locals (both Muslim and Christian). There were very few hostile actions against the Milbuk Christian community from the local Muslims during his stint as the security chief (in 1964-1976). The peace and order of Milbuk, however, was suddenly shattered in 1974, when the first massacre occurred by elements of the new Muslim secessionist group from Jolo/Basilan called the MNLF. This single incident brought so much pain, fear and sorrow to the people of Milbuk.

The succeeding ambushes that took the lives of many Milbukians, resulted in the closure of the logging operation of Weyerhaeuser. They harrassed various Christian communities and during the height of the conflict, several attempts were made to capture Milbuk but they failed because the local Milbukians, aided by the Philippine Military resisted with their homemade guns and whatever arms the Army gave them.

In one incident, a month after the first ambush, my Dad with a handful of his security guards and a few Philippine Constabuary (PC) soldiers escorted a convoy of loggers attempting to resume logging in the mountain area above Palimbang. On their way back from the woods, they were ambushed about 10 kilometers away from Milbuk. It was by luck that the convoy survived that ambush.

Prior to the first salvo of gunfire from the rebels, the company's Cessna airplane made a fly-by over the convoy of logging buses travelling down the road back to Milbuk. The pilot, Capt. Nards Flores tried to warn the convoy of the impending ambush. The rebels fired upon his plane, trying to bring it down. His left foot was hit by the gunfire while flying at low altitude in his vain attempt to warn the convoy. He drew the first salvo of gunfire from the MNLF rebels. Although he was bleeding badly from his injury, he was able to fly back to Milbuk and safely land the Cessna plane before passing out due to shock and loss of blood. The initial upward firing to down the plane gave warning to the convoy of the impending ambush, thereby giving the escorting security forces spearheaded by my dad, a chance to take cover on the side of the road and return fire.

In the course of the firefight, a bullet, fired by a sniper hiding in one of the mango trees behind them, grazed my Dad. Knowing the general direction of the shot, my Dad sprayed that tree with his modified M16 Armalite rifle (in full auto). Nobody knows if he hit anyone, but there was no more sniper fire after that. Although they were outnumbered and out gunned, they remained composed and were able to shoot their way out of that ambush and bring back many of the loggers to Milbuk Alive. A few of his friends had died in that incident and others wounded. In this chapter of his life, he used a gun to defend the lives of his friends and co-workers in Milbuk.

Eventually, the Weyerhauser Company decided that staying in Milbuk was no longer in their best business interest and finally pulled out of the area about two years later. Without local work and fear for their lives, the majority of the Christians left Milbuk and found employment elsewhere. Another logging company in Butuan hired my Dad as the Chief of Security. He never fired his weapon in battle again from that time on.

The 1974 ambushes/massacres happened while I was in Manila and so I have no first-hand knowledge of what transpired there. However, my dad told me the story about the first ambush and the time they went up the mountain to retrieve the dead bodies. When I came back for vacation in Milbuk, my dad took me to the site of the first massacre and pointed out the spot where the bus had been ambushed. He pointed out the places where they found two dead bodies of loggers who tried to escape the carnage but failed to get away. He told me that before they left the ambush site, he ordered the bullet riddled bus pushed over the side of the cliff so that the Rebels could not use it. I was totally stunned by his story and was saddened because the people who died were fathers and brothers of some people I knew.

In Manila, I had the opportunity to visit Capt. Leonardo (Nards) Flores while he was confined at the Makati Medical Center for his foot reconstruction. Although my dad sustained a slight injury on his face, he was very lucky to come home Alive. Since then, I look at Capt. Nards with a different sense of respect for a man who was ready to sacrifice his safety for his fellow Milbukians. To me he was not just a top notch pilot but a big hero who saved my father and the fathers of many fellow Milbukians. My fervent wish is that the graduates of the old Notre Dame that we knew and loved would be able to provide the present children of Milbuk with the kind of education that we had in the past."

-Gerry Dorotheo -

*(The following is an e-mail sent to me almost six years ago by the former Weyerhaeuser Resident Manager of Milbuk, whose tour of duty coincided with my own assignment as parish priest in Milbuk. I was quite surprised to receive the letter and more amazed at the content of the message.)*

"I guess you will always be known as Father Art to me. I was surfing the Internet recently, and found Milbuk. As you know, I spent 4 years there with my young family as Logging Manager and then Resident Manager for Weyerhaeuser. Milbuk was my first international assignment. I was there during the buildup of the Blackshirts and Ilagas during 1971-72. I returned to the states six weeks before the first ambush in the logging area and several weeks before our Wasag log pond supervisor Wil Ramchand and forest engineer Melacio Bajada were ambushed.

Like you, I experienced many highs and lows at Milbuk. I will always fondly remember working with the Weyerhaeuser employees and enjoying their company. Dealing with the infamous mayor, Druz Ali, and most of the ne'er do well PC personnel was part of the assignment that was most difficult. Trying to balance the interests of the company and the welfare of the community was always a challenge. Some things we did well and some things, as is always the case, could have been better.

The losses of personnel at Weyco's Basilan Island operation and the virtual loss of the whole island to the insurgents coupled with the loss of our attorney Jun Meija in a Zamboanga plane hijacking and the close call during the same event suffered by my old friend and boss Andy Macs were most unnerving.

It was interesting for me to remember that over thirty years before I arrived in the Philippines, my own father was the executive officer on a US Navy destroyer that patrolled the Moro Gulf, near

Jolo and other parts of the Sulu Archipelago, keeping the Japanese at bay during WWII.

The Milbuk experience has had an effect on me as it has on you. I read your book with great interest and fascination and was able to see things in a way from your viewpoint that I had either forgotten, not been aware of, or had overlooked in the passage of time. Thirty-five years later, the time in some ways feels like it only happened yesterday and some ways was so long ago that details have faded. However, Milbuk will never go away from me."                   - Lloyd Roberts -

Living in Milbuk during the 60's to mid-70 were "glorious years". Food was abundant. The sea and forest were pristine. Jobs were plentiful. I remember joining my late brother in the logging concession area for one day to see what it was like to perform such dangerous work. He worked as a scaler. That was my first and last experience of a "rain forest".

In the early part of 1974, stories had been circulating for weeks before the massacre that training camps were being set up far up in the mountains beyond Milbuk. Elements of the rebel group sent "extortion letters" to the key people of the company by way of the loggers. However, it appears that the logging management ignored these letters for reasons not known to the ordinary people.

When word of the massacre in the mountains was making its round of the camp, truckloads of loggers and security personnel were already in route to retrieve the dead bodies from the ambushed bus. Scores of women and children flocked to the entrance of Campo Uno to await the arrival of the slain. Great anxiety and fear seized the large crowd as the security guards received word that the trucks were approaching the checkpoint. The security guard struck the alarm bell continuously, as the company flatbed truck, loaded with the dead loggers and native Manobos approached the entrance to the camp. A great noise erupted from the crowd, mingling with the harsh blowing of truck horns as the flatbed truck opened up a path through the crying, shouting crowd toward the clinic. The bodies of the dead loggers lay intertwined upon the bed of the truck indicating how hurriedly their fellow loggers had retrieved them from the ambush site.

The days and weeks following this tragic event were horrible. Some of slain loggers were family friends and some were parents of my friends. That was the first ambush. The situation was serious and very critical. At night, we would sleep in the veneer mill for fear of an attack by the rebels. Every now and then, we would hear the sound of gunfire from nearby Baliango or the shores of Tibulos. Some of the women and children evacuated to Basilan or Zamboanga and from there proceeded to their respective places of origin. My family belonged to the first group of "evacuees" who took a slow moving barge to Zamboanga and Basilan, our hometown. The pain of separation was the saddest part of the story. It was not easy to say goodbye to people you have grown up with, people who were your friends, colleagues and most especially, the memory of the place that is Milbuk. What made this more painful was saying "farewell" under very tense and difficult situations.

Life was difficult at first, in the attempt to rebuild dreams, attend to the family matters and so forth. It was like "starting life all over again. Our saving grace was the help and support from friends and relatives of both my mother and father who were all from Zamboanga. I was a newly married man then. My wife was able to get a seat on the company plane bound for Basilan. She left ahead of me and stayed with my sister in law in Basilan. She finally got a teaching job at the national high school in Isabela proper. I stayed behind in Milbuk to finish the school year at Notre Dame and promised to follow her after the end of the school year. Notre Dame of Milbuk High School was my first teaching job.

After the school year of 1974, I proceeded to Zamboanga where my wife was living. I was already eyeing a teaching job at the Ateneo. I was happy to get a very favorable letter of recommendation from a former friend, an American missionary of the OMI congregation. This was the start of my professional life in the academe. I did not imagine at that time that this was going to be the place where I would spend the rest of my professional life teaching at the college level. My wife accepted a teaching position in an exclusive school for girls run by the RVM, (Religious Sisters of the Virgin Mary) at Pilar College. My brothers and sisters who left Milbuk and "resettled" in Zamboanga have their own families now. Three of them finished college under some form of "merit" scholarship grant.

One of my nieces whose father (my eldest brother) died in Milbuk is teaching in New York. She is based there now with her own family. I continued my academic teaching career at the Ateneo until my appointment as principal of the High School, a post I have held for 18 years. My involvement in this new program of the university has exposed me to the realities of basic education in this part of the country. The challenges were immediate. I designed modules on governance and management of the school, educational leadership, curriculum development and basic educational planning. I performed this type of work until I retired in 2011.        –Oscar F. Carzada -

My family lived close to the Weyerhaeuser camp in Milbuk at 52 Mayapis Street. We resided there for 12 years, from 1962 to 1974, the year of my graduation from Notre Dame. I first took Marine Engineering at the Iloilo Maritime Academy, Iloilo City and had one-year experience on board a ship. I later decided to quit the life of a sailor because of the lifestyle. After two years, I joined the congregation of the Oblates of St. Joseph (OSJ), Philippine Province in Lipa City, Batangas, Philippines for 8 years. I spent 21 years of teaching at Consolacion College of Binan, an extension school of La Consolacion College in Manila near Malacanang Palace.

My mother and sisters left Milbuk in the middle of 1974 because of continuous war during that time between the Military and the Muslim separatists. My father who was then the captain of the towing barge of the company decided to continue working, hoping that this terrible situation would end. During the early part of the Milbuk conflict, my uncle Wilfredo Sillo was a victim to the bus ambush of the loggers in the mountains. My father was furious over the incident and the death of his cousin. In fact, my late father secretly admired and believed in the group, "ILAGA", who prided themselves as "barrio militia" and almost decided to join. I remember then, that our house became a meeting place for these strangers from other provinces, people I did not recognize. I heard someone calling one of the group members, "Commander".

Part of my curiosity at that time was seeing my father with many bottles of different sizes around his waist, an "anting-anting" (magic potions/charms) commonly used by these people who called themselves "ILAGA" to ward off injuries and death in battle. They believed that the "anting-anting" made them invincible from hurt by the bullets of their enemies.

There was also a new and strange house policy implemented in our home during that time. My mother placed a red cloth in front of our house to give warning to members of the "ILAGA" that a woman was having her monthly period. They were afraid to lose the charms/power of the "anting-anting". Another strange custom occurred during mealtime. The "ILAGA" who were wearing their "anting- anting" would place themselves in areas where nobody could pass around their back. How weird!

When my mother and sisters arrived in Iloilo City without any assurance of my father's monetary support, we started to beg and ask help from our relatives just for food. They provided us with a small place to start a "banana-que" stand for us to survive. We received letters from our father telling us that he was trying to return to Milbuk, hoping to receive some compensation and refund from the Milbuk Coop. He lost patience in waiting and decided to proceed to Davao to seek a temporary job. However, after three years he had a CVA that caused his sudden death. The death of my father and our experience in Milbuk perhaps was God's way of awakening my sisters' vocation to religious life, because right after high school (a year after the death of my father), they decided to enter the religious life. I worked as a security guard to help my remaining sister finish her college degree.

After her graduation, we moved back to General Santos City and were fortunate enough to find banana-que area at the plaza circle. There my mother put up our survival store. It was then that we were reunited with some Milbukians, like Bebot Astorga Penuela, parish secretary of our Lady of Good Voyage, Mrs. Gaviola, former NDM Principal. Presently, my mother is with my sister in Koronadal City and half paralyzed due to a stroke. My two younger sisters are full-fledged members of the Reparatrix Sisters of the Sacred Heart, an Italian congregation.

Of course, one of the happiest moments in Milbuk, especially to my mother, was, when the parish priest of our Lady of Perpetual Help Parish accepted an invitation to have dinner in our home. An incident on this occasion, that is still very vivid in my memory, was the moment that Fr. Art bumped his head on the upper part of the entrance as he entered doorway because of the low height.                                        —Samuel Sortido—

# CHAPTER 38

# *A Journey of Remembrance*

M y last departure from the Philippines as a missionary was on June 4, 1976. I arrived at Newark International Airport in New Jersey and was picked up by my friend Barry Ward, the former parish priest of Kiamba. He welcomed me into his home where I lived for about one month until I was able to secure an apartment. Barry had arranged for me to work in a substance abuse program for youth, of which he was the Director. I remained there for the next three months. Each week I was interviewing for employment in areas where I could best use my education, training and experience. It was then that I obtained a position as a Social Worker at the Youth Correctional Facility, Yardville, New Jersey in September of 1976.

In the meantime, I was anxiously awaiting a decision from Rome concerning my status as a priest and religious. I had earlier requested permission to be dispensed from my vows and be permitted to marry in the Church. In December of this same year, I finally received permission in writing from the Office of the Holy See in Rome granting me dispensation from my vows and permission to marry. I was married on January 6, 1977 to Maria Ana Codilla in a simple ceremony in the Church of Our Lady of Sorrows in Hamilton, N.J., with eight of my closest friends in attendance at the Nuptial Mass.

During the next four years, we were blessed with the birth of three boys. All during that time, Mary and I never stopped thinking about the Philippines and our desire to return with our growing family and settle there. In fact, we taped a large travel advertisement of the Philippines on our refrigerator door to remind us of our goal to return there soon. Then in November of 1980, we made plans to leave the United States and travel with our three young sons to the Philippines. I sold my car and other belongings and purchased tickets for me and my family … round trip tickets in case this venture was not successful.

We left the United States on December 23, 1980 and arrived in Manila on Christmas Eve. Friends of ours afforded us lodging for several days until we left by plane for Davao. We stayed at the Apo View Hotel for several days while we contacted my wife's family for a reunion. I had never met any of Mary's family. It was truly a happy occasion. We lived in Digos, where we rented a small house. It was there that Dra. Mariano, formerly of Milbuk, visited us one day and truly made us feel welcome. It was like old times again. I interviewed for the teaching position at the Jesuit Ateneo University in Davao. The position was available but the salary was not sufficient enough for me to support my family. Mary and I decided to return back to the United States where I still had a job at the Correctional Facility.

It was necessary for me to return first to the States and prepare a place for me and my family to live. Mary was already pregnant on our fourth child. It was suggested that she remain in the Philippines until the birth of the child at which time, I would return to assist her in bringing back the other children. In the meantime, I would be busy obtaining an apartment that was large enough to accommodate our growing family.

Two months later, just before my birthday in April, Mary phoned me with the urgent request to return to the United States with the three boys. When my family arrived at the airport, we went to the home of my best friend where we stayed for a month while I completed plans to purchase a house. We moved into a small home and began digging deep roots in establishing ourselves as a family. Mary was able to continue her college studies, with the help of her mother who came to the United States as an immigrant. Our four children now numbered five with an unexpected arrival in August of 1988. All the children received Catholic education, from the elementary grades through High School. And three of our sons graduated from College. My career with the Department of Corrections advanced and was quite successful until my retirement in July of 2002.

Down through the years, Mary and I continued to dream of returning again one day to the Philippines and to visit family and friends and those precious places in which so many memories lay. Now with time on my hands, I decided to write down the story of Milbuk. When the book was published in February of 2007, and initial contact began with the former residents of Milbuk, by means of the internet, the desire of journeying again to the Philippines became more and more intense and urgent.

Mary wanted to wait until she was able to retire from her job with the State of New Jersey. And so it was. Mary retired from State service on December 31, 2013, and three months later, on March the 25th, we left Newark Airport in New Jersey and arrived in the Philippines on March the 26th, 2014. There was a time lapse of 33 years and 3 months since I last stood on Filipino soil. I was so excited even after the long journey of 10,000 miles.

Mary and I left Newark Liberty Airport at 1:50 AM on March 25, 2014. We arrived in Hong Kong on March 26th, which was a Wednesday at 10:30 AM. It was a very long flight of 15 hours or more in the air. I should have broken up the trip into shorter flight times since the total hours of flight time came to over 20 hours' time. We were met at the airport by Boyting Serrano, a former resident of Palimbang.

We were brought to the home of Wilfredo 'Boyting' Serrano, a retired colonel with the Philippine National Police (PNP). He had a distinguished career with the PNP and was rewarded for his fine service with a plot of land here in Makati. The former President and Dictator of the Philippines, Ferdinand Marcos, had given his trusted national police and military, portions of land in the Makati area that belonged to the government as a reward for their loyalty during martial law and as insurance for their continued fidelity to his wishes and commands. Each person received enough land on which to build a home. Thus the whole area quickly became a burgeoning series of connected villages or 'barangays' with a maze of narrow streets, wide enough for two tricycles to pass each other, leaving just room enough on either side for pedestrians to ease carefully along the alleys of homes and small stores.

Boyting's home was situated down a quiet lane. In this area of the development, the streets were named after familiar Philippine flowers like Sampaguita. The larger homes had a massive steel gate that opened into a garage area at the front entrance of the house. Boyting's home is a three-story building with the main portion of the house on the first floor. The entrance to the home opens into a medium-sized living room with beautiful, wooden furniture and continues into a large dining area and kitchen. There are two bedrooms that lie just to the right of the dining area, one having its own bathroom. A common bathroom is situated just off the kitchen area.

Mary had not slept well before leaving the States and was unable to really sleep on the plane. When we arrived, the only thing she wanted to do was to sleep and nap and sleep again. I had not slept at all on the plane but was quickly revived after resting a day at the home of Boyting. All I wanted to do was hop in a car and ride through Metro Manila to see what I could recognize. Everywhere I looked seemed strange and unfamiliar. Manila Bay did not disappear nor did the wide expanse of Roxas Boulevard. However, there had been a huge, huge reclamation project begun by Imelda Marcos in the late 60s, at the far end of Roxas Boulevard going to Pasay. The first major development of the reclamation project was the now famous Cultural Center which still stands majestic and beautiful along the Bay. The shallows of Manila Bay at this point was broadened by continued land-fill operations to such an extent that it now houses some of the most beautiful buildings in the Philippines, including the largest Mall in Southeast Asia. The size of the reclamation project astonishes the mind.

As we passed the City Hall in Manila heading toward Quiapo, we traveled over the famous Pasig River Bridge. This part of crowded

Manila had not changed. It seems that all the major growth in the Metro-Manila area was actually taking place in the surrounding areas of Makati, Taguig, Pasay and Quezon City. These areas had vastly surpassed Manila in the number of skyscrapers, high-rise apartment buildings and huge shopping centers, all of which, for the most part, had been constructed beautifully.

On our third day in Makati, I asked Boyting to bring me to Loyola Heights, to the place where I resided for almost three years as Vocation Director of the Passionists. There had been two facilities in this neighborhood one of which housed the Theology students attending the Jesuit College called the Ateneo. This large two story house was home to seven of us Passionists and bordered the main, two lane road. It was a sparsely populated area that was residential by nature with few commercial establishments along the road. I used to exercise by jogging down this avenue for several kilometers and observed how little traffic there was on this road. The other house was a new one story construction similar to several barrack-like buildings fashioned like a horse shoe. This dwelling housed the Philosophy students who also attended the Ateneo. This other house was about a kilometer away from the older facility.

And so Boyting and I went on our quest to find the locations of the Passionist houses somewhere on B. Gonzales Street near the Loyola Heights section of Quezon City. When we arrived at Loyola Heights, Boyting assured me that this was the place. He was stationed near this area as a member of the Philippine National Police and knew the area very well. I couldn't believe what I saw. My memory of this area just did not fit to the reality set before me. Let me describe to you what I saw. We were deeply embedded in a colossal traffic jam. Cars, motorcycles, and trucks of all shapes and sizes moved slowly on this three lane highway going East, while a similar three lanes of traffic traveled West on this same street that I remembered as two-lane forty years ago.

Our original student house bordered on the main boulevard of Loyola Heights. There was only one, two lane road running along Loyola Heights and you could clearly see the buildings of the Ateneo

University and even the Convent complex of the Maryknoll Sisters. I used to jog down this empty boulevard for a mile or two each day and jog back on the other side. Our student house was a large two story, old fashioned New England type home, housing about six students, three priests and a cook. I lived on the first floor at the back of the house with 2 large windows looking out on a large ¼ acre piece of lawn with a low, four foot stone wall surrounding the whole ½ acre of property. On the back porch, the students were raising chickens from baby chicks. There were a half dozen cages filled with about 30 baby chicks each, gaily chirping away in their cages. Their chirping put me to sleep at night and awoke me at dawn. This place really existed some 40 years ago.

I could not recognize any landmarks because of the wall of buildings on both sides of the avenue. This maze of concrete and glass blocked any view of the Ateneo University or the Maryknoll Convent that I used to see in the distance from the backyard of the Theology House. I finally figured out where this fabled piece of property actually stood. In the ½ acre piece of land that I described above, there now stood a tall 10 story apartment building surrounded on all sides by similar behemoths. And so it was, down the whole length of this boulevard in Loyola Heights...buildings, buildings and more buildings. Had I landed in another country or on a different planet?

We were still looking for B. Gonzales St. and with the help of a traffic officer, we were directed to go West on the avenue for several streets and there we would find B. Gonzales St. Once we reached the street, we turned right and traveled about half a kilometer and came to a security checkpoint. We finally found B. Gonzales St. Luckily, the area had been incorporated so that only residential units could be built. We passed a security checkpoint at the entrance to the village and with some help in directions, we were able to catch sight of the familiar Passionist Sign.

We finally arrived and I excitedly opened the car door and went directly to the front entrance. There was a large metal sign to the right of the main entrance that depicted the Passionist Sign as worn on the religious cassock, with the words PASSIONISTS. I had finally arrived and was anxious to meet the religious members of this community. The former Seminary as I remembered it then had been built around 1974-75. Previously, the Seminary was a combination of several single story units of modular type buildings that housed the students and priests. Evidently, there had been much expansion during the last 40 years so that the present day building was now two stories tall and quite expansive. The property was about one acre in size, with ample room in the back for light recreational facilities. I looked about for a bell or buzzer on the front gate, but could find none. I opened the gate and slowly entered, searching the front door and looking about the property for any sign of human life, but there was nobody that I could see. I, then, called out in a loud voice but there was no reply. I went up to the front door of the convento and knocked loudly and even shouted out…but no voice answered. How disappointing! I was never able to enter the building nor speak to anyone. There must at least be a caretaker for the property and where was he? Questions, questions, questions! I later learned that all the students and supervising staff had been sent away on vacation or on mission assignment since classes at the Ateneo for seminarians had just closed for the summer. Well anyway, I did have Boyting take a photo of me standing next to the sign in front of the Theology house that read … PASSIONISTS. At least I have proof that I was there to visit.

What massive changes had taken place in Manila and the surrounding cities! There has been an explosion of building during the last 40 years. The landscape has been dramatically changed. The Makati I knew doesn't exist anymore nor do many of the areas of Metro Manila that I remember. It is like being on a spaceship that left earth forty years ago. When you finally return back home to earth, you eagerly look about for some familiar land mark and find none. All that you remember of the former planet just doesn't exist anymore. Another planet has taken its place. This is how I felt. I am not joking!

There are so many huge buildings, skyscrapers, office complexes, apartment buildings, massive shopping centers. And then there is the traffic. Vehicles of all makes and models: SUVs, luxury cars, vans, and trucks of all sizes crowd the streets and highways of the cities. The traffic is so intense that drivers are only allowed to use their vehicles on particular days as regulated on their license plates (odds vs evens). Within the maze of streets that make up the old neighborhoods, there is the onrush of the tricycles, which like army ants billowing out of their nests, weave in and out along the narrow lanes, defying the physical law of the universe that states that "no two beings may occupy the same space at the same time". How wrong I was. One more word about the beloved tricycle … please, in the future, build and construct these vehicles a bit larger so that the size and the frame of the foreign devils who visit the Philippines may fit in them more comfortably.

**Thursday, April the 10th** … The highlight of my trip to the Philippines was, of course, my brief visit to Milbuk. Mary and I had been living at the home of Thelma Juaman Hansen in Marbel (Koronadal) for almost a week during which we were able to visit Lake Sebu and act like tourists. Then on Wednesday, April the 10th, we left Marbel at 5:30 A.M. in the transportation of Fr. Boni, the Director of Catholic Education for the Diocese of Koronadal.

Heading south to General Santos City on the four lane cement highway, we passed the churches of Tupi and Polomolok where I had resided for a month or so, taking the place of the resident pastors who had been on vacation. In less than an hour, we arrived at Gen San and headed north-west on the coastal highway to the town of Maasim. It was a very scenic journey with the mountain ranges to our right and to our left the deep waters of the Celebes Sea. The 'Maasim' that I remembered was far different than the resort town that I was traveling through. The former barrio used to sit among a forest of coconut trees in a 'bowl-like' piece of land that would flood each year during the monsoon season. But like so many other places where I lived and traveled, this too was completely new to me.

Our journey continued unimpeded on this smooth, concrete road. We must have been traveling at least 50 miles an hour or more. There was little or no traffic, perhaps because it was still too early. Before I knew it, we were by-passing the town of Kiamba and within twenty minutes of so, we came upon the ever growing and prosperous town of Maitum. As we left Maitum, the road left the coastal plain for a time in order to snake its way around some low lying hills that ran along the coast of the Celebes Sea. Then, after a half hour or so, we approached the outskirts of Malisbong. I was hoping that we might be able to take the alternate route through the town but to my disappointment, we continued on toward Kulong-Kulong. Again, the main road did not pass through this small town but by-passed it altogether. The military that were stationed in the area of Milbuk/San Roque did not want us to remain more than a few hours. They would hardly have approved my visit to Malisbong. Nevertheless, the desire remains with me.

On this journey to Milbuk, I remembered a conversation I had on the milbuklegacy.com website several years ago with one woman, a former resident of the town. She had become a nurse and shortly after, she accepted employment at a hospital in Saudi Arabia. In the course of time, she married a young man from Palestine and converted to Islam. She and her husband returned for a visit to Milbuk and to the property she still owned in the township.

Dear Fr. Art, she wrote. "I hope to see and meet with you personally on your forthcoming vacation to the Philippines. Insha Allah. I will pray for that day to come. I just visited Milbuk and my farm in Tibulos, three weeks ago. The roads are being cemented and there are lamp posts along the hi-way. My husband was with me all along from Milbuk up to Palimbang. I had to pay my land taxes. He fell in love with Tibulos, especially upon seeing the white sand on the shore. The Marines have tried to communicate with me because they wanted to put up their camp on my land. Negotiations are underway. There are a lot of new faces in Milbuk too. They come from neighboring towns. I am contemplating about settling on my farm."

Dear Evelyn, I replied. Thank you for thinking about me. The story of your visit to Tibulos/Milbuk was so interesting. I could imagine myself being there and looking around with curious eyes to see what I could recognize. I know that so many of the homes and buildings have been destroyed by war, tsunami, and the ravages of time itself. But the physical place still remains as do some of the people, the remnants of the great migration. One way or the other, I will attempt to return to Milbuk to honor the people who remain and to pray for all who have passed on from this life to the joys of heaven.

You will appreciate what I am about to tell you. Often in my reveries of Milbuk... during those quiet times when I think about all that had happened during those days in August/September of 1974, I find myself traveling back to Malisbong ... visiting the ruins of the town's Mosque. Nestor Juaman sent me photos of Malisbong during a trip he made there several years ago. Those photos have haunted me, as it were. I cannot remove from my mind the sight of those imprisoned men, huddled tightly together within the Mosque. I felt so sad and helpless, since there was nothing I could do at the time to free them. The fear that I had at the time concerning their safety and well-being was borne out by the events of the next two weeks. So many had been killed. A great injustice had been done.

Now as I plan for my return to the Philippines and hopefully Milbuk, the same desire comes over me, namely, to visit once again Malisbong. Why? I want to be able to kneel within the ruins of the Mosque, if permitted by the Imam, to pray for the souls of all those men who had been tragically killed. I want to express my sorrow and to ask forgiveness for not doing more to save those men.

Some may be surprised that I speak this way since I am a Catholic Priest. There is only one Creator of us all, no matter what we call Him. When Moses went up Mount Sinai at the request of God to receive the Ten Commandments, he inquired of God, "Whom shall I say sent me? that I may tell the people." God only replied, "Tell the people that "I AM WHO AM" has sent you." God did not give Moses a name. It was the thinking of the time that knowing a person's name gave you power over him. The Infinite and Eternal Creator has no name over which men can have any power. We are all sons and daughters of the same God (Allah).

I didn't know any people living in Malisbong. I only wanted to visit the old Mosque where so many had died forty years ago. The ruined Mosque still stood in the very same place that I had visited so long ago. This time, I only wanted to come and pray at the site for all those who died at Malisbong and in the neighboring villages.

When I arrived from the Philippines on April 30, 2014, I still felt that my trip was somewhat incomplete. My fascination with Malisbong led me to "surf the net" and in the process, I came across a website called "Malisbong Massacre". What I found there was very interesting. It seems that the Muslims of the area and those living in other towns of Sultan Kudarat and in the General Santos area had formed an association for demanding from the government an acknowledgement of the massacre of 1974 and also asking compensation in reparation for the massacre.

As I further researched this subject, I came across an article from a newspaper called MindaNews, dated September 26, 2014 – General Santos City. The article begins, *"The national government has finally recognized around 1,500 Moro residents of a village in Palimbang town in Sultan Kudarat province who were killed in a massacre 40 years ago as martial law victims."*

Loretta Ann Rosales, Chairperson of the Commission on Human Rights, personally gave the recognition to the victims' families on the 40th year commemoration of the infamous September the 24th, 1974 Malisbong Massacre. She personally met with some of the survivors and relatives of the victims in a visit at a mosque in Barangay Malisbong in Palimbang town where the massacre happened. Mrs. Loretta Rosales is quoted as saying, "We will give dignity to each one of them (victims) because there is this measure of justice that, although not total, ensures some kind of justice for which we have been hoping."

The CHR chief was referring to the inclusion of the survivors and the families of the massacre victims as among the claimants of a P10-billion fund that was set aside by the government for the monetary remuneration of human rights victims during the martial law regime of the late President Ferdinand Marcos. This was provided in Republic Act 10368, or the Human Rights Victims Reparation and Recognition Act of 2013, a law recognizing and providing reparation to victims of human rights violations during Martial Law. CHR personnel facilitated the filing of the claims with the Human Rights Victims' Claims Board of the Malisbong Massacre victims.

How surprised I was and very pleased at such good news. This did not bring back the dead nor comfort the families of the victims, nor remove their sorrow and impoverishment. It did, however recognize the humanity of the victims and the justice that was denied them. We as Christians need to keep our focus on the teachings of Jesus and follow them.

*"But I say this to you who are listening: Love your enemies, do good to those who hate you.*
*Bless those who curse you, pray for those who treat you badly.*
*Treat others as you would like people to treat you.*
*Love your enemies and do good to them, and lend without any hope of return. You will have a great reward, and you will be children of the Most High, for He himself is kind to the ungrateful and the wicked.*
*'Be compassionate just as your Father is compassionate."*

Luke 6:27-36

As we approached Milbuk, the road was interrupted by a check point and some construction work. The cement highway was not yet completed. The laborers were hard at work laying down the steel frames and pouring the concrete cement. It would be another month or so before this fine highway was able to reach Milbuk and beyond … right up to Palimbang itself.

As I anxiously awaited to enter the area referred to as 'Milbuk', we first traveled through the heavily populated and somewhat prosperous barangay of San Roque or 'Barrio Kalamunggay', as some use to call it. Later in the day, the former Vice Mayor of Palimbang,

Mr. Abary, would give us a tour of the area, but now we only gazed out the car windows as we quickly passed by, heading with great purpose to our destination.

Now we were in Milbuk! We finally turned off the main road and headed directly for the Notre Dame Campus and the Church of Our Lady of Perpetual Help. I noticed that there was no check point at this juncture, nor neat rows of homes that formerly marked the area known as *Campo Uno*. The village was gone! Now there were scattered homes here and there, nestled beneath the shade of various trees and palms. We passed the **Milbuk National High School** that was now closed for the summer and in the distance stood the tall, majestic form of the Catholic Church, decorated, high on the front side, with the painted image of Our Lady of Perpetual Help. We drove up to the Church and stopped at the new convento next door and quickly dismounted the vehicle. We were greeted by the parish priest and his staff with a great welcome. Signs of our coming was evident by the large colorful tent that stood in the large open space directly in front of the convento and parish hall with a large sign welcoming us. I was quite impressed.

My feet hadn't touched the ground for almost two and half hours during our journey and here I was now standing in a place where I had not stood for almost 40 years. It all seemed so unreal. I greeted everyone and thanked them for their evident hospitality and kindness. My eyes swept the area to see if there was anything that I recognized. It all looked so different. Almost everything I remembered, except for the Church itself, was all gone! I was not discouraged. I wanted to see everything that I could in the short time that I would be staying here in Milbuk

Milbuk was truly unrecognizable as I rode into the town. Gone was the Veneer Mill and Power Plant: gone too was Campo Uno and Campo Dos. The Notre Dame of Milbuk had been completely destroyed by earthquake, tsunami and the ravages of time. Gone were the huge boulders that formed a wall of protection from the battering waves of the sea, sunken beneath the ever shifting sands. The only vestiges of this magnificent building that were left was one old classroom, the concrete steps that once led into the Administration section of the building and library and the septic tank that sat beneath the girls and boys bathroom at the end of the school's main corridor. This concrete monument (septic tank) sat strangely on a large stretch of sand, indicating to me just how far the erosion had advanced and the extent to which the sea had claimed the land on which the High School had once stood. And as I rounded the last remains of the old N.D. high school building, there to my great surprise was the old statue of Our Lady of Perpetual Help, standing in a small shrine that sits in front of the wooden office building.

As Mary and I continued to stroll the property, we came upon the 'old convento', the place where I had lived for almost three years…one of the best homes in which I was privileged to live. I did recognize it, but it had deteriorated greatly into a ruinous, ugly hulk of a building, looking at any time to collapse onto the sand and mercifully wash out to sea. It pains me to even see that building still standing. *"Tear it down and free the space. Bring beauty once more to this part of the Milbuk campus"*, I thought to myself. I noticed the many attempts to save the noble structure, but each attempt made the building look grotesque. It is definitely an eyesore. Please do not think that I am critical of anyone's attempt to rescue such a place and make it once again habitable. I am simply narrating my impression of what I see.

What impressed me most were the improvements that have taken place to the parish of Our Lady of Perpetual Help. The Church itself has become more beautiful over the years in spite of war, earthquake, tsunami and time itself. The pastors of Our Lady of Perpetual Help are to be commended for aiding, supporting and increasing the Catholic faith of the community. Milbuk has become a place of retreat for many other Catholic communities who travel several hours to attend training seminars and retreats. The pastors of Milbuk have used well the donations that have been given by former Milbuk parishioners and Notre Dame graduates living in other parts of the Philippines and overseas. The community of Milbukians, those who attended the Notre Dame High School from 1962 to the present, has come alive, and has invigorated itself, becoming vital to the lives of hundreds.

After Mary and I had seen the "ruins" of where we once lived and worked, we returned to the company of our companions, now gathered in front of the new convento and parish center. We narrated the experience of our brief tour and mingled with the parishioners. I was introduced by the pastor to one young man who was a teacher at the Notre Dame of Milbuk. I asked him if he could bring me on a tour of the Notre Dame High School so that I could see first-hand what the place looked like. I must say that I was not impressed by the physical layout of the buildings.

The new Notre Dame of Milbuk is now located across the campus where former students marched as cadets, played softball during recess and ran merrily after each other in one form of tag or another. The new Notre Dame has taken the form of the old "Marcos-type" school houses of former days…namely, one story concrete classrooms, covered with G.I roofing, and linked to one another in a straight line. No architectural marvels here, just plain rooms, shelter from out of the weather to study and prepare for the future. There is no home economics building with facilities to teach the young men and women how to properly cook good, nutritious food and manage a budget. There's no band room or library to supplement the curriculum of studies and enhance the learning experience of the students. And there are no computers! How are the students to survive in the real world of higher education if they lack such common tools like computers?

At the end of this line of four or five classrooms, workers were busy completing the construction of a two story concrete building to accommodate two additional classes of students. These classrooms would accommodate seventh and eighth grade students. The Philippine government had mandated that elementary education would now consist of eight grades instead of the customary six grades of studies before entrance into High School. These additional classrooms would benefit Notre Dame as a feeder unit for the High School. Notre Dame High School will be in need of continued financial assistance for some time to come, a project that we as Milbukians should adopt as our way of paying back all that we have received.

And then there is the Milbuk National High School nearby, which is amply funded by the government. However, it was surprising to me to learn that the Notre Dame High School has attracted so many Muslim students to its classes. Out of the more than 200 students, half are Muslim. What a witness to the world and to the country itself that a Catholic High School should welcome into its classrooms, all students regardless of how they worship God. There is no distinction made among the student body concerning this matter. The traditions of old and the legacy of the Notre Dame of Milbuk are present today. I again congratulate and thank all the pastors of the parish of Milbuk, who as Directors of Notre Dame are defending the rights of all peoples.

After the tour of Notre Dame High School, I did not want to return to my companions. So I asked the young teacher if he would accompany me through the village of Milbuk and all the way to the Baranggay of San Roque. I wanted to see everything that I could, especially the people and the places in which they lived. I told no one of my plan.

We walked along the staff manager's row. Those fine bungalows that once overlooked Milbuk bay and the Celebes Sea were now gone except for one ancient building that still was habitable. The family that occupied this one remaining relic of former days, was gracious enough to permit me to photograph them in front of their home. On the front side of the faded green house, you could still see the small, white painted sign attached to the house that read: "S-1" … (Staff House #1).

Across the street was the large open field that used to host softball games and the venue for viewing the Saturday night movies. We all remember those days. But today, the field was crowded with young boys playing soccer. Two make-up teams were kicking the soccer ball up and down the field under the watchful eyes of a half a dozen marines from the Marine Battalion stationed just outside the village of Milbuk. They were using this opportunity to teach the young boys the fine points of soccer and to promote cooperation and good will among the people of the town. I spoke with one young Marine whom I approached on the sidelines, commending him and his fellow Marines for taking the time to organize recreational activities for the children and showing them how much they cared. I must say that I was quite impressed with the whole experience.

We continued along staff row until we reached what used to be the end of the road. I remember that here there was a wire fence that separated Campo Uno from the Veneer Mill and the Power Plant complex. This area was a large, barren, wide open space of uneven ground that led along the shore for some distance. There was a hole in the fence guarding the Weyerhaeuser industrial complex from unwelcome intruders. I used this passageway once, on the day of the invasion in September of 1974, when I was brought by Rudy Alameida to the floating dock where the Army was holding a group of Muslim men and women from Kulong-Kulong. On this day, however, there was no fence and the large open space was now overgrown with coconut trees and other types of foliage. The whole area that used to be cordoned off with high wire fences for security was now a disorganized grouping of various styles of homes under a huge canopy of green. There was no order among the houses, as you would find in a town with named streets and numbered houses. There was no trace that a Veneer Mill or Power Plant ever existed except for the concrete flooring on which some of the more fortunate homes were built. All of this was VERY STRANGE indeed and quite beyond my imagination.

We wandered through this maze of dwellings beneath the large cover of green, greeting people as we came across them. I chose to walk along the shore area where most of the people seemed to gather. All along the waters' edge, there were numerous bangkas scattered here and there. Some of the fishermen had returned from their night's work on the sea several hours before and they were now sitting around in conversation with one another after having cleaned and prepared their bangkas for later this evening. I asked if I might take their photo and they were all happy at the request. No one asked me who I was and why I was here. They may have secretly inquired this information from the teacher who accompanied me. Nevertheless, everyone seemed so happy and relaxed.

After close to an hour, we walked out of this fishing village to the nearby market place. There to my surprise was a rather nice, open air market complex built of concrete and very neat and clean indeed. It was already past 10:30 A.M. in the morning and the place was deserted except for the few young attendants still manning the large complex. I started a conversation with the attendants and took their photos much to their delight. How I wished that I could have arrived much earlier when the market was in full swing.

As I was looking around at my surroundings, I began to realize where I was. This was the main road to Baranggay San Roque *("Baranggay Kalamunggay")* where I had often traveled on my motorcycle to celebrate Holy Mass. Excitedly, I proceeded down the road with the teacher and we soon came to the Baranggay Hall of San Roque. The teacher told me that the former Vice Mayor of Palimbang, Mr. Rolando Abary, lived in the house opposite to the Baranggay Hall. He had returned from the States to manage some property affairs. "Really!" I said. "How lucky for me if he is home now." I saw that the home of Rolando was behind a high wall, guarded by a steel gate. I asked the teacher to inquire from the guard if the former Vice Mayor was at home. If he was at home and available, please inform Mr. Abary that Fr. Art Amaral is outside and would like to speak with him.

While I was waiting, I engaged in conversation with some of the men gathered at the steps of the Baranggay Hall. I remarked how surprised I was at the surroundings. Everything looked so different, in the good sense. San Roque is definitely much larger in population than I remembered, in fact, it appears to be a very prosperous village. From the ground, I wasn't able to really appreciate the size and flourishing population of this barangay. Only months later, while I was searching some Google satellite photos of Palimbang, I zeroed in on San Roque and was blown away at what I saw in the photo. The place is so overcrowded with homes and various other structures. The shore line along Milbuk Harbor is teeming with bangkas of every size and shape especially in the San Roque area. This place has become the mecca and fishing center for the entire town of Palimbang. I am sure that the great catch of fish from the toil and endeavor of the San Roque and Milbuk fishermen are shipped daily each morning by trucks destined for the City of General Santos or to the many fishing companies doing business along Sarangani Bay.

The result of the teacher's inquiry concerning Mr. Rolando Abary was quick in coming. Within a matter of a few minutes, the guard at the gate of Rolando's compound, quickly called to us to enter. As I proceeded toward the house that was about 100 feet from the main gate, Rolando came walking out of the house toward me and we both met mid-way in the yard. We greeted each other happily with smiles and embraced each other as long lost brothers. I introduced the Notre Dame teacher to him. Rolando led us to a small porch at the entrance to the house and invited us to be seated at a round table while he requested his cook to prepare some coffee and cake for us. Then we began to talk.

Right away, the conversation centered on the events of August/ September 1974. It was as if the years had been stripped away and we were re-living once again the happenings of those tragic days. As the conversation continued, Rolando began apologizing for whatever role he had played during the conflict and the resulting tragedies of those days. I quickly interjected by stating that I had come to visit him here in San Roque to inquire about his health, the happenings in his life and whatever projects he was planning for Milbuk and of course to renew old friendships. The past no longer exists, I commented. It is the present moment that is important. But he would not be persuaded. Rolando needed to tell me his story … and I listened.

There were many issues of that tragic past that he wanted to explain to me. Some of the more personal matters will remain hidden deep within me, not to be shared with anyone. This hour long conversation with Rolando was truly a gift from God for both of us. I came to appreciate this man during my personal visit with him. In the past, I was not kind to Rolando in the opinions that I held. I apologized to him for my past behavior and assured him that the Lord Jesus forgives both of us for any and all sins that we may have committed in thought, word, deed and omission. Truly, I did not know the whole story. And so it is with so many of the negative opinions and harsh judgements we make against one another.

I believe that the Lord Jesus led me to San Roque and to the home of Rolando. I did not know beforehand that he was even in the Philippines, much less living in San Roque. And I never thought that I would even be able to travel to Milbuk because of the possible problems with security. This meeting with Rolando Abary was the highlight of my trip to Milbuk, resulting in a renewed experience of peace in my mind, heart and soul.

Then, as if on cue, Boyting Serrano and Oca Carzada arrived at the house of Rolando on a motorcycle and walked straight into the courtyard through the open steel gates. Rolando at once recognized them and quickly stood up and waved the two men toward us. The conversation came to an abrupt end and I was satisfied. Rolando was able to communicate all that he needed to say and I had listened with understanding and compassion.

We all greeted each other noisily. Oca then remarked how worried Mary had been at my two hour absence from the group at the convento. Boyting had told her not to be concerned since he knew exactly where I was. (Did Jesus let him in on His secret?) Both men had driven directly to the compound of Rolando with the surety that I would be there. How did they know? This was not my plan as I explained earlier. I was being led to this special visitation. We all briefly sat down at the table and then arose to take a series of photos for posterity. Rolando then suggested that we all accompany him in his van for a tour of San Roque and other scenic venues.

The first place that we drove to was the old air field. Many homes had been built at the far end of the airport toward the mountains. Along each side of the airfield, other homes had been set up sparsely along the perimeter. A small plane could still possibly land here as long as the pilot stayed straight in the middle of the runway and avoided the carabao, dogs, chickens and pigs and of course the people. On second thought … not a good idea!

We continued to tour the area, stopping only to take photos. Returning back to Rolando's house, Boyting asked my traveling companion, the Notre Dame teacher, to take the motorcycle back to the convento. We then all headed back to the Church area where lunch had been prepared for all us visitors and was about to be served. Everyone was so happy to see Rolando and to see him joining in our festivities.

2:00 P.M. arrived and Fr. Boni reminded all of us that we had to leave Milbuk soon according to the recommendations and arrangements made with the military. The Marine Battalion did not want us to remain in Milbuk after 3:00 P.M. *TRANSLATION: Get the Americans out of Milbuk on time! We don't want any trouble.*

After this memorable trip, we still had three weeks left on our vacation here in the Philippines. We continued to visit so many interesting places and people, but I will not bore you with the details. We are so grateful for the five mini-reunions we celebrated with Milbukians in Davao, Marbel, General Santos City, Milbuk and Manila. God has truly blessed us all.

Mary and I have so many people to thank, especially those who made our trip so successful. And so before I bring to close the ending of this story, let me thank those responsible in caring for us and keeping us well fed and safe.

We thank, first of all, Wilfredo 'Boyting' Serrano for taking such good care of us from the first moment that we arrived at the Manila International Airport on March the 26th, right up to the moment of our departure for the USA on April the 30th. He opened his home to us in Makati and really treated us as family and honored guests. There was no request that he failed to fulfill. When we arrived in General Santos City from Davao, he was there to meet us. His Manokan restaurant became our 'hangout' and his trademark barbequed chicken still makes my mouth water. He and his inseparable classmate, friend and companion, none other than Oscar 'Oca' Carzada, accompanied us to Marbel and spent the week with us at the home of my now good friend, Thelma Juaman Hansen.

There are no adequate words to describe the grand hospitality that Thelma provided for me and Mary. A "Thank You!" seems so insufficient for the tireless and dedicated attention she gave to our every need. She surrendered up her very own room with the only air conditioner in the house, so that our stay would be comfortable. Early in the morning, breakfast was always there upon our arising from sleep. She and her family members shared with us their lunch and dinner at the same table. We felt so much at home there. Again, thank you is really not adequate at all.

Behind the scenes of all these preparations, there was an invisible master of organization whose name is Beth Didulo. Beth, I really never had the time or opportunity to speak with you privately in order to commend you on your continued dedication to the Milbuk community both in the Philippines and abroad. I thank you especially for making our trip so truly epic and memorable. You have taught me a profound lesson on humility. Your contribution to the success of our trip did not go unnoticed.

There are several other people whom I want to acknowledge for the sacrifice they made to provide for us and make us feel so welcomed. When we arrived in Davao, Boyette Mariano met us at the airport and transported us to the home of Mary's classmate, friend and kababayan, Fortunata 'Atang' Magno. We also were placed in the only air-conditioned room in the home for the entire time that we spent in Davao, almost a period of two weeks. 'Atang' was the perfect host. Boyette organized a Davao Milbukian 'reunion' on April the 6th at the Chapel and Hospital where he works. There is a collage of the event which brought together two people special to me, namely, Mrs. Capacite and Dra. Mariano, the mother of 'Boyette'.

Hospitality is a characteristic trait of most Filipinos, known and acknowledged by the world. Therefore, to the many other people who have also shown their love and concern for Mary and me and whom I have not mentioned, thank you all very much. Please accept my apologies for not including your name in this brief acknowledgement. I would have to write another book just on this subject. Know that Mary and I will always keep you in our thoughts, heart and prayers. Maraming, maraming salamat!

# THE END

Journey of Remembrance: The Church of Our Lady of Good Counsel at Milbuk has greatly improved in beauty. So much has been done to enhance the celebration of the liturgy resulting in an enthusiastic participation on the part of the parishioners. (Lower left): This photo is one of my favorites. I was so fortunate to have spent enriching and valuable time with these three men, all of whom have made my journey so memorable. (Wilfredo "Boyting" Serrano, Macgoon Valle and Oscar "Oca" Carzada). (Lower Right): My companions on this wonderful trip to Milbuk and some of the parishioners who welcomed us so genuinely. Thank you all!

# Epilogue

Memories continue to flood my mind. It seems as if I am watching a movie. How many wonderful adventures I've had...and all the time while working in the service of the Lord Jesus. I look back over my life and see the humor of the Lord and His love in all the strange and astonishing places He has led me. I was further blessed by the special people he sent into my life and so many graces, especially in those moments of trial and suffering. I can only gaze upon the now dim and fading memories with awe at the way Jesus took care of me and those I love. Silently, I whisper a prayer of thanks, knowing how unworthy I was but nevertheless loved.

"I have been crucified with Christ, and I live now not with my own life, but with the life of Christ who lives in me. The life that I live now, I live by faith in the Son of God, who loved me and gave his life for me." Galatians 2:20 (Jerusalem Bible translation)

Printed in the United States
By Bookmasters